ETHNICITY, BORDERS,
AND THE GRASSROOTS INTERFACE WITH THE STATE

Studies on Mainland Southeast Asia
in Honor of Charles F. Keyes

Edited by John A. Marston

ISBN: 978-616-215-072-2

© 2014 Silkworm Books
All rights reserved

No part of this publication may be reproduced, stored in a retrieval system, or transmitted, in any form or by any means, electronic, mechanical, photocopying, recording or otherwise, without the prior permission in writing of the publisher.

First Published in 2014 by
Silkworm Books
6 Sukkasem Road, T. Suthep
Chiang Mai 50200 Thailand
info@silkwormbooks.com
http://www.silkwormbooks.com

Cover graphic adapted from Darunee Paisanpanitchakul, "The Right to Identification Papers in the Thai State" (unpublished MA thesis, Thammasat University, 2005).

Typeset in Arno Pro 11 pt. by Silk Type
Printed in Thailand by O. S. Printing House, Bangkok

5 4 3 2 1

CONTENTS

Acknowledgments v
Introduction 1

THE STATE AND PUBLIC CEREMONY

1 The Tenth Day of March and Contingent Lineages of
   Vietnamese Statehood 23
   Allison Truitt

2 Rock Your Religion: Shan Buddhist Ritual and Stage-Show
   Revelry in a Contested Zone at the Thai-Burma Border 45
   Jane M. Ferguson

3 Reestablishing the Cambodian Monkhood 65
   John A. Marston

THE GRASSROOTS NEGOTIATION OF MODERNITY

4 Alterity to Modernity: Village-Based Self-Sufficient
   Farm Production in Northeastern Thailand 103
   Ratana Tosakul

5 Christianity, Modernity, and Creativity: The Construction of a Lahu Baptist Identity 125
   Judith M. S. Pine

6 Contested Citizenship: Cards, Colors, and the Culture of Identification 143
   Pinkaew Laungaramsri

CROSSING BORDERS OF STATE AND NATION

7 Narrating Legitimacy, Narrating Agencies: Citizenship Negotiations among Internationally Displaced Laotians in Northeastern Thailand 165
   Suchada Thaweesit

8 Temporary Lives, Eternal Dreams: Experiences of Viet Labor Migrants in Savannakhet, Laos 191
   Duong Bich Hanh

9 Cross-Border Hypergamy and Gendered Agency: *Farang* Husbands and Isan Wives on the Global Cultural Stage 215
   Suriya Smutkupt and Pattana Kitiarsa

Charles F. Keyes: His Life and Work 245
Questions for Charles Keyes 251
Selected Publications of Charles Keyes 263
Contributors 277
Index 281

ACKNOWLEDGMENTS

The present volume grows out of a conference in honor of Charles F. Keyes held at the University of Washington on October 5–6, 2007. Thanks in particular are due to Sara Van Fleet for her key role in the organization of the conference, and to Cecilia Lowe and Sara Curran, the other members of the organizing committee. In addition to the contributors to this volume, I would like to thank the other participants who gave papers at this stimulating conference: Nazif Shahrani, Oscar Salemink, Diane Fox, Peter K. Moran, Amara Pongsaphich, Hoang Cham, Phan Ngoc Chien, Pornprapit Phoasavadi, Yasuko Takezawa, Eric C. Thompson, Maureen Hickey, Jennifer Leehey, Tami Blumenfield, Le S. Tran, and Shihlun Allen Chen. Thanks are also due to Laurie Sears of the Southeast Asian Studies Program of University of Washington for her help in shepherding this book toward publication.

INTRODUCTION
John A. Marston

Charles Keyes, Ethnicity, and the State

Charles Keyes's earliest writing about ethnicity primarily focused on ethnicity as group identity and made very little reference to the state. His 1976 article, "Toward a New Formulation of the Concept of Ethnic Group," in the journal *Ethnicity*, which is still a theoretical milestone, developed the idea of descent and its implications for ethnicity. While on the basis of this key article he is sometimes identified with what is called the "primordial" school of ethnicity, what was important to scholars of ethnicity (Andaya 2009, 8)—was not so much the *actual* descent and other primordial traits (as would have been the case in kin-based societies), but the *idea*—what he would later call the "social construal"—of a primordial bond.

The growing salience of the state in Keyes's writing about ethnicity represented the logical development of his own thinking but also reflects changes in the field of anthropology itself, and in the broader sphere of the social sciences, especially the appearance since 1980 of key works on nation and on state, some by scholars of Southeast Asia.

Keyes's introduction to the volume *Ethnic Change* in 1981 drew on many of the ideas of his 1976 article, which he elaborated to include, in particular, a discussion of the ways ethnicity could change over time. Although not yet central to his argument, he begins to talk about the role of the state in the context of ethnic change, where confrontations between ethnic groups and expanding state bureaucracies illustrate the kind of radical change in political-economic contexts that can result in ethnic change.

By 1987, his contribution to the book *Southeast Asian Tribal Groups and Ethnic Minorities*, "Tribal Peoples and the Nation-State in Mainland Southeast Asia" (1987a), while not theoretical in orientation, actively engages the question of the role of minority groups in the Southeast Asian nation-state, evoking Benedict Anderson's 1983 book, *Imagined Communities*. In fact, Anderson contributed the introduction to the 1987 book.

Keyes has said that a key factor in the development of his thought was an article by Brackette Williams in *Annual Review of Anthropology* (Williams 1989).[1] Keyes was one of three theorists of ethnicity whose work she analyzed in great detail in the process of developing her own synthesis, which finally emphasized the need for any viable theory to show ethnicity as existing in a context of the state and the nation.

By 1997, in his entry on "Ethnic, Ethnic Groups" in *The Blackwell Dictionary of Anthropology*, a relationship to the nation-state was very much part of his expanding vision of ethnicity:

> Whereas an earlier generation of anthropologists and other social scientists viewed the persistence of ethnic identities in the modern world as atavistic, students of ethnicity today recognize that, very much to the contrary, ethnicity has become a much more significant factor in social relations since the emergence of the nation-state.

Keyes was now very much concerned with the ways state-sponsored education, in promoting national identities, affected ethnic identity, and how different forms of state-sponsored ethnic classification have related to peoples' formulation of their identity. He also discussed the complications related to the increasing ease with which populations cross state borders. These themes also came to feature in the research of scholars he taught and conversed with, as we can see in the essays in this book.

His presidential address to the 2002 annual meeting of the Association for Asian Studies continued in this vein, containing as it did a careful study of the ramifications of state classification of peoples in China, Vietnam, and Thailand.

> While biological, linguistic, and ethnological sciences can generate significant work about the differences among human beings, they cannot determine the differences between "peoples" or "ethnic groups." Such determination, as I will now attempt to show, has been a product of politics, especially the politics of modern nation-states. (2002a, 97)

Citing the ways in which the ideas of Foucault, Benedict Anderson, and James Scott have influenced his thought, he speaks of ethnic classification as a technology of power of modern states:

> While I certainly do not dispute the observation made by other scholars that ethnic differentiation is rooted in premodern distinctions, I maintain that ethnic classification has been deployed as a technology of power only by modern states; in other words, modern states have set out to make legible, in James Scott's (1998) term, the "motley crowds" located on their frontiers. (2002a, 100)

For Keyes, and for many other scholars, the workings of the state, then, in combination with complex processes simultaneously shaping group self-identity, comes to be seen as essential to how ethnicity is conceived and practiced in the real world.

Ways of Looking at the State

The purpose of the above retrospective is to show how, over time, the concept of the state has assumed more and more prominence in Keyes's thought, as it has in the field of anthropology as a whole. In a brainstorming session following the conference in honor of Keyes, which is the basis for this volume, Keyes, Michael Duckworth (then a University of Washington Press editor), and I came up with the working title, *Asian Legacies and the Inscriptions of the State*. Our inclination to emphasize the state may have been influenced by the way certain conference papers, such as those of Pinkaew Laungaramsri and Suchada Thaweesit, stood out in our minds and, perhaps, shed light on other papers with less explicit references to the state. In adapting their conference papers for the volume, contributors were asked to try to underline the connection to the state, and in some cases, such as the chapters by Allison Truitt and Judith M. S. Pine, this significantly affected the ways they came to articulate their arguments. In the end, although I have decided that the contents are better reflected by a broader title, this, in many ways, is still a volume organized around the concept of the state.

"State" as I use it here means state authority. Modern state authority is intrinsically linked to the ideology of the nation-state, and some readers may prefer to see the overarching theme in these terms, which are so central to the work of Keyes himself; one cannot in a simple way isolate state from nation. However, despite the frequent reference in this volume to ethnicity, a concept inevitably linked to the problematic of nation, the chapters in this book are, in the final analysis, less about the imagined community of nation than the ways a population finds itself in dialogue with the state—the state as a body which defines categories of citizenship, prescribes the setting of official ceremony, provides education, or encourages economic systems—or the state that affects people simply by how profoundly their lives are changed by crossing borders. As Truitt's chapter reminds us, it is often through statecraft that a conception of nation is inscribed.

Pinkaew Laungaramsri's chapter deals specifically with the state apparatus for classifying degrees of citizenship or non-citizenship; John Marston deals with the putting into place of a state apparatus for monastic ordination in Cambodia in 1979; Truitt is concerned with the state's cultural construction of its own lineage. Other chapters are less concerned with the state apparatus itself than with the shadow of state authority in a more general way as it is experienced at the local level.

In *Strong Societies, Weak States*, Joel Migdal, drawing on Weber, provides what he calls an "ideal-type" definition of the state, which, although open to argumentation, can provide a basis for discussion. Thus the state is, an organization, composed of numerous agencies led and coordinated by the state's leadership (executive authority) that has the ability or authority to make and implement the binding rules for all the people as well as the parameters of rule making for other social organizations in a given territory, using force if necessary to have its way. (1988, 19)

While state institutions may act differently from each other and may vary in their actions over time, state authority will consistently be perceived by local actors as "making and implementing the binding rules"—systems and rules which are at least perceived as having consistency over time. As such, it also sets the field for the contestation of its authority.

Some of the chapters of the book—perhaps Pinkaew, Suchada, and Marston more than others—approach their topics with an implicit *distrust* of state authority—where the state is seen as an obstacle to the grassroots populations they are concerned with. Among Southeast Asianists, this distrust is closely associated with the work of James Scott, the keynote speaker at the conference that generated this volume and a frequent interlocutor of Keyes.[2] His celebrated book, *Seeing Like a State: How Certain Schemes to Improve the Human Condition Have Failed*, is about how the state, in the context of modernity, envisioned roles for itself that proved unrealistic. (The book followed other key works on peasant resistance, including *Weapons of the Weak: Everyday Forms of Peasant Resistance*, and anticipated *The Art of Not Being Governed: An Anarchist History of Upland Southeast Asia*, all contributing to an overall vision of state authority and how it can be resisted.) The title refers to state projects intended to make society more "legible," and the book goes on to discuss historically important projects of massive state management. He states in his introduction that he is not simply anti-state:

> The state, as I make abundantly clear, is the vexed institution that is the ground of both our freedoms and our unfreedoms. My case is that certain kinds of states, driven by utopian plans and an authoritarian disregard for the values, desires, and objections of their subjects, are indeed a mortal threat to human well-being.

> Short of that draconian but all too common situation, we are left to weigh judiciously the benefits of certain state interventions against their costs. (1998, 7)

Nevertheless, the overall effect of the book is to call into question the desirability of state capacity; the author is concerned with the inherent logic of the state and its implicit costs in environmental and human terms, especially in the more extreme contexts where an ideology of modernity has been allowed free reign. The early modern tendency for states to systematically map what they govern evolved into the more elaborate state projects which began in the mid-nineteenth century in the West and the twentieth century elsewhere—what he calls "high modernism."

> What is high modernism, then? ... At its center was a supreme self-confidence about continued linear progress, the development of scientific and technical knowledge, the expansion of production, the rational design of social order, the growing satisfaction of human needs, and, not least, an increasing control over nature (including human nature) commensurate with scientific understanding of natural laws. *High* modernism is thus a particularly sweeping vision of how the benefits of technical and scientific progress might be applied—usually through the state—in every field of human activity. If, as we have seen, the simplified, utilitarian *descriptions* of state officials had a tendency, through the exercise of state power, to bring the facts into line with their representations, then one might say that the high-modern state began with extensive *prescriptions* for a new society, and it intended to impose them. (Ibid., 89–90)

Scott begins with discussion of modern state projects of forestry, urban mapping, and the registration of populations, and goes on to write about more far-reaching plans of urban planning, political organization, collectivization, and large-scale agriculture—cases, as his title indicates, of "how certain schemes to improve the human condition have failed."[3] Pinkaew Laungaramsri's chapter about an increasingly involuted system of Thai identity cards is the one most clearly in the tradition of Scott. Others—Marston, Suchada, and more subtly Jane M. Ferguson and

Ratana Tosakul, illustrate in more general terms the growing reach of the state.

None of the contributors go to the opposite extreme, as some scholars do, of valorizing the state and bemoaning its power to function in "failed" or "weak" states. (This despite a scholarly tradition of describing the instability of the *premodern* Southeast Asian state—of it pulsating in and out of power or representing more theater than substance [Wolters 1982; Geertz 1980; Junker 1999]—although this perspective has perhaps been more often applied to island Southeast Asia than mainland.)

The critique of weak states has also applied to more *modern* situations. Joel Migdal's 1988 book, *Strong Societies and Weak States: State-Society Relations and State Capabilities in the Third World*, for example, is concerned with the degree to which many states govern "web-like" societies consisting of many different organizations, each with its own rules and inner logic, which sometimes clash with the rules and inner logic of the state.

> Non-compliance here is not simply personal deviance or criminality or corruption; rather, it is an indication of a more fundamental conflict over which organizations in society, the state or others, should make these rules. These struggles are not over precisely which laws the state should enact or how the state's laws or constitution should be interpreted; these, after all, are decided within *state* organs, legislatures and courts. Instead, these struggles are much more fundamental, reaching beyond marginal deviance and beyond the formal roles of any existing political institutions in the society. These struggles are over whether the state will be able to displace or harness other organizations—families, clans, multinational corporations, domestic enterprises, tribes, patron-client dyads—which make rules against the wishes and goals of state leaders. (31)

This vision of the state is historically situated. Migdal is concerned in particular with the period following World War II when many countries were emerging from colonialism and others were crystalizing as nation-states in ways they had not previously. It was a period of great faith in the powers of the state—a faith that was associated with the same ideologies of modernity that Scott is concerned with. The book explores the circumstances under which that faith was so often disappointed, in a wide-reaching pattern that extends across much of the "Third World."

Migdal indicates that he does not consider a strong state always good—and in charting the historical complexities of the post–World War II state he is distancing himself from scholars who took that position too simply. All the same, it is still hard to escape the feeling that the book, following the political science models it draws on and reacts to, regards state weakness as in some way problematic. It ranks states according to their capacities and, however much it attempts to describe and explain those that lack state capacity, those who have it seem at an advantage.

This approach is worth mentioning, I believe, because it is relevant to the chapters in this volume, that states sometimes, contradictorily, can be weak and strong at the same time—for example when some state institutions consolidate because of fear of disarray. The description Marston offers of Cambodia following the Pol Pot period, for example, when more spontaneous grassroots ordinations were finally suppressed by the state and replaced by a single ordination regime, might be explained in these terms.

In other chapters in the book, the shadow of the state is presented less clearly as something negative or positive but instead as a constant in everyday lives with which people simply know they have to deal: the government representatives at the Shan initiation in Ferguson's chapter, an ongoing history of Christians coming to terms with the Buddhist orientation of the Thai state in Pine's chapter, changing Thai policies toward agriculture in Ratana's chapter, and the ways lives are affected by immigration agreements in Duong Bich Hanh's chapter.

The studies in this volume take place in the historical context of the modernizing nation-states of mainland Southeast Asia. Thailand's process of modernization has been documented in several well-known studies (Keyes 1987b; Tambiah 1976; Thongchai 1994), both its development as a nation-state and the systemization of a state bureaucracy extending to more clearly defined borders. Although it is not central to the rural studies presented here, Thai modernization has also entailed industrialization and ever-deeper links to global capitalism. The projects of modernization in Vietnam, Cambodia, and Laos following

French colonialism, were, by contrast, socialist, although they, likewise, in the terms Scott has used to describe modernization, entailed state penetration and systematization. The studies of these three countries in this volume are set in periods when they have withdrawn to varying degrees from earlier socialist strategies.

What the new forms of modernization—evolving into postmodernity?—really mean has been subject to debate. Since the 1990s there has been increasing scholarly attention to global interconnectedness and its seemingly undeniable intensification. Appadurai writes that,

> It has now become something of a truism that we are functioning in a world fundamentally characterized by objects in motion. These objects include ideas and ideologies, people and goods, images and message, technologies and techniques. This is a world of flows. It is also of course a world of structures, organizations, and other stable social forms. But the apparent stabilities that we see are, under close examination, usually our devices for handling objects characterized by motion. The greatest of these apparently stable objects is the nation-state, which is today frequently characterized by floating populations, transnational politics within national borders, and mobile configurations of technology and expertise. (2001, 4)

Whether or not we can justifiably argue that the nation-state in its most characteristic "modern" form has now been surpassed, or that, rather, its role has in some ways been intensified, scholars continue to struggle to come to terms with the different levels at which transformation is taking place.

Migdal and James Scott in *Seeing Like a State* are very much writing about the modern state as defined by national borders, but it has become increasingly difficult for anthropologists to ignore cross-border population movements. This has also been a concern of Keyes in some recent work as well, and it is not surprising that it has taken on even more prominence in his students' work, as we see in several of these chapters.

Some people in the ethnic system of one country see themselves and are recognized as belonging to border-crossing communities.

Others trace their history to migrations across borders. And yet others are connected by language, kinship, or culture to peoples in another country. The classificatory systems predicated on the assumption that peoples belong within borders are thus rendered problematic by the connection of peoples across borders and peoples who cross borders. (Keyes 2002, 113)

One attempt to theorize cross-border communities in anthropological terms has been Sharma and Gupta's introduction to *The Anthropology of the State: A Reader*. They stress the risk of reifying the state, seeing it not so much as the source of power itself but, instead, as one point at which social relations of power are embodied. Their vision of power is less a Marxist one than a Foucauldian one, where multiple sources of power come to play in relation to each other. The state is the "super-coordinator of governance."

Once we see that the boundary between the state and civil society is itself an effect of power, then we can begin to conceptualize "the state" *within* (and not automatically distinct from) other institutional forms through which social relations are lived, such as the family, civil society, and the economy. Such an analysis of state formation does not simply assume that the state stands at the apex of society and is the central locus of power. Instead, the problem becomes one of figuring out how "the state" *comes to assume* its vertical position as the supreme authority that manages all other institutional forms that social relations take, and that functions as the super-coordinator of the governance of social and individual conduct by these other institutions. (2006, 9)

This gives them a means of discussing ways of framing the state in the context of globalization. We note that even Migdal included multinational corporations in his list of what states have encountered in their struggle to realize compliance along classical Weberian lines. However, Migdal, writing in 1988, was still primarily concerned with the problematic of what the state encountered within national boundaries. By 2006, the question of how states come to terms with transnational processes had become a much more salient issue. Again, Sharma and Gupta stress that the state is only one of many nodes of power coming into play. Transnational nodes of power touch on the state in many ways, not only in terms of the impacts of multinational corporations, but also in terms of the ways international organizations and NGOs interact with the states and, most dramatically, the effects of foreign intervention or UN peacekeeping missions. These are issues that figure tangentially in some of the essays of the current volume. A theme very much at the heart of this volume is state governance in relation to the cross-border movements of population.

> One way to approach these processes of transnational governance is to examine migration, to ask why people move, who moves, from where, and to where. Human migrations are not only articulated to the needs of global capitalism, they are also transforming how we think about the nation, citizenship (or belonging, more broadly), and the state. Diasporic movements point to how the space of the nation, or "home," and the affective ties that bind this imagined community are expanding across the boundaries of the nation-state. For this reason, citizenship too is being imagined, practiced, and regulated transnationally and flexibly. Citizenship is unevenly experienced and spatialized—both transnationally and nationally. People inhabiting different circuits of the global capitalist economy are subjected to different regimes of rights and citizenship. (2006, 25–26)

The chapters in this book can be seen as case studies in the relationships of power between institutions of state and society. These relations which show the kind of state ineffectiveness described by Marston and Duong, but which, contradictorily, can also show the state developing its authority—"inscribing" itself—to the kinds of extremes that Scott would describe (Pinkaew, Suchada), perhaps in reaction to the fluidity of the situation it encounters. This is a fluidity that is accentuated by processes of globalization, characterized, among other things, by increasingly common movements of populations (Duong, Suchada, Suriya and Pattana). We see the clash with grassroots institutions and traditions, which have their own momentum (Ferguson, Marston); and one chapter even shows the state encouraging greater rural autonomy in the face of global economic penetration (Ratana).

The Chapters

The organizers of the original conference out of which this book grew encouraged participants to focus on three themes central to Keyes's work: religion, modernity, and ethnicity. I have altered this organization slightly in dividing the volume into three sections, The State and Public Ceremony, The Grassroots Negotiation of Modernity, and Crossing Borders of State and Nation.

Virtually all the essays here make some reference to ethnicity. Ratana and Marston only refer to it in passing, as a way of clarifying the identity of the people they describe although it is not key to their arguments. Some contributors are clearly discussing the negotiation of ethnic identity by groups as groups: Pine in her discussion of Lahu pursuing modernity, Ferguson describing the ordination ritual as a Shan rallying call; Truitt in describing the alternative nationalism of Vietnamese in Louisiana. Just as important, at the same time, we see throughout the book *individuals* negotiating their status in relation to social categorization: categorization they themselves have made, categorization assumed by other social groups, and categorization as promoted by the state.

The State and Public Ceremony

The three chapters in this section, while quite different from each other in style and methodology, have in common a concern with public ceremony. Allison Truitt's chapter is about ceremonies surrounding myth rather than religion itself—the myth of national origins and a continuing lineage of the state. One recalls Keyes, Hardacre, and Kendall's 1994 introduction to the book, *Asian Visions of Authority:*

> The process of creating modern nation-states has, thus, entailed two rather contradictory stances toward religion. While the

modernizing stance leads to a deemphasis of ritual practices, the nation-building one leads to the promotion of selected practices and even the invention of new rites. (1994, 5)

The quote resonates with the chapters by Jane M. Ferguson and John Marston, as both are more specifically about religion. These two chapters are about ordination ritual but take different perspectives—Ferguson describes the enactment of ethnicity and "Shan nationalism" at the local level. Marston focuses on ordination rituals with and without the stamp of state approval, in the immediate aftermath of the Pol Pot period (ultimately concerned, like Truitt, with the way the state authenticates lineage). The three essays in this section are not so much concerned with rituals through which the state functions, like the theater of elections, or judicial procedure, or state ceremony, and are not concerned with the kind of rituals aimed at accentuating state loyalty, such as that written by Bowie (1997). The section concerns rather the state's controlling or supervisory role in public ceremony—to varying degrees "religious" and to varying degrees contested—as it may articulate with and affect historical change.

Allison Truitt's chapter makes an interesting shift on a theme that has become core to the discipline of anthropology, the use of myth and ritual in the construction of national identity; in this case she is concerned more specifically with the state, and how the mythology surrounding it projects its continuity into the past. In "The Tenth Day of March and Contingent Lineages of Vietnamese Statehood," she explores the continuing significance of the Hung Kings' Death Anniversary, a holiday based on myths of the pre-Chinese origins of Vietnamese identity. Her chapter is about how this seemingly royalist holiday, based on the idea of ancient royal lineage, has been made by the government headed by a communist party to figure in the modern construction of Vietnamese state identity alongside narratives of revolutionary struggle for independence. She tracks the historical ups and downs of the celebration and how it inscribes different meanings in the north and south of Vietnam, as well as in Vietnamese diasporic communities in the United States, where it has come to be associated with opposition to the current Vietnamese government.

Truitt describes rituals of national and state identity with reference to what is unquestionably a sovereign nation—however complicated matters become as the ritual extends to diasporic communities. Jane M. Ferguson, in contrast, describes rituals of national identity among minorities struggling to achieve sovereignty, in her chapter, "Rock Your Religion: Shan Buddhist Ritual and Stage-Show Revelry in a Contested Zone at the Thai-Burma Border." In classic anthropological mode, Ferguson—like Keyes in his 1986 article about novice ordination in northern Thailand—chronicles in detail a novice initiation and the accompanying celebrations in a village on the Thai-Burmese border. Going beyond the classic mode, she situates her description in the context of insurgency and the role of border populations with respect to "Thai state surveillance and ethnic pluralism within Thai national-sanctioned narratives of ethnicity," a context in which ritual becomes carnivalized in ways that throw into relief larger social relations.

The Buddhist ordination ceremony in a highly politicized context is, likewise, the topic of John Marston's chapter, although in a markedly different socio-historical context. In "Reestablishing the Cambodian Monkhood," he investigates the ways monastic lineage in Cambodia was re-created in the immediate aftermath of the Pol Pot period. The chapter describes ordinations found at the grassroots level that characterized the initial revival of Buddhism and the politics surrounding the process whereby these practices gave way to a single "official" ordination in September of 1979. At this time a group of Theravada monks were brought from Vietnam to perform what was conceived of as a charter ritual of the new state. This was intended as an affirmation of sovereignty but has nevertheless over the years called attention to the degree to which, at this moment of historical transition, Cambodian sovereignty was ambiguous and subject to considerations of political power.

The Grassroots Negotiation of Modernity

If the chapters throughout this volume deal with local people coping with authority and social change, it is perhaps the three chapters in this section, all about Thailand, which most explicitly show grassroots populations confronting different aspects of what has been called modernity. Ratana

Tosakul describes how farmers in northeastern Thailand act rationally in response to the rise of NGO-inspired movements, which, at first glance, seem to be in opposition to "state-led capitalism"—what she calls in her title an "alterity to modernity." In very different ways, Judith M. S. Pine and Pinkaew Laungaramsri deal with the ways in which ethnic categories are negotiated in Thailand. Pine offers a historically framed description of how an ethnic group, the Lahu, reach their own definitions of modernity and how their ways of fitting into it may differ from that of state ideology. Pinkaew, evoking a much darker side of modernity, treats the complexities of Thai categories of citizenship in the very practical terms of identity cards.

"Alterity to Modernity: Village-Based Self-Sufficient Farm Production in Northeastern Thailand," by Ratana Tosakul, details some of the effects of the arrival of "modern" institutions in a village in northeastern Thailand. While modernity in this context is closely linked to the penetration of capitalist systems, it also results in a counter, NGO-influenced movement focused on the idea of promoting the "sufficiency" economy—an idea which has come to be part of the Thai national discourse on economic development options. Ratana considers the implications of the discourse, and its successes and failures in practice—including the question of the degree to which it, too, has been incorporated into the larger capitalist system.

Judith M. S. Pine, in "Christianity, Modernity, and Creativity: The Construction of a Lahu Baptist Identity," is concerned with ways modernity figures in ethnic *identity*. She studies the inherent ambiguities in the formulation of an identity that is at once "modern" and Lahu, an identity that is closely associated with the historic role of religion: Protestantism as it came to represent a forward-looking, linear approach to change and the role of the school; Lahu supporting their children attending Thai state schools, but also the use of more Lahu-oriented Baptist Sunday schools. She postulates a kind of hybridity along the traditional/modern dichotomy—one that allows Lahu to exercise creativity in working out new identities.

Pinkaew Laungaramsri's chapter, "Contested Citizenship: Cards, Colors, and the Culture of Identification," takes theories of state surveillance in a new direction in her original and far-reaching study of identity cards in Thailand. She shows elegantly the details of one way a state inscribes categories by use of identity cards, but a practice very much in keeping with the surveillance techniques of the modern state, which nevertheless has specifically Thai elements and generates its own peculiar practices of negotiation at the grassroots level. After giving a brief history of identity cards, she delves into the very real complexities of the Thai system for persons of ambiguous citizenship, most clearly exemplified by members of a number of groups living near the borders of Thailand.

Crossing Borders of State and Nation

The last section focuses on an issue discussed above, the problematic of populations crossing state-defined borders, an increasingly conspicuous state of affairs as mobility becomes seemingly more natural (in correspondence to more global economic integration and communication), even as, borders come to be more rigidly defined. Though studies of border-crossing communities fall naturally into the larger field of ethnic studies, they have their own dynamic, colored by varying degrees of unity among immigrant communities, the range of motivations prompting their migration, and the peculiarities of their relationships to two states. Duong Bich Hahn's chapter describes Vietnamese immigrants to Laos.

The remaining two chapters study immigrant populations in Thailand. Suchada Thaweesit looks at a group that is particularly vulnerable in Thai society, the stateless Lao population in northeastern Thailand. In contrast, Suriya Smutkupt and Pattana Kitiarsa write about the more privileged population of Western men who settle in Thailand after marrying Thai women, whose situation can nevertheless be extremely complicated. These three chapters are based on stories of individuals negotiating their status with the residents of the new country (including those they marry) and with the state.

Suchada Thaweesit's chapter, "Narrating Legitimacy, Narrating Agencies: Citizenship Negotiations among Displaced Lao in Northeastern Thailand," overlaps to a degree with the concerns of Pinkaew's chapter but approaches these issues not so much from the perspective of the state's technologies of inscription as from that of the experience of people struggling with the status of "statelessness." She discusses the experiences of one group of people, displaced Lao in northeastern Thailand, documenting in great detail the experience of "suspended citizenship" and the strategies adopted by individuals in this situation. The chapter explores the ironies connected by the fact that many northeastern Thai are in fact ethnically "Lao," and that ethnicity easily blurs the distinction that the states in question seek to clearly separate.

Duong Bich Hanh, in "Temporary Lives, Eternal Dreams: Experiences of Viet Labor Migrants in Savannakhet, Laos," describes, somewhat more positively, the position of Vietnamese immigrants in Laos. These communities again divide according to their relationship to the state—the Viet Kieu, who have citizenship or permanent residency, and the Viet Lieu, who have come recently with passes that allow them to remain for thirty days (but who often overstay). Duong's research, focused on Vietnamese in residence in Savannakhet, provides an overview of the kinds of immigrants, the work they pursue, their motivations for coming, and their social networks. She shows how agreements between the two governments, as well as improvements in transportation and communication, have facilitated this process.

A very different category of immigrants are the European and American men who marry northeastern Thai woman and take up residence with them in the women's home districts: the topic of Suriya Smutkupt and Pattana Kitiarsa's chapter, "Cross-Border Hypergamy and Gendered Agency: *Farang* Husbands and Isan Wives on the Global Cultural Stage." It is worth noting that, by many definitions, these men would not constitute an ethnic group. They do not, for instance, meet Keyes's criteria of a group with a shared sense of descent. Their situation may nevertheless shed light on the growing phenomenon of flexible citizenship. Building on the research of other Thai scholars focused more exclusively on the wives and the effects of the cross-national marriages on village economy, Suriya and Pattana approach the phenomenon from a more global perspective. They draw heavily on interviews with the *farang* men (previously unstudied) as well as the Thai wives, using their personal narratives to convey a complex sense of the on-the-ground realities for the persons involved. They conclude finally that the marriages are "deeply rooted in the unequal and stereotyped relationship of power across global cultural economies."

Notes

1. Personal communication, June 2010.

2. The keynote address for the conference drew on ideas that would later be published in his 2009 book, *The Art of Not Being Governed: An Anarchist History of Upland Southeast Asia*.

3. The subject of the book is the capacity of actual government—of state in its most commonplace sense—although he acknowledges that the problematic he explores of states acting on what they govern in such a way as to make it more easily accessible and manageable can also be found in the power extended by corporations.

References

Andaya, Leonard. 2008. *Leaves of the Same Tree: Trade and Ethnicity in the Straits of Melaka*. Honolulu: University of Hawaii Press.

Appadurai, Arjun. 2001. "Grassroots Globalization and the Research Imagination." In *Globalization*, edited by Arjun Appadurai, 1–21. Durham; London: Duke University Press.

Bowie, Katherine. 1997. *Rituals of National Loyalty*. New York: Columbia University Press.

Geertz, Clifford. 1980. *Negara: The Theatre State in Nineteenth-Century Bali*. Princeton, NJ: Princeton University Press.

Junker, Laura Lee. 1999. *Raiding, Trading, and Feasting: The Political Economy of Philippine Chiefdoms*. Honolulu: University of Hawaii Press.

Keyes, Charles F. 1976. "Toward a New Formulation of the Concept of Ethnic Group." *Ethnicity* 3: 202–13.

———. 1981. "The Dialectics of Ethnic Change." In *Ethnic Change*, edited by Charles F. Keyes, 6–30. Seattle: University of Washington Press.

———. 1986. "Ambiguous Gender: Male Initiation in a Buddhist Society." In *Religion and Gender: Essays on the Complexity of Symbols*, edited by Caroline Bynum, Stevan Harrell, and Paula Richman, 66–96. Boston: Beacon Press.

———. 1987a. "Tribal Peoples and the Nation-State in Mainland Southeast Asia." In *Southeast Asian Tribal Groups and Minorities: Prospects for the Eighties and*

Beyond. Proceedings of a conference co-sponsored by Cultural Survival, Inc. and the Department of Anthropology, Harvard University. Cambridge, MA: Cultural Survival, Inc.

———. 1987b. *Thailand: Buddhist Kingdom as Modern Nation-State.* Boulder and London: Westview Press.

———. 1997. "Ethnic Groups, Ethnicity." In *The Blackwell Dictionary of Anthropology*, edited by Thomas J. Barfield. Oxford: Basil Blackwell.

———. 2002a. "'The Peoples of Asia'—Science and Politics in the Classification of Ethnic Groups in Thailand, China and Vietnam." *Journal of Asian Studies* 61: 1163–203.

———. 2002b. "Weber and Anthropology." *Annual Reviews in Anthropology* 31: 233–55.

———. 2007. "Remembering Anthropology at University of Washington." Talk given at University of Washington, May 16.

Keyes, Charles F., Laurel Kendall, and Helen Hardacre. 1994. "Contested Visions of Community in East and Southeast Asia." In *Asian Visions of Authority: Religion and the Modern States of East and Southeast Asia*, 1–16. Honolulu: University of Hawaii Press.

Migdal, Joel S. 1988. *Strong Societies and Weak States: State-Society Relations and State Capabilities in the Third World.* Princeton, NJ: Princeton University Press.

Scott, James C. 1985. *Weapons of the Weak: Everyday Forms of Peasant Resistance.* New Haven: Yale University Press.

———. 1998. *Seeing Like a State: How Certain Schemes to Improve the Human Condition Have Failed.* New Haven: Yale University Press.

———. 2009. *The Art of Not Being Governed: An Anarchist History of Upland Southeast Asia.* New Haven: Yale University Press.

Sharma, Aradhana, and Akhil Gupta. 2006. "Introduction: Rethinking Theories of the State in an Age of Globalization." In *The Anthropology of the State: A Reader*, 1–41. Blackwell.

Tambiah, Stanley J. 1976. *World Conqueror and World Renouncer: A Study of Buddhism and Polity in Thailand against a Historical Background.* Cambridge: Cambridge University Press.

Thongchai Winichakul. 1994. *Siam Mapped: A History of the Geo-Body of a Nation.* Honolulu: University of Hawaii Press.

Willlams, Brackette F. 1989. "A Class Act: Anthropology and the Race to Nation Across Ethnic Terrain." *Annual Review of Anthropology* 18: 401–44.

Wolters, O. W. 1982. *History, Culture, and Region in Southeast Asian Perspectives.* Singapore: Institute for Southeast Asian Studies.

THE STATE AND PUBLIC CEREMONY

THE TENTH DAY OF MARCH AND CONTINGENT LINEAGES OF VIETNAMESE STATEHOOD

Allison Truitt

In March 2007, the Vietnamese National Assembly approved a resolution to declare the Hung Kings' Death Anniversary (*Giỗ Tổ Hùng Vương*) an official state holiday. Workers would receive an additional paid holiday and "the entire nation would have a day to turn together towards history and experience the sacred essence of life" (Tuổi Trẻ 2007e). Popularly depicted as the founding dynasty of Vietnam, the legendary kings were mediators of a national patrimony. The celebration of their anniversary on March 10, by reckoning of the lunar calendar, has been called the most important anniversary for Vietnamese people (Trương Thìn 2007, 151).

The decision to recognize the anniversary as a state holiday was more than a move to add one more official holiday. It was also part of a larger campaign to rewrite the national script. As the "fatherland anniversary" (*ngày giỗ tổ quốc*), the legend of the Hung kings provided an alternative origin myth of Vietnamese statehood to Ho Chi Minh's declaration of independence in 1945. Unlike holidays that commemorated the revolution and national independence, the Hung Kings' Death Anniversary promoted genealogical continuity by addressing all Vietnamese people, including those who lived outside the state's territorial borders. As popular verse declared, "Remember the tenth day of March and return home." Despite the appeals to a common prehistoric past, the staging of the Hung Kings' Death Anniversary exposed the contingencies of Vietnamese statehood. In so doing, the anniversary served as a peculiarly appropriate national script for modern Vietnamese nationhood.

Modern Nation-States in Southeast Asia

States in Southeast Asia have sought to contain diverse groups of people under the rubric of nationalism and popular sovereignty. In his work on nationhood in Southeast Asia, Charles F. Keyes (2002, 1174) convincingly argues that ethnic groups did not precede the modern nation-state; rather, the classification of peoples into discrete groups is better understood as a technology of modern state power. Both modern state power and ethnic classification in Southeast Asia are generated through invocations of pre-modern aesthetics (Keyes, Hardacre, and Kendall 1994; Tanabe and Keyes 2002). Political leaders in Thailand have drawn on Buddhist metaphors, idioms, and practices to domesticate their power, status, and privilege. Leaders in Vietnam, in contrast, domesticate ethnic diversity by reference to a common origin in which different groups once shared similarities that were "a product of a unique national unification of Vietnam that began in the prehistoric period" (2002, 1186). This form of national patrimony fused statecraft with the moral legitimacy of ancestor worship. Yet, even as state officials detach events from their particular localities and circumstances thereby promoting a sense of social memory and peoplehood that is unitary, once the meanings and even sentiments attributed to these events are in circulation, they may be appropriated by others. Thus, the very project of national identity and statecraft can never be contained and the making and remaking of political subjectivity never completed.

In Vietnam, the predicament of nationhood and political subjectivity has been compounded by the legacies of the country's post–World War II territorial division and subsequent formation of diasporic communities. Members of these communities identify themselves as Vietnamese in ways that problematize the official national ideology that "all the peoples of Vietnam are united within the boundaries of the country" (Keyes 2002, 1190). It is in this appeal to a transnational Vietnamese identity that we may situate the Socialist Republic of Vietnam's renewed interest in the Hung Kings' Death Anniversary. In the 1990s, the state's sponsorship of the festival showcased its efforts "to re-integrate itself with the pre-revolutionary past," by elevating legendary kings to their prominence in social and ritual life (Malarney 2007, 540). Even in distant lands, Vietnamese communities gather to celebrate the anniversary on March 10, thus paying tribute to the mythic origins that tie them to the homeland. The anniversary offered a form of national mediation that addressed Vietnamese subjects both within and beyond the territorial state.

The concept of lineage or collective membership is intrinsic to the understanding of personhood in Vietnam. I use the term "lineage," in the anthropological sense of descent, but also in terms of fashioning a self-conscious historical subject. People are expected to maintain proper relations both within their household and in society at large, an expectation that is extended to the spirits of deceased ancestors. Like classifications of peoples, the historical continuity of Vietnamese statehood has been framed in terms of unity rather than division or disruption, a unity that is often conceived in terms of lineage. I contrast the Socialist Republic of Vietnam's renewed interest in the Hung Kings' Death Anniversary with an alternative vision associated with Vietnam's diaspora. By analyzing these stagings in terms of their physical location, the symbols of political authority, and the deployment of culturally specific narratives of heroism, I demonstrate how even the commemoration of ancient kings makes visible the multiple and contingent lineages of Vietnamese nationhood. In so doing, I argue that the lineage of Vietnamese statehood is neither unified nor singular, but emergent in the movements of history and the politics of the present. Summoning the Hung kings makes visible these contingent lineages.

Genealogies of the Vietnamese State

The Hung kings are a potent source of national mediation. They are personalized as a named dynasty of eighteen kings. The dynasty of kings is identified with the Hồng Bàng period (2879–258 BCE), and grounded in the kingdom of Văn Lang located in what is today Vĩnh Phúc and

Phú Thọ in northern Vietnam. The site was later consecrated by kings who performed rites in Phú Thọ. Today, the legacy of the Hung kings is associated with a popular legend of the origins of two special rice cakes: *bánh chưng*, a cake made from sticky rice with a pork and mung bean filling, and *bánh dầy*, a round white cake made from sticky rice. Humble in their ingredients, the two cakes were created by the son of a Hung king as symbols of the earth and sky, respectively.

The Hung kings as mediators of national sovereignty emerged in the *Đại Việt sử ký toàn thư* chronicle compiled in 1479. By initiating his official history with the Hồng Bàng dynasty, Ngô Sĩ Liên emphasized the importance of Confucian ethics, particularly the ruler-subject relationship, as a strategy to assert the autonomy of Vietnam (Yu Insun 2006, 65). By contrast, an earlier chronicle, Lê Văn Hưu's *Đại Việt Sử ký*, inaugurated the kingdom with Triệu Đà's reign in the late third century BCE. The belated appearance of the Hung kings in chronicling the state underscores how political interests motivate genealogical records.

In the early twentieth century, the Hung kings were popularized through the writings of Tran Trong Kim and Tran Huy Lieu. Despite their different political visions, both authors invoked the legendary Hung kings within a discourse of ancestor worship to legitimate claims of popular national sovereignty. Tran Trong Kim's "An Outline of Vietnamese History" (Jamieson 1993, 81), popularized the legends of the Hung kings, while Tran Huy Lieu (1927) conjured up the patrimony of the Hung kings only to claim that it had been lost. By invoking the ancient kings, these intellectuals reordered the meaning of the ruler-subject relationship from a ruling dynasty to a modern vision of nationhood, thereby shifting identification from provincial origins—the family and village—to the nation.[1]

Later, after the 1945 August Revolution, the Hung kings were also appropriated by the provisional government. Vice President Huynh Thuc Khanh made offerings to the Hung kings in 1946 (Malarney 2007, 533). By 1958, the Democratic Republic of Vietnam reordered the ritual calendar, privileging secular holidays that marked the birth of the modern nation (Malarney 2007, 533). While this move did not eliminate the role of the Hung kings in mediating Vietnamese nationalism, it did shift the dynamics of power from the patriarchal clan to that of science and the production of knowledge. Scholarly efforts in Vietnam subsequently attempted to reconstruct the existence of Văn Lang state in order to establish northern Vietnam as an early center of civilization independent from China (Han 2004; Taylor 1983). The existence of the Văn Lang state was no longer recreated through the performance of ancestral rites but through the techniques of codifying cultural heritage and social memory through rational knowledge.

Contemporary scholars remain divided on the place of the Hung kings. Some scholars argue that the *Hùng Vương* is best understood as a historical period associated with the Bronze Age, rather than a specific dynasty like the Lý or Trần dynasties (Lê-Kim Ngân 1974, 33). Other scholars prefer *Lạc Vương* instead of *Hùng Vương*. The characters for *Lạc* and *Hùng* are easily mistaken for each other, thus sparking debate and reminding us that even visual inscriptions confound attempts to anchor understandings of the past (Taylor 1995, 5).

By the 1990s the Hung kings were once again elevated on the stage of national culture. The National Assembly debated whether their anniversary should be recognized as an official holiday but deferred the decision. Still, the considerable state funding dedicated to renovating the temple site and making infrastructure improvements demonstrated how claims of ancestry and heritage were increasingly linked to processes of commoditization (Malarney 2007, 533).

The state's investment in the Hung Kings' Temple can be interpreted as a strategy of public control in the face of the commodification of national identity. Today, the Hung kings are again popular subjects for national histories and video productions. Their place has been codified within the national curriculum. Even cartoon series depicting national history for popular consumption pay tribute to the Hung kings for establishing a distinctly Vietnamese national culture.[2] It is also a strategy of harnessing the moral legitimacy of ancestor worship for remaking its own claims of legitimacy.

From Kings to Ancestors

The Hung kings are transformed from the first sovereigns of the Vietnamese state into the ancestors of the Vietnamese people through the legend of *Lạc Long Quân* and *Âu Cơ*. Some versions of the legend claim *Lạc Long Quân* was the son of Kinh Dương Vương, the leader of *Xích Quỷ*, a principality governed by Chinese officials. More fantastical versions mythologize the union of *Lạc Long Quân*, a dragon lord, and *Âu Cơ*, a fairy princess. In this mythological version, *Âu Cơ* gives birth to a sack of one hundred eggs from which sprang as many children. Most versions claim that *Lạc Long Quân* longed to return to his native land and so informed *Âu Cơ* that fifty children would follow the father to the sea, and fifty children would follow the mother to the mountains. The story hinges on *Lạc Long Quân's* promise that should they ever met with difficulties, each would come to the aid of the other. The separation of *Âu Cơ* and *Lạc Long Quân* initiated a metaphoric division of the social landscape drawing on what Thien Do (2003, 5) has called the "metaphoric landscape" of hills and streams that unites the imagined and the historical embodied by *tổ quốc*, or "ancestral land."[3] Out of this division, the eldest son, *Hùng Vương*, established the first Vietnamese state.

This origin myth for Vietnamese peoplehood is reaffirmed in colloquial sayings of national identity. People often refer to the undivided nation by the term *con rồng cháu tiên*, "children of the dragon, descendants of the phoenix." As people invoke the expression, they rejuvenate a sense of sentimentality and collective identity based on mythic origins. Yet, most people invoke the phrase to express solidarity rather than difference, unity rather than division. Foreign scholars have argued that the term is productive in other ways as well. Charles Keyes (1977, 2) argued that the legend depicted the symbiotic relationship between people in the lowlands who organized into a state, and others living in the uplands. Other scholars interpreted the legend in terms of a malleable gender system: *Âu Cơ's* return to the mountains with fifty children served to legitimate a bilateral family system in which women enjoyed a relatively high status (Taylor 1983, 13).

In spite of the division, most people emphasize unity by the cultural term, *đồng bào* (literally, "same sack" or "of the same womb"). The term, *đồng bào*, often translated as "compatriot," circulated in the nineteenth century and was invoked by twentieth-century Vietnamese intellectuals harnessing national consciousness to family consciousness. In contrast to *dân tộc*, or "ethnicity," the term *đồng bào* casts a moral net of obligation and care that spans difference. The extent to which ancestral rites actually support a national cult remains questionable. On the one hand, the household remains a powerful metaphor for maintaining proper relations: "the image of the altar of the family ancestors easily transformed itself into the image of the altar of the founders of the nation" (Woodside 1971, 490). More recent studies (Kwon 2006; Malarney 2001) of ritual practice in postwar Vietnam emphasize the structural contradictions between the localized and personalized ancestral rites and state-sponsored efforts to memorialize the dead. By locating ancestors within specific lineages, these rituals work against the models of self-sacrifice commemorated by the Vietnamese state. Does then the term *đồng bào*, by proposing an identity prior to division and dispersal, offer a different model of belonging, one that both acknowledges and reaffirms that difference and division is central to the project of national identification?

The term *đồng bào* is usually accompanied by an attribute of social difference or geographical distance, such as *đồng bào vùng rét* (people of impoverished areas), *đồng bào dân tộc miền núi* (highland people), or *đồng bào dân tộc thiểu số* (ethnic minorities). Vietnamese people who live abroad are also marked by the term, *kiều bào*. Unlike the term, *Việt kiều*, which carries a meaning of sojourning or temporary residence, *kiều bào* marks an identity based on descent even though it still carries the idea of a subject position outside of, or external to, the state. As the Vietnamese state renovates its own scripts—as foreign aggression yields to global integration—the festival provides an occasion by which to solicit people abroad to return their homeland bringing their talents and resources. The Hung Kings' Death Anniversary provides a spectacle of popular culture to solicit those people who are not "of the state" but "of the womb" (*đồng bào*). Herein lies the productiveness of the Hung Kings' Death Anniversary. It is a tale of statehood, but a tale of statehood initiated by division, separation, and dispersal.

A National Holiday

In the days leading up to the official celebration of the Hung Kings' Death Anniversary in 2007, cultural commentators and historians provided competing rationales for the official holiday (Tuổi Trẻ 2007a). Some accounts focused on the distant past, framing the anniversary in terms of historical continuity. During the Minh period people honored the Hung kings in village temples and shrines. Lê Thánh Tông (1442–97) recognized the anniversary as a national holiday and established its date as the tenth day of the third lunar month during the Nguyen dynasty. Other accounts framed the importance within revolutionary terms. Some commentators recalled that in 1946, Ho Chi Minh visited the Hung Temple and declared the anniversary a national holiday so that people could remember the contributions of past heroes. Others claimed he visited following the battle of Dien Bien Phu in 1954 (Tuổi Trẻ 2007d). Some officials argued that another day of rest was now warranted in order to boost consumption and promote tourism (Tuổi Trẻ 2007d). A few detractors, however, worried that recognizing the anniversary as an official state holiday risked codifying "legends" (*truyền thuyết*) into law.

The Hung Kings' Death Anniversary appeared to transcend revolutionary narratives even as its celebration commodified a distinctive national heritage. Nevertheless, its celebration was still authorized within the moral framework of the revolution. Ho Chi Minh's quotation, "The Hung kings made contributions to the country. Our people young and old together should preserve our country!" (*Các vua Hùng đã có công dựng nước. Bác cháu ta phải cùng nhau giữ nước!*) appeared printed in newspaper articles and school textbooks and was even engraved on a bronze stele-like tablet at the front of the Hung Temple in Ho Chi Minh City. Thus, the commemoration of the Hung kings was framed by the revolution even in a historical moment of increased global integration and economic expansion.

By invoking the Hung kings, Vietnamese statecraft is transformed into a transnational project with commemorations carried out in multiple locations, including Ho Chi Minh City and Washington DC. By invoking the Hung kings as ancestors to all Vietnamese peoples, the Socialist Republic of Vietnam appears to construct a transnational Vietnamese identity, one that transcends political divisions and territorial borders. Does then the legacy of the Hung kings transcend particular lineages of statehood? By way of addressing this question, I consider how the anniversary has been celebrated from the perspective of South Vietnam (1954–75) and its diaspora.

A View from the South

On April 26, 2007, celebrations of the Hung Kings' Death Anniversary were organized in almost fourteen hundred locations (Tuổi Trẻ 2007e). While the prime minister visited the Hung Temple in Phú Thọ, city officials in Ho Chi Minh City (formerly known as Saigon) staged the festival at the Hung Temple in the Botanical Gardens. The temple was the primary stage for officials and included representatives from the City Party Committee, the People's Committee, and the Fatherland Front. Other locations competed for audiences, especially Suoi Tien Amusement Park,[4] which boasted a recently constructed Hung Temple and sponsored a spectacular show honoring the kings.

The temple at the Botanical Gardens was not always dedicated exclusively to the Hung Kings. Built in 1926, the temple was designed by French architects and named the "Temple of Memory," to honor the ancestors of the Vietnamese, which included the Hung Kings as well as Confucius, Trần Hưng Đạo, and Lê Văn Duyệt.[5] The architectural motifs of the temple reflected the associationist ideology of the 1920s, which promoted greater Vietnamese participation in colonial affairs to legitimate the regime. The Temple of Memory thus provided a visual landmark to identify the ancestry of the Vietnamese people in distinctly Asian terms in contrast to earlier colonial efforts to assimilate colonial subjects. While dedicated to memory, the temple was also a reminder that "tradition" was in the service of modernity (Wright 1989).

Tradition in the service of modernity was not only a colonial project. The Republic of Vietnam drew on the signs of national patrimony and historical continuity to legitimate its claims to sovereignty. In the Republic of Vietnam, the Hung Kings' Death Anniversary was a national holiday in which all civil servants and employees enjoyed a day off. The

Hung kings were not relegated to the distant past but invoked as part of the visual culture of the nation. The kings were featured on a series of postage stamps. They were not, however, included in the 1966 series of currency that featured prominent historical figures including Lê Văn Duyệt and Trần Hưng Đạo. The commemoration of the Hung kings then dramatized the regime's claim of continuity with its dynastic past, in contrast to North Vietnam where officials emphasized overcoming that past to create a revolutionary society.

After 1975, the Hanoi-led regime consolidated the repertoire of national signs. The capital of Saigon was renamed Ho Chi Minh City and the Temple of Memory was rededicated as the Hung Temple to eliminate alternative and dangerously foreign origins. The meaning of the temple also changed as the site served as an extension of the Museum of History. On display in the temple were the symbols of *đất nước*, or national substance: two pots, one containing *đất* (soil) and the other *nước* (water) from Phú Thọ, as well as two bronze drums enclosed in glass display cases. Today visitors to the temple can still see dioramas of the Hung Temple in Phú Thọ as well as two bronze drums on display.

The Hung Temple, unlike other sites in Ho Chi Minh City, has not become a site of popular religion. People lit incense as a sign of respect to the kings, but they did not present offerings or solicit the approval of the kings to grant their prayers. Unlike in temples around the city, people did not attempt to personalize their relations with the kings. Visitors behaved in the temple much as they did in the museum, respectfully reading the captions on the wall, and nodding appropriately in front of the bronze drums. The absence of more elaborate prayers was not due to lack of interest but rather to the state's own surveillance. On a visit to the temple in 2007, one of the guards explained how they prohibited people from carrying out other forms of worship classified as "superstitious." While the guard invited visitors to the temple to light incense, they did not allow them to toss coins or sticks, practices used to determine whether spirits would fulfill a request. Yet, the guards themselves were still invested in other rites. In the corner of the temple, I noticed a small altar to the gods of land and wealth with offerings of fresh fruit and a small packet of spirit money.

Contingent Lineages

In the Socialist Republic of Vietnam, the Hung kings have been ritually resurrected into "exceptional dead," (Malarney 2007) worthy of emulation, and venerated as the ancestors of all Vietnamese people. The annual celebration of the *Hùng Vương* kings invokes an ancestral sovereignty not divided by religious differences or political affiliation or provincial origins. Yet, rituals that construct historical continuity also produce the specter of ghosts—the unassimilated, the abject, and the excluded. What then does the tenth day of March signify for Vietnamese diasporic communities? How do these communities resolve the predicaments of ancestral sovereignty and peoplehood?

The Hung Kings' Death Anniversary, for both the Socialist Republic and its diaspora, is a political project, a "calculated and ritualized act of forgetting [that] produces a new genealogy" of the state (Rafael 2005, xvi). Like other ancestral rites, this anniversary is reckoned by the lunar calendar, usually falling in mid- to late-April. While the Hung Kings' Death Anniversary invokes the distant past, through the coincidence of the lunar and Gregorian calendars, the day falls quite close to April 30, which marks the fall of South Vietnam. The predicament for Vietnamese in the United States is "mourning the dead, remembering the missing, and considering the place of the survivors in the movement of history" (Nguyen 2006). It is this predicament that turns the legend of *Lạc Long Quân* and *Âu Cơ*, not into a celebration of strength, but an explanation for division.

The myth of *Con Rồng Cháu Tiên*, for many Vietnamese-Americans, provides a cultural idiom for expressing their moral and cultural heritage and claims of belonging to a homeland (Safran 1991; Butler 2001).[6] But the myth has also been appropriated to explain the intractable divisions between two different lineages. In an essay entitled, "Double Diaspora of Vietnamese Catholics," a college-aged woman framed the experiences of her father and uncle who were forced to flee North Vietnam in 1954, and then South Vietnam after 1975, with a reinterpretation of the myth:

> The Vietnamese fought bravely and eventually forced the barbarians out of the luminous mountains of the north. But at length, new

barbarians with strange features and exploding guns arrived by sea, in wave after wave. Again, after many hardships, the Vietnamese pushed them out. But this time the children of the dragon and the phoenix did not regain their harmony; instead they turned against each other. Thus, in victory was defeat, and harmony was broken (Nguyen 1995, 491).

In the United States, the cohesiveness of "Vietnamese" has been destabilized by intergenerational shifts and the varying degrees of identification with and relation to Vietnam as a "homeland" (Espiritu and Tran 2002). Since the initial resettlement of more than 130,000 refugees in the United States, Vietnamese-American scholars have begun to rewrite their own historical narratives. Most Vietnamese-American residents in New Orleans are no longer "refugees," but the category is still difficult to escape, especially for Vietnamese-American scholars (Trinh 2003). Moreover, the experiences of Vietnamese in the United States cannot be disentangled from the systematic exclusions of Asians within the United States' political imaginary (Lowe 1996; Nguyen 2006). The predicaments of diaspora and transnationalism are not resolved through commemoration events like the Hung Kings' Death Anniversary; rather, they are staged and celebrated.

Staging the Festival in Louisiana

The Hung Kings' Death Anniversary staged in Louisiana has not been transformed into a spectacular tourist event. In 2006 and 2007, the celebration in New Orleans did not attract large crowds. Much larger audiences attended the festivals for the lunar New Year organized on the grounds of Buddhist temples and Catholic churches. For these events, people were attracted by performances of Vietnamese singers from California and the chance to win prizes in a lucky raffle. By staging the Hung Kings' Death Anniversary, participants asserted their membership, status, and belonging in South Vietnam. The Hung Kings' Death Anniversary was an occasion for community leaders to gather and proclaim their allegiance to South Vietnam. Like festivals in

Vietnam, the organizers drew on the nation's visual symbols—offerings of *bánh chưng* and *bánh dầy*, solemn recitations of prayers by men in long mandarin robes, a procession of Vietnamese leaders and representatives from different social organizations—symbols that also appeared for celebrations of the Lunar New Year.

The Hung Kings' Death Anniversary in New Orleans is not an official holiday. However, it has in past years been included on the city's official calendar, and on one occasion, the mayor of the city even attended the event. The sponsoring organization of the event, the Vietnamese-American Community of Louisiana, was promised financing from the City Council of New Orleans to build a national temple on a plot of land in New Orleans East. The municipal government's support for the cultural lives of the Vietnamese-American community could be interpreted as an example of "cultural citizenship." This interpretation overlooks the performative dimensions of the ceremony in terms of US statecraft. Such performances still have political value in that the successes of Vietnamese and other Southeast Asian groups demonstrate how the war in Indochina was still a victory, even in defeat (Espiritu 2006).

For many Vietnamese-Americans, although by no means all, national identity is entwined with their experiences with the Republic of Vietnam (1954–75). Vietnamese-Americans draw on the symbolic inventory of the Republic of Vietnam to reclaim their inheritance. Vietnamese commercial areas in the United States are made visible by the symbol of the South Vietnamese flag, which is also raised over churches, temples, and other community organizations. These flags are often raised alongside the US flag, displaying the historical arrangements and alliances that gave shape and meaning to this particular lineage.

For almost ten years, the Hung Kings' Death Anniversary has been organized by the Vietnamese-American Community of Louisiana, a mutual assistance organization that spans religious differences and parish boundaries. In previous years, the celebration was held on an undeveloped piece of land owned by the community and earmarked as the site for a national temple on the easternmost edge of New Orleans.[7] In 2006 and 2007, following Hurricane Katrina, the celebration was organized on the other side of the Mississippi River. The first year after the storm, the celebration was held on the grounds of a Buddhist temple.

One member confided to me that he was surprised that the organizers, many who were also Buddhist, had served roasted pig on the temple grounds. In 2007, the event was held in a Catholic church.

Scholars often describe ancestor worship as place-based religion, but the mobility of the Hung Kings' Death Anniversary suggests that notions of place are not bounded geographically, but rather produced within particular social and political configurations. The event's mobility indicates the greater stability of religious identities, certainly the investments of time and resources that households dedicate to maintaining these organizations. The Hung Kings' Death Anniversary momentarily converted social space—the stage at a Buddhist temple or a Catholic church community hall—into ritual space for venerating the nation's ancestors.

In many respects, the mode of commemoration resembled how the ceremony was celebrated in Vietnam. In 2006 and 2007, a table had been set up on an elevated stage for offerings of special dishes, flowers, and incense. On each occasion, three male members of the organizing committee carried out the ancestral rite. Below the stage, another man pounded rhythmically on a large drum dedicated to this ceremony, while the men on stage recited prayers to the kings. Below the elevated stage were men dressed in military uniforms from different divisions of the army of the Republic of Vietnam. These men dressed in uniforms of South Vietnam represented the military, whose role was to protect the kingdom, thus ensuring people could prosper and culture could develop. This explanation was offered to me by the president of the community in 2006. While people who live outside Vietnam are often discursively constructed as having betrayed the country, in conversations with me, these same participants are adamant in distinguishing the nation from the state. In honoring the kings and donning their military uniforms participants reclaimed their status as Vietnamese subjects, not from the position of exteriority, but from within a zone of social life in which claims of political subjectivity could be produced. In this ritual, participants produced themselves as rightful bearers of ancestral sovereignty. As in Saigon, sovereignty was no longer vested in locality; it instead operated through the power of representation and was thus mobile and multiple.

Yet, the staging of the ceremony in Louisiana also demonstrated the diasporic community's indebtedness to foreign sources of authority. The military officers held several flags: the five-colored dynastic flag associated with Vietnamese kings, the yellow flag with three horizontal red strips representing the Republic of Vietnam, and the US flag. This display demonstrated the complex staging of South Vietnamese identity, which must continually reproduce its allegiance to the United States. The event was suffused with self-conscious awareness, evident in both the display of the military guard as well as the chosen guests. The event included honored guests, including city officials and former army officers. On both occasions, the invited guests also offered incense to the Hung kings.

The deliberately self-conscious invocation of South Vietnam does not appeal to everyone who claims Vietnamese as part of their selfhood. It is not simply that kingship is uneasily reconciled with other practices of political authority, although this may be one reason that the ceremony does not draw the same crowds as religious events and celebrations such as the mid-autumn festival. Still, the sponsorship of the Hung Kings' Death Anniversary offers a staging for a unified national identity that might otherwise splinter into religious and regional differences among Vietnamese-Americans. Through the invocation of cultural signs of multiple regimes—military uniforms, mandarin robes, ancestral offerings to the founding kings—the Vietnamese-American community of Louisiana claimed its place as rightful descendants within the historical continuity of the Vietnamese state.

In 2007, the day for celebrating the Hung Kings' Death Anniversary fell on April 26. Because the day fell so close to April 30, the organizing committee combined the two anniversaries. In the morning, the ceremony for honoring the Hung kings was staged in the community hall, and celebrations to mark April 30 were planned for that afternoon. On the walls of the church were laminated photos of the 1954 land reform, which prompted nearly eight hundred thousand Catholics to move from North Vietnam to the South. Behind the raised stage was a large flag of South Vietnam. The president of the community passed out fliers with a brief history of "Vietnam's National Day" in English. The coincidence of these two anniversaries signaled that Vietnamese subjectivity is not easily reconciled by traditionalism. The recent past figured by the commemoration of April 30 is simply too close to be forgotten. By first venerating the Hung kings and then marking April 30, the community of Vietnamese gathered for the celebration marked their irreconcilable lineage of Vietnamese statehood.

Of Wombs and War

Ancestral spirits are powerful material for displaying the politics of the present. In this chapter, I sought to demonstrate the various modes for appropriating the legacy of the Hung kings. From nationalist discourses in Saigon, to the recreation of the Hung Temple in an amusement park in Ho Chi Minh City, to the festival held in a Catholic church in Louisiana, the Hung kings offer potent cultural material for invoking Vietnamese subjectivity. While the commemoration of the kings as ancestors is a project of statecraft—basing its claims of sovereignty in the display of historical continuity and genealogical identity—I have argued that the origins of peoplehood cannot be reduced to the claims of statehood. Legend tells us that statehood was inaugurated only after division and dispersal. The claim to a primordial and unitary identity expressed by đồng bào is thus available to subjects within and outside the territorial borders of the Socialist Republic of Vietnam.

The commemoration is intended to produce a collective national subject, one "of the womb." The promise of a unitary national subject was, and continues to be, split by the contingent lineages of Vietnamese statehood. In North Vietnam, state officials privileged the use of rationalized and secularized knowledge to overcome the past; in South Vietnam, officials promoted a sense of national consciousness in a regime otherwise beholden to foreign sources of power. Today, there are still limits to the reconciliation of postcolonial divisions. These limits, I argued, are visible in the staging of the commemoration. By examining how the ancestral rites are staged, we may understand how the event reinscribes, rather than transcends, the divisions of Vietnamese modernity. Government officials in the Socialist Republic of Vietnam perform ancestral rites to the kings in a context of increasing global integration, but the commemoration is still framed by the words of Ho Chi Minh. In Louisiana, Vietnamese community leaders reinstall the South Vietnam regime, drawing attention to the politics of difference, division, and dispersal that have underwritten Vietnamese statecraft (Tanabe and Keyes 2002, 23–24).

I have sought to demonstrate how the Hung Kings' Death Anniversary demonstrates the power of ritual to make and remake political subjects. Lineages of Vietnamese statehood are not uninterrupted lines of descent, but contingent on the forces of history and the politics of the present. In 2007, the Hung Kings' Death Anniversary was declared an official paid holiday in Vietnam. All Vietnamese people would have the opportunity to look back in history and experience the sacred life stream of the nation. In Louisiana, the commemoration was followed by an act of mourning. As people looked back in history, they were reminded of the ruptures and discontinuities that defy the promise made by *Lạc Long Quân* to *Âu Cơ*.

Notes

1. A similar argument is made in studies of state-sponsored commemoration in Europe following World War I. Britain and France sought to replace particularistic ties to family with ties to the nation through tombs honoring unknown soldiers (Anderson 1998).

2. The first volume in *Theo dòng Lịch Sử Việt Nam* published by Nhà Xuất Bản Giáo Dục, begins with "Legends of the Hồng Bàng dynasty." Another series, *Lịch sử Việt Nam bằng tranh*, published by Nhà Xuất Bản Trẻ, includes three volumes of the "Legends of the Hung Kings," and includes photos of the Hung Temple and Gate in Phú Thọ as well as depictions of traditional festivals.

3. A popular poem invokes the metaphorical landscape of hills and streams and calls for people to return to their origins through such acts of remembrance. In the poem below, the named Hung kings give way to the claim of ancestral sovereignty, whose worship domesticates contemporary state power:

Dù ai đi ngược về suôi	Whoever travels far and wide,
Nhớ ngày Giỗ Tổ mồng mười tháng ba	Remember the Ancestors on the tenth day of March
Dù ai buôn bán gần xa	
Nhớ ngày Giỗ Tổ tháng ba thì về	Whoever trades near or far, Remember the ancestors in March, and return home.

4. In 2007, the amusement park Suối Tiên invested 4 billion dong (approximately US$260,000) in building a Hung temple and a stage for performances (*Tuổi Trẻ* 2007b). The performance included one thousand performers and representatives from twenty-five ethnic groups. Tickets were discounted 50 percent in anticipation of drawing crowds because of the holiday.

5. Lê Văn Duyệt is an example of a historical figure whose contributions were reevaluated after 1975. A diplomatic liaison between the Nguyen rules and the French, he was also an advocate for Catholic missionaries.

6. One Vietnamese-American described her heritage through the mythic union: "The dragon and fairy have been national symbols in Vietnam for thousands of years. The dragon represents a grand, imperious force, undefeatable perseverance, and ingenious talent. The fairy represents grace, beauty, freshness, delicacy, gentleness and vivaciousness. Those two beings symbolize a distinctive Vietnamese philosophy—to live powerfully and gracefully"(Chan 2006, 150).

7. Only a sign marks its use for a national temple to Vietnam's ancestors. In April 2006, many businesses in New Orleans East, including the Kim-Anh reception hall, were still closed. That project has been indefinitely postponed as people attend to more immediate needs—rebuilding their homes, businesses, and regular places of worship after the flooding from Hurricane Katrina.

References

Anderson, Benedict. 1998. "Replica, Aura, and Late Nationalist Imaginings." In *Spectre of Comparisons: Nationalism, Southeast Asia, and the World*, 46–57. London and New York: Verso.

DiGregario, Michael, and Oscar Salemink. 2007. "Living with the Dead: The Politics of Ritual and Remembrance in Contemporary Vietnam." *Journal of Southeast Asian Studies* 38 (3): 433–40.

Do, Thien. 2003. *Vietnamese Supernaturalism: Views from the Southern Region*. London and New York: RoutledgeCurzon.

Espiritu, Yen Le. 2006. "The We-Win-Even-When-We-Lose Syndrome: U.S. Press Coverage of the 25th Anniversary of the 'Fall of Saigon.'" *American Quarterly*: 329–52.

Espiritu, Yen Le, and Tran Thom. 2002. "'Viet Nam, Nuoc Toi' (Vietnam, my Country): Vietnamese Americans and Transnationalism." In *The Changing Face of Home: The Transnational Lives of the Second Generation*, edited by Peggy Levitt and Mary C. Waters. New York: Russell Sage Foundation.

Flores, William V., and Rina Benmayor. 1997. *Latino Cultural Citizenship: Claiming Identity, Space, and Rights*. Boston: Beacon Press.

Glover, Ian C. 1999. "Letting the Past Serve the Present—Some Contemporary Uses of Archaeology in Vietnam." *Antiquity* 73 (281): 594–602.

Gustafsson, Mai Lan. 2007. "The Living and the Lost: War and Possession in Vietnam." *Anthropology of Consciousness* 18 (2): 56–73.

Hall, Stuart. 2006. "Popular Culture and the State." In *The Anthropology of the State*, edited by Malden Aradhana Sharma and Akhil Gupta, 360–80. MA and Oxford: Blackwell Publishing.

Han, Xiaorong. 2004. "Who invented the Bronze Drum? Nationalism, politics, and a Sino-Vietnamese Archaeological Debate." *Asian Perspectives* 43 (1): 7–33.

Insun, Yu. 2006. "Lê Văn Hưu and Ngô Sĩ Liên: A Comparison of their perception of Vietnamese History." In *Việt Nam: Borderless Histories*, edited by Nhung Tuyet Tran and Anthony J. S. Reid, 45–71. Madison, WI: The University of Wisconsin Press.

Jamieson, Neil L. 1993. *Understanding Vietnam*. Berkeley: University of California Press.

Jellema, Kate. 2007. "Returning Home: Ancestor Veneration and the Nationalism of Doi Moi Vietnam." In *Modernity and Re-enchantment: Religion in Post-Revolutionary Vietnam*, edited by Philip Taylor, 57–89. Singapore: Institute of Southeast Asian Studies.

Keyes, Charles F. 1977. *The Golden Peninsula: Culture and Adaptation in Mainland Southeast Asia*. New York: Macmillan.

———. 2002. "'The Peoples of Asia'—Science and Politics in the Classification of Ethnic Groups in Thailand, China, and Vietnam." *The Journal of Asian Studies* 61 (4): 1162–203.

Keyes, Charles F., Helen Hardacer, and Laurel Kendall. 1994. "Contested Visions of Community in East and Southeast Asia." In *Asian Visions of Authority*, edited by Charles F. Keyes, Laurel Kendall, and Helen Hardacre. Honolulu: University of Hawaii Press.

Lê-Kim, Ngân. 1974. *Chính-Trị và Xã-Hội tại Việt-Nam thời Hùng-Vương*. Sài-Gòn: Tủ-Sách Khảo-Cứu Đại-Việt.

Lowe, Lisa. 1996. *Immigrant Acts: On Asian American Cultural Politics*. Durham and London: Duke University Press.

Malarney, Shawn Kingsley. 2001. "The Fatherland Remembers Your Sacrifice: Commemorating War Dead in Northern Vietnam." In *Country of Memory: Remaking the Past in Late Socialist Vietnam*, edited by Hue-Tam Ho Tai, 46–76. Berkeley: University of California Press.

———.2007. "Festivals and the Dynamics of the Exceptional Dead in Northern Vietnam." *Journal of Southeast Asian Studies* 38 (3): 515–40.

Mitchell, Timothy. 2000. "The Stage of Modernity." In *Questions of Modernity*, edited by T. Mitchell, 1–34. Minneapolis: University of Minnesota Press.

Nguyen, Thi Lien Hang. 1995. "The Double Diaspora of Vietnam's Catholics." *Orbis* 39 (4).

Nguyen, Viet Thanh. 2006. "Speak of the Dead, Speak of Vietnam." *CR: The New Centennial Review* 6 (2): 7–37.

Rafael, Vicente L. 2005. *Promise of the Foreign: Nationalism and the Technics of Translation in the Spanish Philippines*. Durham, NC: Duke University Press.

Safran, William. 1991. "Diasporas in Modern Society: Myths of Homeland and Return." *Diaspora* (1): 83–99.

Tanabe, Shigeharu, and Charles F. Keyes. 2002. "Introduction." In *Cultural Crisis and Social Memory: Modernity and Identity in Thailand and Laos*, edited by Shigeharu Tanabe and Charles F. Keyes, 1–39. Honolulu: University Hawaii Press.

Taylor, Keith Weller. 1983. *The Birth of Vietnam*. Berkeley: University of California Press.

———. 1995. "Preface." In *Essays into Vietnamese Pasts*, edited by K. W. Taylor and John K. Whitmore, 5–8. Ithaca, NY: Cornell Southeast Asia Program.

Taylor, Philip. 2007. "Modernity and Re-enchantment in Post-Revolutionary Vietnam." In *Modernity and Re-enchantment: Religion in Post-Revolutionary Vietnam*, edited by Philip Taylor, 1–56. Singapore: Institute of Southeast Asian Studies.

Toloyan, Khachig. 1996. "Rethinking Diaspora(s): Stateless Power in the Transnational Moment." *Diaspora* (5): 3–36.

Trinh Vo, Linda. 2003. "Vietnamese American Trajectories: Dimensions of Diaspora." *Amerasia Journal* 29 (1): ix–xviii.

Trương Thìn. 2007. *101 Điều Cần Biết về Tín Ngưỡng và Phong Tục Việt Nam*. Hà Nội: Nhà Xuất Bản Hà Nội.

Tuổi Trẻ. 2007a. Chất men kết nối lòng người. April 26. http://www.tuoitre.com.vn/tianyon/Index.aspx?ArticleID=198412&ChannelID=3. Accessed March 15, 2008.

———2007b. TP: HCM: Nhiều nơi tổ chức lễ giỗ Tổ. April 25. http://www.tuoitre.com.vn/Tianyon/Index.aspx?ArticleID=198253&ChannelID=10. Accessed March 15, 2008.

———. 2007c. Câu hỏi hôm nay: Nghỉ lễ, Tết--Người lao động được hưởng các quyền gì? April 25. http://www.tuoitre.com.vn/Tianyon/Index.aspx?ArticleID=198201&ChannelID=3. Accessed March 15, 2008.

———. 2007d. 26–4 năm nay, được nghỉ Giỗ Tổ Hùng Vương. March 28, 2007. http://www.tuoitre.com.vn/Tianyon/Index.aspx?ArticleID=193627&ChannelID=3. Accessed March 15, 2008.

———2007e. Thiêng Liêng cội Nguồn "bọc trăm trứng!" April 26, 2007. http://www.tuoitre.com.vn/tianyon/Index.aspx?ArticleID-198413&ChannelID=330. Accessed March 15, 2008.

Woodside, Alexander. 1971. "Ideology and Integration in Post-Colonial Vietnamese Nationalism." *Pacific Affairs* 44 (4): 487–510.

Wright, Gwendolyn. 1987. "Tradition in the Service of Modernity: Architecture and Urbanism in French Colonial Policy, 1900–1930." *Journal of Modern History* 59 (2): 291–316.

Vo, Thu Huong Nguyen. 2005. "Forking Paths: How Shall We Mourn the Dead?" *Amerasia Journal* 31 (2): 157–75.

ROCK YOUR RELIGION:
Shan Buddhist Ritual and Stage-Show Revelry in a Contested Zone at the Thai-Burma Border

Jane M. Ferguson

There is a Burmese idiom that states, "Shan shin laung pway a-lway ka lay" (Dayaikta Seya Myint 1969, 97), which means, "The Shan novice ordination ritual is easy and simple." What I find so striking about this expression is that the ritual, in Shan called a Poy Sang Long, is hugely elaborate, laborious, and expensive. Why such a Burmese saying about this ritual would circulate, either in irony, or seriously, could speak more of Burmese perception of the Shan as a minority, a hill people without the complicated traditions and rituals of the lowland Burmese. Leaving this paradox on the back burner, I would like to turn my attention to one such Poy Sang Long ritual and examine its broader meaning within the cultural milieu of Wan Kan Hai, a community of former insurgents and stateless Shan migrants.

The Shan constitute one of the largest ethnic nationality groups in mainland Southeast Asia, with the majority of them located in Shan State, in the northeast of the Union of Burma (Myanmar). Although Shan politicians were promised autonomy following ten years' initial membership in the union, this was never realized, and some groups of Shan separatists have been fighting the Burmese military in one of the longest-running internal conflicts in modern history. Since 1969, the village of Wan Kan Hai has been an important strategic nexus for this Shan insurgency, as its location at the Thai-Burma border allowed for the trafficking and sale of goods necessary to fund the operations of insurgency. At present, the village is under the authority of the soldiers of the Thai state and is bureaucratically incorporated into Thailand, although neighboring mountaintop encampments are occupied by Burmese, United Wa State Army, and Shan State Army (South) commandos. Returning to the initial quotation: what does a novice ordination ritual mean to these people in this contested political context? In order to tackle this issue, first I will give an overview of the Poy Sang Long in its central function as a merit-making ritual for young boys to ordain as novice monks, and then I will examine how, in contentious times, the ritual one-upmanship of merit-making has been carnivalized and has taken on outside ideological significance. Paying special attention to the bracketing of certain events both within and outside the ritual, I will flesh out how it transgresses the orthodox intent of the novitiation and speaks directly to broader national concerns of Thai state surveillance and ethnic pluralism within Thai nationally sanctioned narratives of ethnicity and investiture in the hope for a future prosperous Shan nation. While parts of the ritual explicitly engage Thai interlocutors, I will argue that it is through rock stage-show revelry that the reverberations and syncopation of Shan nationalist sentiments, foregrounded by economic and political marginalization, are transfused through the Shan community at large. The excitement of collective merit-making, and the sheer joy of participation in this massive, all-consuming event is most palpable by day, as dozens of small percussion ensembles play their Shan gongs and long drums incessantly throughout the various parts of scheduled (and non-scheduled) activities. However, the Shan rock music played during the evening stage show gives language, thus symbolic meaning, to a specific kind of rich future: a future in which there is a place at the cosmo-political table for the Shan people. The Shan nation, which is currently denied realization, and its people are politically and economically marginalized by two larger nations. It is through these tropes that nation-building sentiments are transmitted through ritual practice but articulated via rock music. It is the Shan culture's industries, predicated on an insurgency, that hardens these sentiments into symbols and diffuses them in the ether. Part of what makes this point so energizing might partly have to do with the fact that this notion of Shan militancy, which emerges during the evening activities of the ritual, is largely lost (or ignored) by Thai interlocutors.

The Ritual Itself

The Poy Sang Long is the Shan counterpart to the Burmese Shin Laung Pwe, and its nomenclature and symbolic vestments are indicative of the centuries-long interrelationship between Burmese and Shan Theravada Buddhist practice. The ritual itself is a mass ordination ceremony for young boys who are being ordained as novice monks. The *sang long* (in Thai called the *luk kaeo*, or jeweled prince) refers to the boy himself, dressed up in the ornate costume that represents Prince Siddhartha Gotama, who would later become the Buddha (Tirapap 1995, 113). Siddhartha was prince of a small area in northern India. He sought truth and meaning, and one night stole away from his palace and discarded his fancy attire, cut his hair, and became a wandering ascetic. In the Shan (and Burmese) ritual, the princely status of the former life of the Buddha is expressed in the ornate costuming of the young boys, as their elaborate, colorful outfits and laboriously applied makeup and headdresses make them appear vibrant and other-worldly. The significance of becoming a novice monk is derived from the prince's renunciation of worldly possessions and riches, so the Shan ritual simulates this wealth in the ornamentation and indulgence of the boys.

Within Theravada Buddhist practice, this ritual is particularly important, as it is a simulation of a biographical narrative of one of the lives of the Buddha. The little boys embody the prince and his renunciation; it is biographical narratives like these, taught through ritual performance, that also constitute one type of Buddhist pedagogy. Woodward (1997) has even suggested that it is the biographies of past and future Buddhas that frame the tradition of the teachings of the Buddha (Woodward 1997, 50). So, taking Siddhartha's renunciation as the example, the Poy Sang Long becomes a kind of festivalized biography.

The elevated status of the boys is demonstrated throughout the ritual, as their feet never touch the ground. Whereas the prince rode a horse when he left his palace, these Shan boys are carried atop the shoulders of men, usually male relatives or friends of the family. These men represent Siddhartha's horse. In the Burmese counterpart ritual, the Shin Laung Pwe, the boys ride on horses, and sometimes in the mass ordination of little girls as novice nuns the girls ride in ox carts. For this ritual in Wan Kan Hai, although nearly all of the boys were carried atop the shoulders of men, one rode on a pony.

It is believed that the *sang long* is able to make more merit, or *kuso*, for his family, since he is still a child and thus better capable of transmitting Buddhist merit than an adult becoming a monk (Tirapap 1995, 112). This marks an interesting departure from the biography of Siddhartha or Gotama Buddha: Siddhartha was already an adult with a wife and a child when he stole away from the palace to renounce his worldly wealth and become an ascetic. Returning to the Shan Poy Sang Long, although the focus is on the boys, the novice ordination is much more of a rite of passage for the sponsoring adult than it is for the boy (Eberhardt 2006, 90). Although the ritual can be, and often is, deeply meaningful to the boy himself, for a Shan mother, having her son become a *sang long* is the most important way for her to make religious merit, and to mediate the merit-making act between the religious, spiritual realm, and the logistical social world that is necessary for the event's successful execution. Viewing the boy himself as the symbolic epicenter of the network (where actually his mother is most likely the logistical and social epicenter), spokes radiate outwards from him, extending into circles of reciprocity and obligation, kinship ties, be they blood or social, and other forms of beholden-ness to the spiritual health of the network at large.

This year in Wan Kan Hai, with the eighty-six little boys initiated as novice monks come eighty-six donation networks comprising relatives and friends that sponsor each boy and the six days of ceremony and festival that each boy's ordination ritual entails. Contributing to the individual *sang long* signifies more than just donating money so that the family may most effectively sponsor the boy's merit making. To give money to sponsor a fellow community member's novitiation is to make merit through the indirect sponsoring of an auspicious act. By taking on this symbolic capacity to influence a higher future, the boy, as is shown through his peregrinations throughout the six days of the ritual, comes to signify the Shan past through the conservation and preservation of specific aspects of Shan expressive culture, and also points toward a vibrant Shan future free from despair. The themes of the events are distinctly Shan in nature, and their work for an ethnic future, in their terms, supersedes without negating their claim to a glorious past. In these senses, ethnicity does not derive exclusively from a cultural interpretation of descent, as argued by Charles Keyes (1981, 5), but also from a cultural interpretation of future rebirth.

In Thailand, the Poy Sang Long is seen as a ritual demonstrating unique Shan expressive culture, and in the long-established Shan communities in Mae Hong Son, where a large proportion of the Shan population consists of Thai citizens, the Poy Sang Long is exploited as an important event in the many festivalized nodes of tourist attractions in the Thai national landscape. This is particularly true in the Mae Hong Son provincial capital town. Unlike the Poy Sang Long in Mae Hong Son, the ritual at the border town of Wan Kan Hai is not advertised or heavily marketed for international or urban Thai tourists. Aside from becoming a locus for many people from the Shan diaspora working in urban areas such as Bangkok or Chiang Mai, the principal outside interlocutor for this borderlands event is the Thai government. Its various branches directly and indirectly restrict and manage circumstances of the event, because the fact is, the majority of the Shan population participating in this event lack full citizenship in Thailand.

For many Shan people who lack citizenship in Thailand, traveling outside of their district requires state-issued travel documentation. This can make a trip to the borderlands very difficult and makes state surveillance an inevitable factor in the event. For the six days of the festival, however, revelers reincorporate geographic territory into the cosmography of the Poy Sang Long ritual. According to tradition, the event need merely to include the temple and the community, but the specific framing of this Poy Sang Long extends itself to include the King Naresuan monuments, multiple temples, the school soccer field-cum-carnival grounds, and finally the contested border zone itself. Whereas in big cities in Thailand, at large Shan events Thai police occasionally linger and check attendees' citizenship documents, in the borderlands, this kind of surveillance is not as acute, or at least it was not during Poy Sang Long in 2006.

Listening to some community members' concerns about the tremendous expense of the event, one might expect that only those who were relatively comfortable financially would be direct sponsors of any of the little boys in the merit-making endeavor. This was, however, only partially the case. For most Shan families in this area, if they had a boy above the age of seven, it would be expected that he become a *sang long* to make merit for his family according to the Shan tradition. But what was particularly striking was the way in which the greatest enthusiasm for the event came from those who were in the least likely position to be able to afford it. As the event drew near, the topic of the Poy Sang Long captivated the entire village. It was the only thing that people would talk about.

In addition, according to Buddhist doctrine, greed leads to poverty, whereas generosity (especially in donating to monks) leads to wealth (Warren 1953, 171–72, quoted in Keyes 1983, 263). Ironically, it is those who are most impoverished that are most likely to attribute their situation to their lack of store of *kuso* (merit), and thus express greatest enthusiasm for the merit-making ritual as a vastly elaborate and expensive event. Therefore, their renunciation of worldly wealth (although it is often done on credit) is also a donation in the hope that they will recover, even surpass, the notion of vast wealth that they paradoxically simulate during the days of the ritual. The higher the stakes, the bigger the party.

It seemed that every Shan household had a few, and often many, houseguests during the week of festivities. The organizers began months in advance, and their preparations included setting a date with Thai government authorities and coordinating with other Shan communities in northern Thailand so as not to overlap in the scheduling of the massive ritual. This is similar to the five-day market rotation system of years past: villages do not want to have their Poy Sang Long on the same days as neighboring villages, because this would overextend the resources of the Shan community at large, simultaneously dividing the labor and the donation pool.

In order to provide a base for these eighty-six networks and their stars, the sports field in front of the high school was converted into a parade ground, with eighty-six booths set up with tables and sofas to house the boys and their families. On the first full day of festivities the boys settle into their booths, in their full regalia, after a morning at the temple and a round of photographs with local officials.

Shan revelers come from both sides of the Thai-Burmese border. There are even Shan people from Rangoon who have traveled to the borderlands to attend the event. For the relatively privileged Shan with full citizenship in Thailand, or for travelers with proper Thai visa documentation in their Burmese passports, it is easy to get up to the border town, but for everyone else, even just to travel the two hundred kilometers from Chiang Mai, they must navigate through two, sometimes three, district police and army checkpoints, where officials demand that they show their identity cards and travel documentation. What is striking also, is that this is a diasporic return, and the sounds that are created at the return make a referential creation of a homeland, through merit-making and through carnival. It is these revelries, coupled with millenarian-style hope for the future through merit ritual, that strive to make the Thai-Burma borderland Shanland, for six days that pass all too quickly.

The Ordination Events Commence

On the first evening of the Poy Sang Long, the boys' heads are shaved in anticipation of the religious rituals the following morning. The eighty-six little boys are accompanied by their bearers, their umbrella bearers, their mothers, and other assorted parts of a true retinue to every event on this extensive six-day itinerary. The first full day starts with a ritual meal in which the boys are hand-fed twelve different kinds of food for breakfast, and following this they chant incantations led by the abbot of Wan Kan Hai Temple. After leaving the temple, the boys are led by prominent members of the community first to honor the village spirit, and then, along with the Shan percussion ensembles, on three clockwise circumnavigations of the temple. (They will do this for every temple they visit throughout the days of the event). Following this, the parade makes its way across the street to the soccer field of the town's public elementary and high schools. The soccer field has been converted into a parade ground of sorts and a stage is set up at the halfway point of the grounds. These grounds, in addition to being the field for high school sports, are also the location of the weekend market, or the *kat nat* (rotating market), where traders come to sell sundry items such as laundry soap, sponges, and children's clothing to the villagers. While the *kat nat* is characterized by its canvas tents, for this festival the area has been transformed by the erection of eighty-six bamboo booths. Each of these booths is for an individual *sang long*, and they are numbered accordingly.

At the front of each booth is a silver bowl, the same kind used to carry items to the temple for merit-making, used to hold water to pour on blessees during the Poy Son Nam or the water throwing festival. The bowl has a piece of paper stretched across the top with a slit cut in it so that it can receive gift envelopes. Many of the gift envelopes are actually hand-delivered to donors in the weeks prior to the event, and now it is into this bowl that the recipients will "return to sender" these envelopes with cash inside. While the donation networks, at least those larger networks of family and friends who receive these envelopes, will not add up to "full" sponsorship for each *sang long*, each envelope is a solicitation for a blessing and one that cannot rightly be refused. As F. K. Lehman (1996, 30) writes, "One who solicits blessing is, to some extent, coercing the blessing, because receiving blessing reciprocally brings increased merit to the blesser—somewhat in the sense of the idea underlying the Biblical parable of casting the bread upon the waters".

Behind the silver bowl located at the front of the booth are some tables and chairs to receive guests. In the middle of the table are plates of oranges, popcorn, sunflower seeds, and sweets. The booth itself, just past the table, has a larger bamboo platform, upon which is a sofa on which the sang long himself sits, facing outwards. In many ways, the booth is not just a "home base" for the events of the six days, but also a makeshift throne, and as the donation networks come to deliver their envelopes they are received by the family of the sang long, invited for tea and snacks, and given an audience with the Jeweled Prince himself.

As part of the introduction to the morning and midday activities of gathering the community around the *sang long*, the ceremony organizers invite all of the district officials, the police, and the Thai army to join with the *sang long* to be photographed in front of a large banner announcing the Poy Sang Long, with the location of the event and the dates. These big signboards are de rigueur for any event in Thailand or Burma, it seems, as is taking photographs of the participants in front of the signboard. Prominently positioned in the center of the display is a picture of King Bhumibol Adulyadej, the reigning monarch of Thailand.

The announcer on the megaphone calls people over to take a picture in front of the banner, "as a souvenir"; first are the Thai officials and the main sponsors of the event, the village politicians, and the village elders. After this picture is taken, the announcer calls over the *sang long*, and they, carried by their bearers, pose for photographs as well. In this case, the photograph is to the event what the completed form is to the bureaucrat: it takes a dynamic proceeding in time-space, which extends over several days, and teases out and flattens certain meaningful key elements, namely what the event is, when it takes place, who participates in it, and who sponsors it. In the bureaucrat's paper form, the mechanism is not interested in discourse, or language about the subject, but rather key variables and numbers to satisfy its machine. The photograph presents the name, date, and place of the ritual as announced on the signboard, the subjects of the ritual, as well as the political figures who have the power to frame and facilitate the ritual.

I would like focus on the Shan announcer's choice of the Thai (not Shan) word, *khong thilaruek*, souvenir. The English word "souvenir" is derived from the Latin *subvenire*, or to recall to the mind. With the growth of the tourist industry, a souvenir has become a specialized niche in a market, and souvenir shops, which we tend nowadays to associate with collections of objects ranging from marginal to negative utilitarian value, have some symbolic name or reference to a place that has been exploited as a tourist sight. From miniature copper-zinc Eiffel Towers, to green plastic erasers in the shape of the Statue of Liberty, to snow globes where plastic chips can be shaken in their mineral oil emulsion slowly to settle once again on the skyline of Tokyo, these objects serve the purpose of recalling to mind the bracketed event of touristic consumption as a tiny commodity. The souvenir provides the market-mediated object that is meant to invoke the memory of the experience. For those who were part of the experience, the souvenir brings it back to them. For the recipient, the souvenir recalls to mind the loved (or otherwise) giver who has chosen to bring back the object. For the recipient, then, the souvenir gift object, like the vacation postcard, says not "remember this," but rather, "remember me." While the undocumented Shan migrant will try to be invisible and slip into the Thai labor market by minimizing difference, here is a key role reversal: the Thai officials are invited to remember the Shan in the form of the souvenir image, in full Shan regalia. While there are gestures toward the Thai authorities, it is interesting that although many Thai emphasize the historic closeness of the Shan and the Thai, and the linguistic similarities, the actual probability that the Thai interlocutors fully understand Shan is very low. On occasion, I have met a Thai person who would tell me how similar the Thai and Shan languages are, but in my experience, Thai people who assert this do not actually speak Shan themselves. For many, this emphasis on a Thai-Shan "brotherhood" is considered to be a liberal, cosmopolitan stance on the part of the Thai, but for some Shan people on the receiving end of such statements by Thai cosmopolitans, there is often a tangible bitterness. In her work on a Shan community in Mae Hong Son Province in Thailand, Nancy Eberhardt (1988, 9) points out that while Thai people often emphasize that they and the Shan have "deep historical and cultural links, it is the Shan themselves who tend to be more aware of (and sensitive to) differences between their culture and that of the lowland Thais." As one of my Shan informants comments,

> The Thai come here and smi-i-i-i-ile, and say, we're *phi nong kan*, (brethren) but then they look down on us as aliens or worse, just because we want to travel to the city or to work for them under humane conditions. It's easy for them to say we're brethren while they're rich and we're poor.

On another occasion, this informant told me that central Thai who would make the *phi nong kan* assertion would leave her speechless. While the quotation above shows marked frustration and bitterness over the assertion and its irony, when the lowland Thai assert this idea, often it is economic inequality and political marginalization that keeps the Shan speaker silent in the interaction. In the context of the Poy Sang Long, this is not the case, but the rebuttal is latent in the ritual. The transgressive act, the mystique of the *sang long*, is that for many Thai it is a manifestation of Shan identity. It is Shan people preserving their "culture," which, in general Thai understanding, entails Shan forms of dress, Shan language, and of course, the Shan's Buddhist rituals. For the Thai, the very reasoning that the Shan Poy Sang Long is ethnically distinct, but somehow, "pretty," "cute," or part of their "identity," in some ways precludes recognition of the potential for a radicalizing consciousness, or one which would even point to the history of Shan militancy, or the economic or political problems faced by Shan migrants in Thailand. The very marginalization of the Shan people is what, in some ways, has discursively created their identity and their culture, at least according to difference, as perceived by Thai spectators. This is the distinction made by the interpreters of the sound of the Shan gong and long drum. And this point is deftly avoided in the framing of the souvenir photograph.

The souvenir photograph, specifically because the Thai government officials are invited to join, is similar to the way which Nicola Tannenbaum (2007, 12) has observed the Shan Poy Sang Long in Mae Hong Son Province, in which Shan people actively perform their ethnicity, particularly when the performance is oriented outward to the Thai state. The photograph displays the Shan men and boys, with their lavish, ornate costumes, together with the officials of the Thai government in their uniforms. The bureaucrats wear their costumes and the *sang long* wear theirs.

After the pictures, the *sang long* are taken back to their respective booths, and for many of them, their earlier costuming is removed so they can relax in their undershirts and silk pants. The groups of people surrounding each *sang long* enjoy lunch together, and after a couple of hours' break, they begin the process of doing the makeup and adornment of the sang long for the afternoon's event.

Sang long number fifty-seven, Jok, is a little boy who lives with his aunt in a neighboring village. His cousin is a woman in her early twenties, who kneels in front of him with foundation cream, spreading it over his face with the foam rubber pad that came with it. Jok is nine years old, and he grimaces with his eyes scrunched tightly closed as she sweeps the pad over his cheeks. They chat and joke about as his cousin applies more makeup. Jok clearly takes being the center of attention in his stride, and when asked to stand to show his relatives his makeup, puckers his lips in a comical way. He may be the symbolic figure of the Jeweled Prince, but he is a nine year old, after all.

When his makeup is finished, another friend of the family, a man in his late twenties who is a very recent migrant from Shan State, attaches more of Jok's adornments. Each of these adorners is especially appointed to this task; in other words, part of the merit-making involves having a designated man attach all of the ornamentation to each individual boy. The adornments are like royal-style cuffs, almost like armor, but they are made of colorful cards, decorative, fin-like accouterments that are attached to Jok's wrists. Another set is attached to his torso. Jok's image starts to become more regal with each addition to his body. The wrist adornments are tied on, and the adornments around his torso are slipped over his head. Although these are relatively lightweight, they look not unlike the elaborate costuming depicted in the photographs of nineteenth century Shan *saopha* (princes, literally "Lord of Heaven"); often, then, the costuming and adornments weighed upwards of fifty pounds. This idea of the powerful, immobile monarch invokes O. W. Wolter's (1999) notion of the Southeast Asian monarch, the "man of prowess," whose supreme power is exerted by his seeming lack of action; in fact it is the symbolic investiture in his position by the social milieu that allows him to be so powerful. This investiture is most tangible in the ornamentation of the monarch. Now the boy becomes a simulated monarch and the symbolic investiture follows suit, literally.

Finally comes the headdress. For Jok, it is a white, pre-sewn, turban-style wrapping, with silver decorative wire in spirals around the top and the sides. The painstaking makeup and adornment process is only summarized here; for Jok it took about an hour and a half. This occurs twice a day for the remaining four days of the festival.

An Evening's Entertainment

As part of the official schedule, for many of the evenings of the Poy Sang Long, starting at 7:30 p.m., there is an "arts and dance show" in both "modern" and "traditional" styles. According to the event flier, this includes Shan national music, bird dance, Shan dance, sword dance, and assorted other performances. As night falls, the thumping of the Shan long drum and the striking of the gongs and cymbals continues in unison, and every corner of the parade ground, it seems, has a small ensemble of men in Shan traditional costumes playing these instruments. Many of these ensembles congregate around the noodle shops where their peers are seated, red-faced and merry around a growing collection of large, empty (and emptying) Chang beer bottles. However, as it is a giant carnival, there are also booths selling snacks, noodle shops, CD and VCD vendors, and myriad and sundry games of skill with prizes. Strolling through any of the three, 150 meter columns of booths, one can hear the competing sounds of the long drums, the rock band warming up, and the hi-fi systems with which many of these booths are equipped. The cacophony of competing sounds signify carnival, and teenagers start to appear in their favorite punk-style outfits, dressed up with their spiky hair, dark glasses, mod-hats, and long, dangling chain wallets.

Two of the *sang long* perch on a table at one of these carnival booths, and as the early 1980s pop song "Hands Up" blares in the background, the attendant hands one of them four darts. With acute concentration and his eyes on the prize (a plastic M16), the boy pulls back and launches a dart at the pattern of numbers on the board on the opposite wall of the booth. He misses the target. He tries twice more and misses both times. Then he starts pulling the shoulder of his bearer's jacket. Without needing an explanation, the older man produces another banknote so that the young boy can play another round of darts. Finally, the little boy wins that plastic M16 that he had been vying for, and as his bearer carries him away from the dart booth, the *sang long* triumphantly tears the prized M16 out of the packaging and soon cocks the weapon with his right index finger on the trigger, the mock militant with his new weapon, weaving through crowds of revelers in the din of carnival games, flashing lights, and blasting hi-fi systems.

After night has fallen and the sky is completely black, the young men in the rock band start to warm up. All the while, the announcer tests out the microphone and welcomes people to the Poy Sang Long. A few people stand around the stage, but there is not yet a full audience of onlookers. The lead guitar player has gelled his hair into a spike, and wears a mechanic's work shirt and jeans. The keyboard player wears a bomber jacket, jeans, and a chain wallet. As the guitar player warms up with the band, he tests out some solos using fuzz distortion. As he hits the high notes, he gyrates his head in a punkish gesture to show that he is "in" with rock music.

The band's first number, as is tradition for all Shan rock concerts on the Thai side of the border, is the song "*Kat jai hai mai soong*," written by Sai Htee Saing. This song is not a Shan national anthem so much as it is a Shan nationalist song used to open all stage shows. The song features a chorus of young men and women all dressed in Shan costumes, lined up on the stage in a U-shape to face the audience.

Prior to starting their song, they bow and pay respect in unison, and when the drums crash and the music starts, they soon begin to sing:

> The sound of the Shan gong and the Shan drum
> Resonates everywhere, When Shan people meet
> They have joy in their hearts and happiness
> For they share a heart, and whatever they do it gives them strength
> Our Shan brethren will be united until the end of history!
>
> Prosperity! Prosperity one day! Our Shan kin will be great!
> The Shan race, don't let it die, the Shan land, don't let it disappear.
> Strive for the future generations, make the Shan people with the times.
>
> Great hearts beat in the Shan people
> Our ideas are farsighted
> Don't let our ancient history be impoverished
> Bear the weight, when we see we can strike back
> We are able to build a great nation!

As the rock band plays the accompaniment, the singers clap their hands to the downbeats of the song. Before the song started, a sizable standing audience had already gathered in front of the stage, including at least two dozen *sang long* being carried by their bearers. Following the trend of the M16-toting *sang long*, at least half of the other *sang long* now hold toy guns. When the band begins to play, the *sang long* bearers start to dance to the music, also shaking the *sang long* on top. The more enthusiastic *sang long* also dance, flailing their arms and guns wildly.

Following the opening song, "*Kat jai hai mai soong*," the band moves on to play other Shan rock songs. As is the routine for many such Shan (or Burmese) stage shows, local people who want to come up and sing a song will be put on a list, though priority is usually given to those who are already established as skilled singers within the community. Social prestige, or relative privilege in the community also often trumps vocal skill in many cases for getting a spot with the microphone.

The band's repertoire is Shan rock songs, ballads, and love songs. There are many politically oriented songs, especially those by the beloved local songwriter and former Shan teacher Sai Mu, such as "*Wan tai tay loat le'o*" ("On Shan day we will be independent"). The revelry continues well into the night, and when popular singers are up on stage it is customary to buy a wreath to place around their necks to show appreciation for their songs. These wreaths are purchased at a booth next to the stage. An audience member generally walks onto the stage and places it on the singer while he or she is still singing, so that the whole audience may see his or her appreciation of the singer. On one occasion a *sang long* bearer and his *sang long* appear on the stage holding a wreath each, with the intention of placing it on a pretty young singer in red Shan traditional costume who is wooing the audience with her sweet voice and classic good looks. This particular *sang long* is the original winner of the plastic M16 gun, and, still holding the gun in one hand, he places the wreath around the neck of the singer, as his bearer dances to the music and the crowd cheers.

Throughout the night, on this stage there is a rotation of bands and singers, and on another competing stage in the carnival grounds there is Shan traditional dancing and verse poetry, which is sung as a dialogue. Some of this traditional Shan verse poetry, such as the poem "*Sao sua khan fa*," is about a famous thirteenth-century Shan monarch. The older members of the audience are less interested in the rock concert and have set out plastic mats on the ground in front of this traditional show so they can sit and watch. Off to the side, the noodle shops and the carnival skill games are buzzing, and crowds wander from the concert, to snack vendors, to the shopkeeper, while local teenagers in their punk garb socialize between the rows of parked motorbikes.

As the night wears on and midnight draws near, the proportion of *sang long* in the crowd of rock aficionados significantly diminishes. I am approached by one local family who asks me if I've seen their *sang long*. I soon learn that this is a typical joke played at the Poy Sang Long. Inevitably a bearer will tire of carrying the boy on his shoulders after a while, and especially during the dancing, so other men will come up and offer to carry the *sang long*. During the night's carnival atmosphere, a flourishing of trickery induces a few men to run off with a *sang long*, if only for a half hour to play a joke on the *sang long*'s family. It is all meant in good fun, and the reunion of the *sang long* with his rightful owners is a moment of laughter and congratulation on a theft well executed.

Later in the evening, the front of the stage is increasingly dominated by very drunk men shouting and singing to the rock music. The members of the household I have taken up with tell me that they are leaving to return home to sleep as the *sang long* must wake up early the next morning. Many revelers' families sleep at the booths of the *sang long*, adjoining the carnival. It is testament to their ability to block outside noise that they are able to sleep at all. Indeed, many *sang long* sleep in the booths, too. Although the family commented that the *sang long* needs his sleep, his bearers and make-up artists, inevitably, have to get up even earlier. As I depart, I notice that three *sang long* and their bearers are still dancing to the music at the stage show.

Sound Transformations

While it is the acoustic environment that crucially forms the ways in which sounds and noise are subjectively appreciated (Smith 2003, 138), the transformative ritual involvement of Shan merit-making and carnivalizing also influences the acoustic environment. The Shan gongs form the rhythms that frame the participants' movements during the day. But by night, when the sound of the gongs is replaced by a gigantic sound system, the reverberations from the speakers, the booming bass out from the mountaintops causes a specific kind of subjective appreciation of Shan rock, and Shan nationhood as well. Prior to forming a basis through which people are moved to social action, symbols of ethnic identity must first be appropriated and internalized (Keyes 1981, 9). For the former Shan insurgent soldiers, they had already been mobilized in one context, and although they are now migrant laborers on construction sites in urban Thailand, the ritual draws them back into the borderlands.The emanating symbolic capacities of the *sang long*, the sounds of the drums, and the presence of Burmese soldiers on the other side of the ravine serve as a certain kind of ethnic preservation. This preservation does not take place under the same terms that the Shan United Revolutionary Army gathered its forces thirty years ago, but rather invokes not only a neo-liberal consumerist "identity" by which Thai interlocutors are thereby appropriated but also a future in which sacrifices of the past are vindicated. For some, it is the rock music, the soundscape, that puts this hope out into the ether, and its very mode of amplification, reverberation, and "everywhere but nowhere" universalism make it an apt vehicle for this kind of nostalgia in anticipation of a modern nation-state.

The sound of the drum in Shan ritual implies both sovereignty and modernity, in terms of its domination of soundscape and the territory of its sound vibration. Although, as iterated earlier, the Shan are governed by the Thai and Burmese states through instruments of state building, how prescient that in Shan nationalist songs and poetry the vitality of the Shan nation is evoked in the sound of the Shan gong and long drum. In one particularly representative example, the popular song, "*Sà tai sà taen Laen Tai Laen Put*" by the songwriter Sai Kham Ti, the younger brother of the very famous songwriter Sai Kham Laek, details the sacrifice of the Shan soldiers, and claims that if the soldier dies, so will the sound of the Shan gong and the long drum (Sai Kham Ti 1991, 111).

When discussing Shan musical genres with my informants, they would often make a very clear distinction between two genres: *wan maé* and *wan gao*, modern and traditional. I translate these as such because I suspect that the Shan nomenclature is similar to the Burmese use of *kit mi* and *kit haung*, which, again, mean modern and traditional, or new era and old era. As one of my informants explained, the Shan drum is *wan gao*, and a guitar, bass, keyboard, and drum set are *wan maé*. Whereas both forms coexist in the Poy Sang Long, it is only metonymically through the lyrics in *wan maé* that one can refer to the instruments in *wan gao*. As shown in the nationalist anthem, "*Kat jai hai mai soong*," the gong and long drum are invoked, but it is guitar, drums, and bass that form the rhythm of Shan rock music. The modern medium of rock music itself evokes the traditional sounds. In other words, instead of being the displaced antecedent to modernity, the traditional is actually discursively created as a primordial "other" to a modern present. What makes this especially striking is that Shan politicians were never able to achieve their vision of Shan modernity, in which they would be in control of an independent Shan nation, using the Shan language and script as the bureaucratic print language of the polity.

As Gluckman famously pointed out, rites of reversal, while they include a counter-narrative to the established order, ultimately strengthen the order itself (quoted in Stallybrass and White 1986, 13). In other words, in spite of the rituals' potentially radicalizing discourse, are there ways in which the Poy Sang Long is actually conservative? For many of the members of this Shan community, economic poverty and daily financial struggle is the cruel reality that is endemic to the plight of any such undocumented worker. The large amount of money spent on the Poy Sang Long must somehow be recuperated later, as private loans are often repaid through a return migration to urban centers to engage in unskilled low-wage labor. For the owners of construction companies, the great expense of the Poy Sang Long punctuates their labor force's work year, and their laborers' wages, which are turned into merit, once again pushes them back to work. Whereas many of the families in the border area are supported through the remittance economy of the urban wage laborers, the Poy Sang Long represents a time where the remittances are accompanied by the wage earner and injected into the local (and trans-local) economy in the form of temple merit-making and carnival merry-making.

While the Thai government might frown upon certain forms of Shan militancy that are expressed in rock music, it is highly unlikely that Thai listeners would fully understand the lyrics in Shan or the political circumstances to which they refer. This, of course, presumes that the Thai officials were interested in attending the Shan rock concert in the first place. I did not recognize a single Thai government official in the audience at the concert, although I did see a small group of them drinking beer at one of the noodle stands at the carnival.

Just as Keyes (1977) agreed with Tambiah in his refutation of Spiro's idea that Buddhism and animism are separate and contradictory religious realms, there is nothing contradictory about rock music played as part of Shan Buddhist practice, although not in the temple itself, but as a key part of the six day event; its messages are incommensurate with the goals of the Poy Sang Long ritual in this context. In describing the Poy Sang Long ritual and its broader implications for a stateless community of Shan migrant workers, I hope that I have provided sufficient evidence to demonstrate that the ritual, as described in the Burmese idiom, is, in fact, neither easy nor simple. While the ritual time-space provides a context through which Shan Buddhists can express great elation over the Buddhist biography, make an emotional investment in merit towards a future rebirth, and anticipate a great Shan nation, the festival itself also draws together recurrent themes of Thai surveillance, and economic poverty and struggle. These themes are amplified, repeated, and syncopated using the instruments of sound production and amplification.

In constructing the meta-narrative of religious tropes incorporating notions of Shan traditions, which alternate with those of a futurity in which the Shan rulers are in control and Shan people are no longer marginalized by two dominant nations, the ritual pulls together notions of history, ethnicity, and economies of subordination. Nowhere is popular culture more apparent than in juxtaposing the ritual acceptance of the precepts with the rocking of the boys to Shan nationalist rock music. They feed the boys Shan food to fill them with Shan traditions. They jostle the boys to Shan rock music to charge them up on the tropes of the Shan nation. And they pose the boys with the Thai officials so that the image will go out and they will be "remembered." Recalling the lyrics to "*Kat jai hai mai soong*," through the rhythm of the ritual is the message transmitted most clearly: The Shan race, don't let it die. The Shan land, don't let it disappear.

References

Bull, Michael, and Les Back, eds. 2003. *The Auditory Culture Reader*. Oxford: Berg.
Dayaikta Seya Myint. 1969. *Shan Pyay Chay Mon*. Yangon: Min Nyunt.

Eberhardt, Nancy. 1988. *Gender, Power and the Construction of the Moral Order: Studies from the Thai Periphery.* Madison: University of Wisconsin-Madison Press.

———. 1988. "Introduction." In *Gender, Power and the Construction of the Moral Order: Studies from the Thai Periphery*, by Nancy Eberhardt, 3–12. Madison: University of Wisconsin-Madison Press.

———. 2006. *Imagining the Course of Life: Self-Transformation in a Shan Buddhist Community.* Honolulu: University of Hawaii Press.

Kammerer, Cornelia, and Nicola Tannenbaum, eds. 1996. *Merit and Blessing in Mainland Southeast Asia in Comparative Perspective.* New Haven: Yale University Press.

Keyes, Charles F. 1977. *The Golden Peninsula: Culture and Adaptation in Mainland Southeast Asia.* New York: Macmillan.

———. 1981. *Ethnic Change.* Seattle: University of Washington Press.

———. 1983. "Merit-Transference in the Kammic Theory of Popular Theravada Buddhism." In *Karma,* edited by Charles F. Keyes and E. Valentine Daniel, 261–86. Berkeley: University of California Press.

Keyes, Charles F., and E. Valentine Daniel, eds. 1983. *Karma.* Berkeley: University of California Press.

Lehman, F. K. 1996. "Can God Be Coerced? Structural Correlates of Merit and Blessing in Some Southeast Asian Religions." In *Merit and Blessing in Mainland Southeast Asia in Comparative Perspective,* edited by Cornelia Kammerer and Nicola Tannenbaum, 20–51. New Haven: Yale University Press.

Sai Kham Ti. 1991. "Sà Tai Sà Taen Laen Tai Laen Put." *Song Le'o* 8: 110–15.

Schober, Juliane, ed. 1997. *Sacred Biography in the Buddhist Traditions of South and Southeast Asia.* Honolulu: University of Hawaii Press.

Smith, Mark M. 2003. "Listening to the Heard Worlds of Antebellum America." In *The Auditory Culture Reader*, edited by Michael Bull and Les Back. Oxford: Berg.

Stallybrass, Peter, and Allon White. 1986. *The Politics and Poetics of Transgression.* Ithaca: Cornell.

Tannenbaum, Nicola. 2007. "Being Shan on the Thai Side of the Border: Continuities and Transformations in Shan Culture and Identity in Maehongson, Thailand." Paper presented at the Shan Buddhism and Culture Conference, School of Oriental and African Studies, University of London. 8–9 December 2007.

Tirapap Lohitakul. 1995. *Khon Tai Nai Usakhane.* Bangkok: Prapansan.

Woodward, Mark R. 1997. "The Biographical Imperative in Theravada Buddhism." In *Sacred Biography in the Buddhist Traditions of South and Southeast Asia*, edited by Juliane Schober, 40–63. Honolulu: University of Hawaii Press.

Wolters, O. W. 1999. *History, Culture and Region in Southeast Asian Perspectives.* Ithaca: SEAP Publications.

REESTABLISHING THE CAMBODIAN MONKHOOD

John A. Marston

A 1994 article by Charles Keyes, an account of Cambodian political history as it relates to Buddhism in recent times, includes a short description of how in September 1979 a delegation of Theravada monks from Vietnam reordained seven Cambodian men who had been monks prior to the Pol Pot period, and how these newly ordained monks then officially reestablished the Cambodian lineage. As my own study of Cambodian Buddhism has deepened, this passage has kept coming back to me, in part because I was present when Keyes conducted the interview with senior Cambodian monks that he drew on for the article, but also because I perceived how Keyes had understood better than me the significance of this event in the history of Cambodian Buddhism. This ceremony, I would argue, can moreover be considered one of the most significant rituals of charter of the new state, the People's Republic of Kampuchea (PRK).

Nevertheless, I see this ceremony as in continuum with the series of more grassroots ordinations that preceded it. The "irregular" ordinations that occurred prior to this key September 1979 ordination have typically been presented in the literature as self-ordinations. I quote Michael Vickery's description of the events as one example of this:

Since all monks had been defrocked under DK, the first step in reviving Buddhism was to renew ordination procedures, for which specific ceremonies conducted by a traditionally defined group of monks are required. No one, even if previously a monk, may simply put on robes and declare himself ordained; and this is a universally-recognized requirement of traditional Buddhism, unrelated to the politics of any state. Apparently in 1979 there were a number of such private resumptions of monk status, but their continued toleration would not only have undermined the policy of having religion serve national interests, but would also have discredited Cambodian Buddhism among the Buddhists of other Asian countries . . . Thus, an initial proper ordination was organized by the Front and the KPRC on 19 September 1979, with a delegation sent from the Buddhist community of Vietnam, possibly from the Cambodian community in Vietnam whose temples had not been closed by the Vietnamese authorities after 1975. Seven Cambodians, all former monks of twenty to sixty years of service, were reordained. (1986, 161–62)

In fact, however, many ordinations prior to September 1979 were far from being simply self-ordinations. Representing the groundswell of interest in the reestablishment of the monkhood, and frequently with the support of local authorities, they were often serious attempts to reproduce traditional requirements. They represent the creative spirit of that time, the widespread determination to make things work after years of chaos. They show, more than standard historical accounts of the September ceremony assume, that the process was not simply imposed from above.

What follows is a work of historical anthropology to the degree that it shows grassroots-level events in counterpoint to the events described in more dominant narratives. I am recounting individual action in pursuit of meaning, but action that would ultimately be affected by an emerging political and social context at a local and national level. My approach is consistent with Bourdieu's strategy of looking behind public formulations of events to find more chaotic realities of practice, with the caveat that, whereas Bourdieu's theory has sometimes been criticized for reducing motivation to the self-interested pursuit of power, the individuals engaging in the "practice" documented were often not focused on its power dynamic but apparently on the pursuit of a transcendent religious vocation, even if considerations of power also came into play.

I approach these ordinations at various levels. If the early ordinations were an expression of how individual men chose a religious vocation, they were most often also communal events. As such, the description of them contributes to the ongoing discussion within Cambodian studies about the nature of rural community and the degree to which, weak to begin with, it was further dispirited by the traumas of the 1970s (Zucker 2007; Ovesen, Trankell, and Öjendal 1996; Marston 2011). These ordinations serve as an example of something that at least *some* rural communities could mobilize around in the immediate aftermath of the Pol Pot period.

There is a fascinating literature on ordination that approaches it as a rite of passage (Van Gennep; Lefferts; Sou et al), and Keyes's 1986 article, "Ambiguous Gender: Male Initiation in a Buddhist Society" is a key work in this vein. François Bizot (1988) has also written a key study of the ritual aspects of Cambodian ordination. Here, however, I am more interested in looking at ordination as a means for the social legitimization of the monkhood—and the monkhood's legitimization of social institutions and beliefs—at points of historical change. We should keep in mind as well that ordination lineage represents in important ways a mechanism of the Sangha's memory, the mapping of a relation to the past—even when it is in fact mythic—and that the ability to define proper lineage is a means of shaping that memory as well as projecting its future continuity. There are historical cases of Theravada lineages that ended and were restarted, often in the context of war or political upheaval. Narapathisithu, the last important king of Pagan, accusing the Sangha of corruption, declared invalid the existing ordination lineage, and sent monks to Sri Lanka to establish a new, pure lineage (Taylor 1992, 166–67). The most extensively documented case is the dying out of the higher lineage in Sri Lanka, which after some time was restored by Siamese monks in the eighteenth century (Gombrich 1988, 139; Blackburn 2003). Looking at the ins and outs of the 1979 events may even shed some light on these historical events. Their basic interest lies, first of all, in the fact that, from a Buddhist perspective, a break in monastic lineage is a major catastrophe, and the reestablishment of lineage becomes, similarly, an event of great historical weight.

I am interested in the tensions generated, perhaps inevitably, as this process works itself out. Roy A. Rappaport (1999) is the scholar who has most systematically worked out the ways ritual relates to the performativities of speech act theory—and ordinations are imminently performative acts. What I am concerned with here is a moment of rupture when different performativities, so to speak, compete with each other, and when the state plays a role in legitimating a central performativity over others.

Let's begin by reviewing what, according to scripture or tradition, constitutes a proper ordination. In core scriptures, the Pali Vinaya calls for a minimum of ten monks to ceremonially bestow ordination on an initiate (Rhys Davids, and Oldenberg 1881, 175), but commentaries allow for there to be only five in outlying districts, which are defined as the entire world outside of the middle Ganges Valley (Thanissaro, chapter 14, 15; Gombrich 1988, 107). For the initiation of a novice in Southeast Asian countries, the presence of a single monk, the preceptor, is often considered adequate. For the higher *bhikkhu* ordination, a common pattern in Theravada Southeast Asia is to use five monks, although the full contingent of ten monks has been required, for example, in northern Thailand (Keyes 1986, 77–78; Swearer 1995, 51). In Cambodia, in the dominant Mahanikay sect, twenty-one monks were traditionally required (Sou et al 2005, 55), and Wells, in a 1939 book about Thai Buddhism, reports the approved number as twenty-eight.[1] An important exception to the rules, as related to me in Cambodia and relevant to this study, is a provision that a statue of the Buddha can take the place of one of the required *bhikkhu*; I have so far found no textual basis for this. The group of monks performing the ordination includes a preceptor (*upajjhāya*, in Khmer pronounced as *kru upachea*), at least one person designated as ceremonial interlocutor with the ordinant, or, in Khmer, *kru sotr*, and the rest of the monks known as *kannekaq sang* (or *hathabat*). According to the Vinaya, the preceptor for higher ordination should be "a learned, competent *bhikkhu* who has completed ten years or more than ten years" (Rhys Davids and Oldenberg 1881, 178).

The need for ordination ceremonies in 1979 stemmed from the fact that the practice of Buddhism was prohibited in Democratic Kampuchea (DK) (1975–79) and monks were disrobed on a mass scale. Common knowledge in Cambodia holds that during this period Buddhist institutions were dissolved and all monks were forced to disrobe, and this is largely true. As we shall see, one issue is the degree to which there can be said to have been some monks who lived through DK without abandoning their vows. This is not easy to judge. Harris (2005, 178–79) describes the process that unfolded after the April 1975 Khmer Rouge victory in which the highest-ranking monks were the first to be purged. Soon afterwards, those who resided in the unliberated zones were forced to disrobe. Finally, in the last three months of 1975, following the rainy season, the remaining monks from liberated zones were asked to leave their orders. Harris gives a range of figures for the number of men who remained monks at the end of the period—from one hundred (which would have included those who fled to neighboring countries) to a number given by the Ministry of Religion of twelve. The issue is complicated by the fact that different monks may have kept their vows to varying degrees.

I have studied four sites where early ordinations (i.e., before September 1979) took place. Two of these are of special importance since they involve the monks Nel Mony and Chan Sang, who performed hundreds of ordinations; these are also the cases where I have the most documentation. However, two other reports of ordinations, each one based on a single interview, seem significant for describing the trajectory of what happened: an early ordination near the border of Vietnam in eastern Kampong Cham and a Thammayut ordination in Takeo.

The information I have about all of these early ordinations comes almost exclusively from interviews, and I recognize that such accounts are subject to the distortion of memory. Where I have been able to interview more than one person involved, I have often found contradictions. However, enough consistencies remain that I feel confident that I have a sense of a larger picture. I would also stress that the information I have comes from a limited number of Cambodian provinces, and more systematic interviews throughout the country might reveal other trends. However, the areas where I conducted my research correspond to the areas that government officials recalled as being the primary areas of "irregular" ordinations.

Eastern Kampong Cham

Ven. Chan Oun is a monk now resident at a Cambodian temple in Rochester, Minnesota, who was a young monk prior to the Pol Pot period. In DK, in his early thirties, he was on a mobile team in Prey Veng Province. He recalls what must have been one of the earlier ordination ceremonies, in February 1979, taking place in Memot, a district in eastern Kampong Cham Province near the Vietnamese border. Memot was one of the places where Vietnamese troops, together with those of the new Cambodian Front, entered Cambodia at the time that DK was overthrown. His story is interesting both because it is early and because it gives a sense of the way, in the first flush of the new era, authorities encouraged reordinations and people responded enthusiastically. He said that at the time the Front entered Cambodia, tracts were scattered from the air giving the people specific directives. They told them to return to home villages; they also said monks should reordain and traditional Buddhist customs be reestablished. A Front official likewise encouraged him to reordain, and he learned of arrangements to have a ceremony in Memot.

As Ven. Chan Oun recounts it, the first obstacle he faced was obtaining cloth for monastic robes. So before going to be ordained, he went to his home region in Prey Veng Province. There the people knew he had been a monk, and when they learned he needed the cloth they were willing to exchange rice to obtain it. White cloth was easily available, but they had to buy saffron dye on the black market.

Ven. Chan Oun said his preceptor was a Cambodian monk named Ta Nep who had fled to Vietnam as a refugee. The ritual was performed by twenty-two monks that came from Vietnam. Only Ta Nep was actually a refugee from Cambodia; the others were from Vietnam. On that occasion only Chan Oung and two other monks ordained, although he knows that over time Ta Nep ordained many others. The ordination, he maintains, had the approval of the Front, even to the extent that they organized military forces to guard the ceremony from possible disruption. Following this he returned to Prey Veng. Although he was later under pressure to disrobe and reordain in the officially approved lineage, he never did so. His story shows the early importance of ordination to the Front and illustrates the fact that by no means all ordinations taking place in the early days were "self-ordinations"; it also shows local community coming together to support the project.

Nel Mony and Wat Sansom Kosol on the Outskirts of Phnom Penh

The most conspicuous preceptor during this period was Nel Mony, and I will discuss him and the ordinations he performed close to Phnom Penh first, even though ordinations may have begun earlier in Takeo. Nel Mony was born in the 1920s in Kampong Thom Province, and studied Pali in Kampong Cham and in the central Pali school in Phnom Penh during the last years of the colonial period—meaning he was probably one of the better-educated monks of his generation.[2] He was appointed to be an abbot and monastic district chief in Tbong Khmum, Kampong Cham, and was well established there by the time war broke out. Held captive by guerrillas briefly in the early 1970s, he eventually fled to Phnom Penh to escape the war. He resided at Wat Unnalom when the city fell and upon evacuation went to a rural *wat* in Kampong Speu where he had friends. One after another, the other monks in residence left the order. In 1976, as he tells the story, DK authorities asked him to disrobe, but he protested that he could not. Villagers warned him that this might result in him being killed, but he persisted. A week later, authorities told him that he did not have to stop living like a monk but they wanted him to dress as they did. He weighed in his mind the rules of the Vinaya and concluded that he could reconcile to himself changing his clothes without changing his behavior. During the rest of the period he was never asked to do heavy labor and, he maintains, was able to follow the lifestyle of a monk. He kept his monastic robes in a bundle that was always on his person.

Immediately after the fall of DK, he made his way back to the area of Phnom Penh. In the early days there were restrictions on entering the city, and large numbers of people returning from the countryside clustered in areas just outside the city's boundaries. He gravitated to Wat Sansom Kosol, just outside the dike road that encircles the city. As is consistent with other observers' accounts, his story makes it clear that authorities wanted at least the symbolic reestablishment of Buddhism in the country. He said Phnom Penh authorities actively sought out former monks for this purpose. Thus, he and four others "ordained" with the support of local authorities on April 7.[3] Thousands of people were present as the five men ceremonially circled the *vihara* on horseback, in traditional fashion, and then entered it for the ordination ritual. While there was no preceptor, the ceremony was justified on the basis that it took place in front of an image of the Buddha, also present was a copy of the *Tripitaka*. Nel Mony, in any case, regarded himself as never having left the monkhood.

Within two weeks, men began arriving from around Cambodia for further ordinations and Nel Mony began to assume the role of preceptor. These ordinations did not have as much support from the authorities as the first ceremony did. They would have liked to stop with five monks, he said, once they had "enough to show foreigners." Thus, a process originally started with the approval of authorities began taking on a life of its own. He describes what must have been negotiation with authorities and claims a sort of success in the fact that they let monks over fifty years old ordain. (In fact, a few men under fifty did ordain at this time, including three from Cheoung Prey District now very prominent in the Sangha.) Since *wat* had begun opening up around the country, more and more men began arriving at Wat Sansom Kosol to be ordained. A commune chief who brought a group to be ordained said that Nel Mony was at that time being called a "patriarch"; it was thus construed, like the later September ordination, as a national project. Nel Mony's claim that he ordained some thousand monks at this time seems credible to me, given the accounts of other people I interviewed. If it is exaggerated, even a fraction of his number would be significant. Two of what are now the highest ranking monks in Cambodia, Samdech Noun Nget and Samdech Loh Lay, were resident at Wat Sansom Kosol at that time and ordained by him. According to Nel Mony, robes were provided by the Phnom Penh party secretary, Vann Sen, and the minister of commerce, Tang Sarim, which indicates a degree of state support. Nel Mony had sufficient state recognition that he was called on to authenticate a document signed by thirty-nine monks that was submitted as evidence in an August 1979 trial in absentia of Pol Pot and Ieng Sary. The text indicates that sixty-eight monks were resident at Wat Sansom Kosol (de Nike et al 2000, 45, cited in Harris 2005, 191, 292n5).

Samdech Loh Lay was one of those who arrived at Wat Sansom Kosol in the period after Nel Mony's initial return to the Sangha. He describes Wat Sansom Kosol as a sort of "wilderness" (*prey*) at that time; none of the buildings were intact.[4] A highly educated monk before the Pol Pot period, Loh Lay was forced to disrobe in 1975 and spent the Khmer Rouge period in the Srey Santhor District of Kampong Cham. After the fall of DK he returned to Phnom Penh, which was, he says, a fearful place; he stayed for a while in the home of a former student. He had hoped to go to his previous temple, Wat Mahamontrey, but found it completely desolate. He soon learned that there were monks at Wat Sansom Kosol and went there. During this period, there "might have been thirty, forty, or eighty ordinations taking place in a single day;" he himself ordained in a ceremony of eighty. The vast majority of these monks returned to their home districts after ordination; he recalls there being only thirty monks permanently resident. He slept in a sort of indentation in the ground under one of the walls of the broken-down *vihara*. While he eventually ordained in the lineage established in the September ceremony, and now readily accepts it, a sense of the importance of this time at Wat Sansom Kosol is perhaps indicated by the fact that, despite being offered positions at more prestigious Phnom Penh *wat*, Loh Lay has continued to stay there. In fact, in addition to Ngun Nget, four more of the seven monks who would ordain in the September ordination—that is, all except Tep Vong and Kaet Vay, had previously been ordained by Nel Mony.

Chan Sang in Trang, Takeo

The case of Chan Sang is much less well known in Phnom Penh and involved fewer currently prominent monks, but purely in terms of the numbers of monks ordained his work is just as important as the ordinations conducted by Nel Mony.

Chan Sang was born in 1940 and ordained in 1964 at Wat Chuos in Trang District, meaning he was significantly younger than Nel Mony. He was in his early thirties when the Khmer Rouge took control of area where he lived. As a monk, he was moved to two different *wat* in Kampot Province and was at Wat Serei Sangkum when, as he tells his story, he learned of a Khmer Rouge plan to make monks disrobe.[5] Thus, sometime in either 1973 or 1974 he decided to flee to Vietnam.[6] He left with a young layman named Rin, then seventeen years old, who had for several years been living with him as a sort of adopted son. They went to a large refugee camp near the border run by a Kampuchea Krom monk, Ven. Om San Nou. However, they soon moved on to Wat Ampil Svay in Svay Ton, in An Giang, South Vietnam, where the abbot gave him a position of authority and he taught Khmer literacy. He spent five years at this *wat*—a period which included the fall of the Saigon government. Eventually Rin, the young man, also ordained. At the time of the Khmer Rouge incursions into South Vietnam, the pair fled further from the border and stayed at several other *wat*. In late 1978, Chan Sang was advised of what was happening by Ven. Oum Son Nou and so moved close to the border. He and Rin went back to Chuos soon after liberation, some time before the Cambodian New Year holidays.[7] At first they only performed novice ordinations. They petitioned Ven. Som Nou for help and he sent a Khmer Krom monk named Mao Ou from Wat Taok Biet; after performing only a few *bhikkhu* ordinations, he returned to Vietnam with the understanding that Chan Sang could continue as preceptor. Rin recalls that the first *bhikkhu* ordinations may have occurred in June. Rin and Kaet, a Khmer Krom monk who was close to them, were the *kru sotr* in the ceremonies, and older monks from the area served as *hathabat*; there were nine of them in total. Their right to perform ordinations was well recognized at the provincial level, Chan Sang claims, although not at the national level.

Chan Sang reports having performed 664 ordinations. In most cases the men came to him to be ordained, often arriving in oxcarts; however, at times he would travel to them, and later he obtained a bicycle for this purpose. The majority of the men he ordained resided in a handful of districts in southern Takeo.[8] Occasionally he traveled considerable distances, including west to Kampot Province and even once to Srey Ambil, Koh Pich, in Koh Kong Province. This was possible because the train from Phnom Penh to Kampong Som passed through the part of Takeo where he was living; he could travel westward on the train, and was taken by car from Kampong Som to Srae Ambil.

The case of Chan Sang, like that of Nel Mony, illustrates how great the numbers of ordinations were in the months following the liberation of the country. And, as in the case of Nel Mony, these ordinations seem to have had legitimacy with authorities; they were far from being simple self-ordinations.

Thammayut in Takeo

The ordinations I have described so far were in the Mahanikay order, but in the early months of 1979 there were also attempts to reestablish the Thammayut order. Of the two major orders in Cambodia, the Thammayut, which originated in Thailand in the nineteenth century, is smaller and considered stricter in discipline, and has more links to the royal family. The two orders have separate ordination lineages. While the ceremony I will describe took place in Takeo Province, it involves another monk from Kampong Cham who claimed he had never left the monkhood during the Pol Pot period. I recount this from the perspective of a small group of monks from Choeung Prey District who traveled great distance by foot to participate in the ceremony. Most of what follows is based on interviews with a single elderly monk who was one of those ordained, but the broad outline of the events as he recounts them is generally known and accepted at the four Thammayut *wat* in what was formerly Cheoung Prey District.

Ven. Kaev Nin, now eighty years old, had been a novice for four years in his youth.[9] While most of his adult life was spent as a rice farmer, the great suffering he experienced under DK motivated him to ordain in 1979, despite having a wife and children who were still living. His preceptor was another monk from the district who claimed never to have left the monkhood during the Khmer Rouge period, a man named Paen Sen (also called Sar).[10] (The current abbot at the *wat* with which Paen Sen was affiliated explained the circumstances with another version of the events that has doubtless circulated in the community. He said that Paen Sen was such an old man that the Khmer Rouge just did not think making him abandon his robes was worth bothering about.) It was Paen Sen who arranged for a group of men to walk to Wat Salong in Takeo Province near the Vietnamese border.[11] It is a journey of well over two hundred kilometers and it took two weeks to get there and back. The ordination was performed by five monks, with Paen Sen as preceptor. The other four had ordained two months earlier in an ethnic Khmer Thammayut *wat* in Vietnam. The monk who assumed the role of *kru sotr* was Maha Phen, a well-known Thammayut monk who later resided for a time at Wat Unnalom and eventually went to France. Seven monks ordained, one a young novice, perhaps in his twenties, from Oudong, and the rest, like Kaev Nin, older men from Choeung Prey District.[12] Upon returning to Choeung Prey District, the contingent of monks performed further ordinations.

The Process as Seen from Rural Areas

The overall pattern of the early ordinations becomes clearer if we look at what happened more from the perspective of those involved in a single district in rural Cambodia. Over the course of several years I have done field research in Batheay District in Kampong Cham Province, which in 1979 was still part of a large single district, Choeung Prey. While what occurred here is definitely not typical of rural areas in the country as a whole, it is suggestive of the possibilities afforded by the historical moment and may have represented patterns found elsewhere, at least in the province. My sense of the pattern of ordinations began to emerge in conversation with Ven. Po Diep of Wat Taprong (also known as Wat Preah Meas), one of the most celebrated monks in this region, considered a major practitioner of non-reformed (*boran*) Buddhism in Cambodia[13] and noted for his esoteric skills in the performance of blessings with water (*sraoch toeuk*). Ven. Diep, who had been a monk prior to the war, said that he ended up reordaining four times in the post–Pol Pot period.

First, he assumed the robes by himself in front of a Buddha image on the grounds of Wat Taprong, which he was instrumental in reestablishing. Then he participated in a group ordination at Wat Cheoung Prey, in the same district, in which the preceptor, Khing Naem, was yet another monk from the district who claimed to have never abandoned his vows. Later, he was ordained in Phnom Penh by Nel Mony. Finally, he was ordained in the official lineage line that was set up after the September 1979 ceremony.

While what I know about the ordination at Wat Cheoung Prey is limited, it seems to have involved several of the monks who, a month later, would go to be ordained by Nel Mony, including Ven. Diep, the future abbot of Wat Tang Krasang, Ngun Son,[14] and two monks who are currently abbots of important Phnom Penh *wat*, Ven. Kroch Saret of Wat Toeuk Thla and Ven. Sim Soyong of Wat Saravan. This event is important in showing that villagers *were* trying to reproduce the conditions for formal ordination at a local level, and suggests what might have been happening in many places in Cambodia.

The monks' early trips to Phnom Penh to be ordained by Nel Mony are now looked upon as important and daring. Sao Sareth, today a high-ranking military officer and chair of the *wat* committee for Wat Saravan, recounts that he was then a commune chief in the district.[15] He says he was motivated to help monks ordain because he himself was once a monk, and because he knew enough Vietnamese to help negotiate the trip. He claims to have brought fourteen monks (including the four mentioned above) to Wat Sansom Kosol, by traveling some sixty-five kilometers by foot.[16] While there were already regulations stipulating that only men over fifty could ordain, at least two of those accompanying him, Ven. Diep and Ven. Soyong, were not yet fifty. Ven. Soyong, present at our interview, laughed that they simply signed papers indicating that he was over fifty, even though it must have been obvious he was not. Sao Sareth claims he was subsequently criticized by authorities for having arranged the trip and even taken to the forest and threatened by Vietnamese troops, although the monks appealed for his release.

What I see here is an unfolding process, where communities and men seeking ordination pursue one strategy after another in order to attain what could be considered an ordination legitimated by society, beginning at the most local level and then by traveling increasing distances. Gradually, more and more men became involved in the process. At the same time the authorities were refining their criteria for ordination.

Given the story of the Thammayut monk Paen Sen, we see there were at least two men in this district who claimed never to have abandoned their vows during the DK period. The enthusiasm among the rural population for ordinations in early 1979 is evidenced by the fact that groups of men were willing to travel long distances on foot to be ordained.

While my research in other regions is quite limited, I managed to talk to several older monks in Stong District, Kampong Thom, the central area of Cambodia. These monks had all been ordained in the lineage established in the September 1979 ceremony. They indicated that there may have been some irregular ordinations in the early months of 1979, but shrugged them off, suggesting that these were isolated cases with few repercussions. All acknowledged that in the early 1980s there were only thirty monks in the district—not enough so that there could have been a monk resident in each of the forty *wat*, which meant that there had to be a system of rotation. We can contrast this with the memory of one monk ordained by Chan Sang who reported attending a meeting of the monks in Trang District in early 1980 in which 273 were present. A contrast between Takeo and Kampong Thom is consistent with the comments of Cambodians in a position to have observed the general pattern.

We can perhaps put the cases of ordination/assumption of robes into five categories: 1) Those who simply put on monastic robes without any attempt at ceremony (if there were any cases of this at all); 2) those who assumed the monkhood in a ceremony in front of a Buddha image (with or without the sanction of local authorities); 3) those who were ordained by men who claimed never to have left the monkhood during the Pol Pot period; 4) those who were ordained by monks who spent the Pol Pot period outside of Cambodia (whether Cambodians or non-Cambodians); and 5) those who crossed national borders to be ordained at *wat* in neighboring countries.

What were the motivations of the men who became monks at this time? Perhaps most of them had previously been monks. A few clearly had a strong sense of personal identity with the Sangha and were returning to what they felt was their vocation. This was certainly true both in the case of Samdech Loh Lay, a Pali-educated urban monk in the reformist tradition associated with Chuon Nath, and Ven. Po Diep, a rural-based monk who identified himself with the Sangha's atrophic "magical" traditions. Their sense of the monkhood's importance to their identity made it inevitable that they should return to it. Others ordained specifically because of the spiritual crisis of the Pol Pot period. We recall that the Thammayut monk Kaev Nin said, movingly, that after the great suffering he experienced during the Pol Pot period he felt compelled to enter the monkhood, even though he had a wife and children. At the opposite end of the continuum were older men who, because of the death of family during DK, looked to a monastic life as a means of subsistence in their old age. The gist of some of my interviews with older monks in Stong District was that after the September ordination, local officials chose trustworthy older men who were in need of support and would have a sense of responsibility toward *wat* property. Doubtless there were many gradations between these extremes. It is evident that many communities were eager to reinstate the activities of a Buddhist temple and that they encouraged former monks to reassume the roles they had once taken.

Early on it was established that only men over fifty years old could become monks. However, we know that some young men were also eager to ordain. Later, some would become monks to avoid military service (as perhaps some had always done in Cambodian history); however, the young men in these early months were probably more motivated by the same reasons that motivate youth today: their feeling (and that of their families) that it was a natural stage in a man's life, that it would provide them with education, and that it would generate merit. Likewise, since what has been reported for young men ordaining on the Thai border is doubtless true inside the country as well, some wished to gain merit for parents who died during the Pol Pot period.

Rationale of the September Ordination Ceremony

Let me start by stating my belief that there was no urgent need for the September ordination ceremony. If the Cambodian authorities had chosen to recognize the ordinations performed by Nel Mony and Chan Sang, and perhaps other preceptors, this would not in itself have created any crisis of legitimacy (and might in fact have avoided some of the problems that came to be associated with the ordination process that grew out of the September ceremony). That is to say, I do not see any risk of the situation described by Vickery in the quotation cited above, whereby the "continued toleration [of these ordinations] would not only have undermined the policy of having religion serve national interests, but would also have discredited Cambodian Buddhism among the Buddhists of other Asian countries." Chan Sang's ordinations could be criticized on the basis of his lack of seniority and scholarship as a monk; Nel Mony had seniority and scholarship, but there were questions about whether he could legitimately be said to have been a monk during the DK period. There is in fact no scriptural basis for saying that merely not wearing robes—perhaps the chief basis for the judgment that Nel Mony had left the monkhood—constitutes in itself an invalidation of monastic vows.[17]

The September ordination raises its own questions. Well-informed Cambodian observers point to scriptural requirements that a preceptor have been a monk for at least ten years, implying that even though the seven newly ordained monks had legitimately become monks, they did not yet scripturally have the right to perform further ordinations. Those who point this out go on to state the obvious: that despite this technical violation of rules, it was reasonable that they do so because of the special historical circumstances. One could argue, though, that if authorities had so chosen, they could have used the same argument in defense of Nel Mony and Chan Sang's role as preceptors. My purpose here, however, is not to dismiss the September ordination, which was a complex event in response to difficult historical and social circumstances. In the end, a performative act, such as that of an ordination, is effective to the degree it has social legitimation—in practice, the sanction of state authorities. On the principle of yielding unto Caesar that which is Caesar's, it had its own justifications.

In a Vietnamese-language account of the ceremony (Lê Húu Dan, 227–47), Do Trung Hieu, a Vietnamese official assigned to work with and unify Vietnamese Buddhist groups, describes the decision to perform the ordination ceremony as the result of discussions between him and Vietnamese Central Committee member Xuan Thuy. His account makes it clear that the February 17, Chinese invasion of Vietnam, over the issue of its presence in Cambodia, was a conscious factor in the decision to hold the ceremony: they were looking for ways to legitimate the newly formed government. Cambodians, Do Trung Hieu argued to Xuan Thuy, would be grateful to Vietnam. The project as he described it was originally conceived as involving monks from other Buddhist countries—and if this plan had been put into effect it might have been more effective than it was. (Vietnamese religious officials contacted Buddhists in Sri Lanka and India, but they were reluctant to participate, doubtless for political reasons. Soviet and Mongolian Buddhists would have participated,[18] but Do Trung Hieu rejected this idea because they were Mahayana.)

Since Do Trung Hieu's account gives the impression that the decision to have the ordination ceremony was largely made between him and Xuan Thuy, we must recognize at least the *possibility* that the event was planned without much awareness of what was happening on the ground in Cambodia, such as the ordinations by Nel Mony and Chan Sang. However, it is equally possible that Do Trung Hieu's account simplified a process that involved consultation with Cambodian and Vietnamese officials at different levels.[19] This is at least partly indicated by an August document cited by Gottesman:

> The leadership feared, accurately perhaps, that newly ordained monks might "take advantage [of the situation] and use Buddhism and the beliefs of the people to go and conduct activities to destroy the principles of the pure revolution to propagate and divide national security." (2002, 71)

The statement suggests that security may have been a major factor in the decision to create a new, unified monastic lineage. If so, officials were probably less concerned with the ordinations by Nel Mony and Chan Sang than they were by the few ordinations performed by monks crossing over from Thailand. Whether or not the more formal plan had yet been put in place in the border camps to make a monk long resident in Thailand, Ven. Buth Ngoy, the preceptor for an ordination lineage, the implications of possibilities of this kind were already etvident on both sides of the conflict.

In fact, the September ordination authorities promoted the idea of a single monastic order that would not distinguish between Mahanikay and Thammayut. By declaring ordinations invalid (all marked as either Mahanikay or Thammayut) they promoted the idea that Buddhism was a single, unified system under the guidance of the Front. Since Do Trung Hieu was already preparing a campaign to unify Buddhists within Vietnam, this plan was consistent with his overall agenda.

Another factor in rejecting ordinations already taken place may have been that, even though there was an early policy that only men over fifty could ordain, this rule was often ignored. In my interviews with them, both Nel Mony and Chan Sang emphasized that they ordained very few younger monks, as though still wanting to emphasize how cooperative they were with authorities—but their statements were belied by the circumstances of the interviews. I interviewed Nel Mony at Wat Saravan in the company of its now well-known abbot, Ven. Sim Sayong, who only a few days earlier had told me how he had ordained with Nel Mony in his twenties. I was directed to Chan Sang by another monk who had been ordained by him in his twenties. And although Chan Sang told me that perhaps only 5 percent of those he ordained were young, he almost immediately produced a photograph of himself standing beside yet another young monk. Preventing ordination of young monks may have been a factor in the authorities' decision to create a new monastic lineage more under their control, although in fact its establishment did not produce that result.

Cambodian and Vietnamese authorities were looking for clearer lines of monastic authority and a monastic bureaucracy, which, if not necessarily dominated by Vietnam, would interface well with emerging Vietnamese religious bureaucracy. They wanted a monkhood that was, to use Scott's term, more "legible" (Scott 1998, 2) than the chaotic one that was emerging. To the extent that what was being invoked was bureaucracy and legibility, it was a very modern process. But it is striking that they felt the need for ceremony: the modern nation always, if sometimes rather cynically, evokes the idea of continuity with the past, and in this case it sought to evoke in ritual a link to the past—one that also, somehow, had to pass through the hands of Vietnamese liberators.

Ordainers and Ordainees in the September 19 Ordination

Do Trung Hieu provides a list of twelve members of the delegation; some of the names are confirmed by other sources.[20] The list includes five Kinh (ethnically Vietnamese) monks from Ho Chi Minh City, four Khmer Krom monks from Rach Gia,[21] a "retired scholar," also from Rach Gia, the poet Hai Nhu, and another member of the delegation from Ho Chi Minh City, Do The, listed only by name.

The fact that key participants in the ceremony were Kinh (that is, ethnic Vietnamese) rather than Khmer Krom (that is, ethnic Khmer from Vietnam) is very sensitive in Cambodia, relating as it does to historical fears of Vietnam dominating Cambodia and resentment of Vietnamese presence in the 1980s, and is systematically avoided if not lied about when the topic of the ceremony is breached. This is one reason it is difficult to find any detailed Cambodian account of the proceedings.

The identities of the preceptors becomes more complicated and concerns about their nationality are perhaps ameliorated if we look more closely at their lives. While the three main officiants in the ceremony probably would have identified themselves and been identified by all those present at the ceremony as "Vietnamese," Theravada is a relatively new and strange practice among Vietnamese, who are more traditionally Mahayana Buddhists. What I prefer to emphasize here is the degree to which any Kinh (Vietnamese) Theravada monk (as opposed to an ethnic Khmer monk from Vietnam) would almost by definition have represented a sort of cultural hybridity.

Scholarly work on the topic of Kinh Theravada Buddhism is only now beginning to appear. As Bourdeaux (2007) points out, it has its roots in the 1930s, a period of religious ferment in Vietnam. Bourdeaux recounts the circumstances behind the creation of the first Kinh Theravada temple, Bu Quang Temple, at Thu Duc near Saigon, in 1940. Bourdeaux tells us a great deal about the founder of the temple, a man named Lê Văn Giang, who after ordaining would take the name Hô

Tông. Born in 1893 to a fish merchant in Phnom Penh, he was trained as a veterinarian in Hanoi, then returned to work in Cambodia and was attracted to the circles surrounding the Buddhist Institute, eventually studying meditation and Pali. In 1935, he decided to found a center for Vietnamese study of Theravada Buddhism in Phnom Penh at Sung Phuoc, until then a Mahayana temple. This led to the founding of the temple in Vietnam; the sima boundaries were established in a ceremony in which the Cambodian Mahanikay patriarch Chuon Nath and thirty other Cambodian monks took part (Binh 1999). Lê Văn Giang ordained in Phnom Penh and went to reside in the new temple the same year.

The two most senior monks in the September 1979 delegation, Buu Chon and Gioi Nghiem, are mentioned by Binh as other monks who had studied in Cambodia and went to Bu Quang Temple in the early years. Do Trung Hieu's account mentions that they both spoke Khmer, and although we don't have as much personal biography for them as we do for Lê Văn Giang, we can assume that like him they were in one way or another products of the colonial bureaucracy, came to identify with Cambodian religious practices, and were caught up by personal fascination with the Pali scriptures. Do Trung Hieu tells us that Buu Chon studied at Wat Lanka in Phnom Penh for twelve years.[22] In 1952 he also studied Buddhism in Sri Lanka. His scholarship is further demonstrated by the fact that he was the author of a Pali-Vietnamese dictionary. Of the Theravada monks in the delegation, he was the one with the clearest international profile, since in 1954 he was the leader of the Vietnamese delegation to the Sixth Buddhist Council and attended meetings of the World Buddhist Federation in 1957 and 1960, holding office with the federation. Radio broadcasts at the time of the ordination ceremony identify him as the delegation leader and "advisor of the Central Commission of Vietnam Theravada Buddhism." His presence lent the delegation international credibility, and the fact, as we shall see, that he was incapacitated and did not participate in the actual ceremony was a major blow to its organizers.

Do Trung Hieu's account describes a third member of the delegation, Sieu Viet, as Cambodian-born and speaking Khmer perfectly. Ven. Thien Tam confirmed that this was the monk known in Cambodia as Nou Choeuy, usually called Ta ("grandfather") Choeuy.[23] Since, according to Samdech Loh Lay, his father was Khmer, there is genuine ambiguity about his ethnic identity; however, Cambodians who remember him refer to him as "Vietnamese." This identity was apparently strong enough that he was at risk when the Vietnamese were expelled during the Lon Nol period, and he went to Bu Quang temple. He had ordained in Cambodia as a young man and was resident for a period of time at Wat Mahamontrey, during which he was under Loh Lay's supervision. His role in the ordination has perhaps been more vivid in the memory of Cambodians than that of other delegation members because he returned to Cambodia frequently in the 1980s. He had his own designated residence at Wat Mahamontrey, where he is remembered with great reverence. By 1990, when he returned permanently to Vietnam, he was so frail that he made alms rounds in a wheelchair.

Do Trung Hieu describes Thien Tam, the fourth Theravada monk, as a disciple of Buu Chon and states that he did not speak Khmer. He was then thirty-three years old and had ordained under Buu Chon in 1963; he came to the events as Buu Chon's assistant and did not originally expect to participate in the ceremony. He is still living and is the abbot of Pho Minh Pagoda in Saigon, a senior member of the Vietnamese Buddhist hierarchy, and a frequent participant in international Buddhist conferences.

Another member of the delegation was the Mahayana monk Ven. Minh Chau, who did not participate in the actual ordination. Like Buu Chon he was a scholar monk with a high profile, having studied in Sri Lanka and India for ten years, from 1952 to 1962 and having served as rector of Van Hanh Buddhist University in Saigon from 1965 to 1975.[24] While we don't know exactly what he was doing in 1979, he would eventually become the vice president of the Asian Buddhist Conference for Peace, and, in 1985, the rector of the Vietnam Buddhist Research Institute. In addition to his high profile, there was an obvious logic in his presence on the delegation as a scholar of Pali who could make judgments about scriptures pertaining to ordination.

The names of the four Khmer Krom monks were Danh Dinh, Ngô Van Âm,[25] Danh Bân, and Danh Dêm.[26] According to Ven. Danh Dinh, they ranged in age from twenty-seven to thirty-one years of age. He said it was almost an accident that they were chosen to participate in the ceremony.

However, according to one Khmer Krom man from the area, there had been a protest in the early 1970s by Khmer Krom monks against the South Vietnamese government, and the ties between Khmer monks and the Communist Party may have been stronger there than in other parts of the Mekong Delta. According to Ohashi (2008, 26), the four monks listed above were ex-members of the National Liberation Front.

The seven Cambodian monks ordained were: Kaet Vay of Kampong Thom Province; Prak Dith of Takeo; Din Sarun of Kandal; Et Sum of Takeo; Noun Nget of Takeo; Kaen Von of Prey Veng; and Tep Vong of Siem Reap. The Cambodian news agency account translated by Summary of World Broadcasts said that those ordained "had been monks for twenty to sixty years before they were defrocked by the Pol Pot–Ieng Sary clique" (SWB 1979). According to Prak Ing, the selection was made by the Central Committee of the Front; the two principle criteria, according to Noun Nget, were that they had been monks for long periods prior to DK and had never married. Some political considerations must have entered into the decisions as well.

According to former Cambodian prime minister Pen Sovan, he found Tep Vong (the eventual head of the Cambodian Sangha) dressed in white on the grounds of a temple in Siem Reap in June 1979 and asked him to come to Phnom Penh. There, Tep Vong stayed for a few days at the headquarters of the Front and then went to live at Wat Unnalom after it was cleaned up. Pen Sovan said he told Tep Vong to assume saffron robes, and insofar as we have any documentation he did so without any further ceremony as soon as they were brought from Vietnam (a controversial issue for those critical of "self-ordination").[27]

According to Prak Ing, all of the monks except Tep Vong and Kaet Vay had probably ordained previously with Nel Mony.[28] Kaet Vay, another figure who had some claim to having never abandoned his monastic vocation during the Pol Pot period, also came to Phnom Penh in robes (according to a Kampong Thom man who claims to have accompanied him; Thien Tam also mentions this detail).[29] Tep Vong had already assumed robes when he traveled to the Soviet Union and Mongolia earlier that same year, and in August when he issued a statement at the time of the trial of Pol Pot and Ieng Sary (Harris 2005, 179). Thien Tam remembers that Tep Vong was already wearing saffron robes when he met the delegation of monks arriving to perform the ordination ceremony in September 2009.[30] Nel Mony was invited to reordain with the other monks, but refused. In his interview with me he suggested that he was unwilling to renounce his previous ordination—a stance that excluded him from the new ordination lineage and alienated him from authorities.

Narrative of the September 19, 1979 Ordination

Like previous English-language students of the ordination, I rely heavily on the short news reports in Summary of World Broadcasts for basic information about the event. I have also been able to learn some details from interviews with persons who, while not present at the ordination, would have been well informed at the time. The bulk of my description, however, insofar as it provides details not previously written about in English, comes from my interview with the lay ritual specialist at the time at Wat Unnalom, where the ceremony took place, Prak Ing, and from a Vietnamese-language account by Do Trung Hieu.[31] These two sources are quite consistent with each other, although they differ on two major points: the name of the preceptor and the circumstances of the death of Buu Chon. (My interview with Ven. Thien Tam provided only a few new details and in general follows the account by Do Trung Hieu.)

According to a Vietnamese News Agency broadcast translated by SWB, the delegation of monks that performed the September 1979 ordination came at the invitation of the KNUFNS Central Committee (SWB 1979). The delegation arrived by plane on September 17.

Chea Sim, the head of the Front (and still a key political figure in Cambodia) headed the event's organizing committee. Do Trung Hieu recounts how Chea Sim prostrated himself before the monks at the airport and how some Vietnamese communist experts who were present expressed their annoyance, muttering, "A communist bowing again to monks!" The delegation stayed at Central Party Headquarters although they took their meals at Wat Unnalom.

On the evening of September 18 there was a minor crisis when Buu Chon and Gioi Nghiem approached Do Trung Hieu and suggested that it would be better to have a Cambodian monk leading the ceremony, given the political sensitivity of the situation. As Do Trung Hieu describes it, there was consensus in trying to accede to this request, and there were discussions about who might possibly fill this role. Under these circumstances the name of Kaet Vay was raised, the man who was said to have never left the monkhood during the Pol Pot period. A helicopter was sent to get him in Kampong Thom and he arrived back at midnight,[32] at which time the members of the delegation met with him for an hour. Since, somewhat like Nel Mony, he had removed his robes and kept them hidden in the woods,[33] they concluded that he really had ceased to be a monk and thus could not serve as a preceptor. He was, however, added to the list of those to be ordained the following day and was put first in order of ordination.

That same night, according to Do Trung Hieu's account, Ven. Buu Chon fell ill and was taken to a Phnom Penh hospital, where he died on September 21. Du Trung Hieu writes that he had suffered from liver illness for some time and had already had an operation for this problem in 1967.[34] His symptoms had recurred before the Phnom Penh trip, but he was determined to go. Prak Ing, on the other hand, told me that Buu Chon was injured in an automobile accident and was taken back to Ho Chi Minh City, where he died. A website critical of Vietnamese policy toward religion also gives the story of an automobile accident (Nguyen and Nguyen 2006). Since Prak Ing said that authorities tried to keep this information from getting out, it may be that he himself was also not privy to what happened, and he based what he told me on stories he heard later. In any case, the secrecy surrounding the event lends it an aura of suspicion.[35]

In the absence of Buu Chon, Gioi Nghiem became the preceptor, in Du Trong Hieu's version of the events.[36] The other two Kinh monks, Sieu Viet and Thien Tam, were *kru sotr* and the four Khmer Krom monks were *hathabat*. The ceremony began at nine o'clock in the morning at Wat Unnalom. The press agency account stated that:

> Chea Sim [vice chairman of the Front Central Committee] made a speech in which he recalled that under the Pol Pot–Ieng Sary regime Buddhist monks had been despised and treated as beasts; monasteries

had been transformed into arms depots, stables, and places of torture and detention; believers had been forced to renounce their faith and monks had been defrocked; those who opposed the regime had been killed. (SWB 1979)

Prak Ing told me that he had experience in sewing and personally prepared the robes for the seven monks. The political authorities attending the ceremony provided food, tea, and sugar. Festivities lasted until two the following morning. As Do Trung Hieu recounts the story, he and Thien Tam stayed behind when the other monks flew back to Ho Chi Minh City and accompanied Buu Chon's body back by land.

The journey was rough and difficult and we were vulnerable to attack by the Khmer Rouge at any time, therefore our security detail was equipped with serious firepower, one group [of them] rode point and another covered our rear and we didn't arrive until two in the morning on September 22, 1979.

Following Events

In the years following the ordination there was some exchange between the Vietnamese and Cambodian Buddhist communities, with monks from Vietnam visiting Cambodia and delegations of Cambodian monks visiting Vietnam—a positive interchange which nevertheless, as it related to Vietnamese political and military dominance over Cambodia during that period, would later sometimes be questioned.

The seven newly ordained monks functioned as a group to perform further ordinations and reestablish the lineage in Cambodia. Initially, according to Prak Ing, Kaet Vay (the oldest) was the preceptor, Prak Dith and Din Sarun were *kru sotr*, and the remaining four were *kannekaq sang*. In addition to his role in ordinations, Tep Vong assumed the role of *viney thor*, meaning that he was in charge of maintaining discipline among the monks. In 1981 (or earlier, by some accounts), because Kaet Vay was growing old, Tep Vong assumed the role of preceptor. Sometimes monks would go to Phnom Penh for ordination; if there were enough men to be ordained in a certain area, the ordination team sometimes might travel there. It took considerable time before the process of reestablishing the lineage was complete, and during this period many *wat* were populated with monks who had undergone unauthorized ordinations, and unauthorized ordinations continued to be performed.[37]

As early as November 1979, Tep Vong declared that those assuming the robes must be former monks, over fifty years old, with "clear" biographies, no "blood debts" (that is to say, no crimes of violence during the DK period), and no responsibilities due toward a wife or children.[38] Under the new procedures, candidates for the monkhood had to be approved by the Front, and those to be ordained received some education about the proper role of the monk in society before the ceremony took place. Also, there was no longer to be a division between the Mahanikay and Thammayut sects. Instead, men ordained as "patriotic monks" under the supervision of *wat* committees linked to the Front, an organizational pattern similar to what was found in Vietnam.

In the course of the 1980s, Tep Vong would emerge as the most senior monk in the country. With later political change and the return of Prince Norodom Sihanouk in 1992, the Sangha would once again be divided into Mahanikay and Thammayut, and royal titles were reestablished. Tep Vong was named Mahanikay patriarch, and a monk who had returned from France, Buu Kri, became the Thammayut patriarch.[39] Over a period of five days beginning on June 2, 1992, some thousand monks were ordained into the Thammayut order in ceremonies performed under a Bodhi tree in front of Wat Batum in Phnom Penh.[40] The ceremony was performed by Buu Kri, as preceptor, and nine other monks—Cambodian-born monks resident in other countries, mostly Thailand. In 2006, Tep Vong was named Samdech Preah Agga Maha Sangharajadhipati, or Great Supreme Patriarch, which gave him authority over the two orders. At the same time Samdech Noun Nget was made patriarch of the Mahanikay order.

Nel Mony continued to perform ordinations for a time after the September ceremony. He reports having been pressed to ordain in the new lineage, and for a three-month period he endured a sort of house arrest in Wat Unnalom. He finally abandoned his robes in 1983, and once policies liberalized in 1991 began to teach Pali in Phnom Penh *wat*, including Wat Saravan. Samdech Loh Lay indicates that both he and Noun Nget provided some financial support to him over the years since he left the monkhood.

Kaev Nim remained a Thammayut monk in Choeung Prey District for three years, but then, like Nel Mony, was brought to Wat Unnalom and held for a period of time while authorities tried to persuade him to ordain in the lineage of the Front. Rather than do so, he simply disrobed. He reordained at the end of the 1980s, when policies began to liberalize.

At least a few monks did manage to resist reordaining in the new lineage, including Ven. Chan Oun, described above, and another monk who asked not to be mentioned by name.

Chan Sang continued to perform ordinations for some time, and as late as 1981 or 1982 was still doing so locally, although not outside his immediate area. As he and Rin describe it, they always felt what they were doing was positive and even that they were helping to enact state policy; when Chan Sang learned he was no longer authorized to perform ordinations there was, as Rin tells the story, a certain bitter shock at having the rug pulled out from under him. He remained a monk until perhaps 1985.[41] His reason for leaving the Sangha was not specifically related to ordination, he says, but to the fact that he was tired of authorities asking him to request money for social projects. He had acquired the not totally justified reputation, he told me, of someone who challenged authorities. Chan Sang's later life was anomalous for an ex-monk of some importance, as some Cambodians accompanying me noted when we first learned his story from relatives. He entered the military, motivated, he said, to learn more about the Khmer Rouge. He rose quickly in rank, but was frustrated by its "injustice and stupidity" and left within months to became a fish merchant on the outskirts of Sihanoukville, where he has remained ever since, a second profession involving the taking of life. He married while in the military and has five children.

Conclusion

Purely in Buddhist terms, the breakdown of a monastic lineage or its restoration are events of historical importance. Perhaps the investiture of a monastic lineage as an enduring social institution can never be totally successful without the implicit or explicit sanction of the state.

Ordination, as ritual, has great personal meaning in the lives of those who ordain, in a web of meaning that extends to the lives of their family members and to the life of the temple community as a whole. At the national level, as Keyes, echoing Weber, has frequently reminded us, religion is deeply involved in the legitimation of both society and the state. The events in Cambodia highlight the degree to which the state is deeply linked to processes of ordination, both in the degree to which the state legitimizes ordination and vice versa. Insofar as ordination is further linked to processes of bureaucratization, it is a very modern institution. In the degree to which the September 1979 ordination was a step in the direction of setting up the state bureaucracies that would continue to provide an organizational structure for religion, it was successful. But insofar as it aimed to be something more—a performative charter ceremony legitimizing the new state—its effect was more ambiguous. Certainly it did not, as Do Trung Hieu had hoped, create in Cambodia a sense of gratitude to the Vietnamese.

The impact of the September ordination was diminished by the fact that the organizers did not succeed in attracting participants from other Theravada countries, and the death of the one Theravada monk in the delegation with an international reputation meant that it was harder to say that the preceptor was chosen for his special status rather than merely because he was Vietnamese. The discussions among Do Trung Hieu, Buu Chon, and Gioi Nghiem the evening prior to the ceremony indicate that there was already some awareness that a Vietnamese preceptor would be perceived negatively. That Vietnamese participation in the event has been kept secret has meant that, in whispered form, it has been part of the discourse used against the state. The Kinh Theravada monks who participated in the ceremony represented, in reality, very complex identities in that they practiced a religion more closely associated with Cambodia than with Vietnam. Their having pointed out the problem is an indication of their sensitivity to the Cambodian perspective. They represent the fluidity of national identity as much as its essentialization—and yet in Cambodian historical memory, to the degree to which they are remembered at all, they are "Vietnamese monks."

In the framework of James Scott's *Seeing Like a State*, the lineage set up by the September ordination may be seen as an attempt to make the Sangha more "legible" to the state. But the process certainly didn't make the state legible to the monkhood, in the sense of accessible and understandable. Rather, the different levels at which the narrative of the ceremony operates—an official version and whispered alternative versions—has tended to obscure the conception of state power and make it appear alien and vaguely corrupt to the Cambodian public.

The ordinations of Nel Mony, Chan Sang, and others show us that there was nothing inevitable about the September ceremony. It was not needed either because of the requirements of Buddhist scriptures or because the general Cambodian population lacked ingenuity in finding ways to re-create the monkhood. While it would be a mistake to overly glamorize their ordinations, they were very meaningful to the people involved at the time. They represent some of the creative communal spirit that flourished in the immediate aftermath of the DK period. The fact that these ordinations traditions were not allowed to continue perhaps merely proves that the establishment of a state-legitimated order will inevitably have human costs—but it is wise not to completely forget those human costs.

Notes

Research for this paper was supported in part by a grant from the Center for Khmer Studies, with funds from the Council American Overseas Research Centers. My fieldwork would not have been possible without the research assistance of Chhuon Hoeur. I owe special thanks as well to Michele Thompson, who helped put me in touch with relevant scholars of Vietnam and reviewed and corrected the translation of a key text from Vietnamese to English. I also thank Thanh Nguyen for generously providing me with a copy of the text by Do Trung Hieu.

For reasons of length, I have deleted sections of the original paper dealing with Long Xim, a monk, or pseudo-monk, who entered with Cambodian troops at the time of the 1978–79 liberation of the country. I have also deleted a section on Buddhist ordination in refugee camps on the Thai-Cambodian border. These can be found in an earlier, somewhat different Spanish version of the essay published by *Estudios de Asia y África* (Marston 2013).

1. "In this case twenty-five monks sit in two concentric semi-circles at a prescribed distance of about twenty inches apart. The ends of the semi-circle are nearest the door. The Upajjhaya sits in the center of the curve, his back to the altar and facing the door and the entering candidate. Just within the ends of the semi-circle sit the two monks who have acted as the tutors of the candidate" (Wells 1939, 123).

2. Interview with Nel Mony, Sept. 16, 2006. My findings are also confirmed in Harris (2007, 186).

3. He remembers only the first names of the other four monks: Chaem, Phon, Mom, and Sot.

4. Interview, March 9, 2007.

5. Chan Sang's account is, in general, consistent with that of Quinn (1976), who wrote about Khmer Rouge activities in Takeo and Kampot in the 1970–74 period, based on interviews with refugees to southern Vietnam. Like Chan Sang, he writes about monks being moved around and concentrated in special locations that the Khmer Rouge designated. While Chan Sang seemed to be saying that he left because he learned of plans to disrobe *all* monks, the Quinn article makes clear that it was only *some* monks who were forced to disrobe (and subsequently expected to join the military).

6. In his interview with me, he reports making this decision on April 7, 1974, but since he showed a tendency to get dates wrong, and since his relatives and the young man who accompanied him to Vietnam said 1973, this seems more likely.

7. Chan Sang gives the date January 24. Rin talks about them arriving in April, shortly before Khmer New Year.

8. I interviewed on March 9, 2007, an elderly man now a monk at Wat Chenchea Trae in Samrong District, Takeo, Ven. Han Tit. He recalled in the period immediately after the end of the Pol Pot period driving an oxcart to take an ex-monk named Pen Pon to ordain with a monk who had returned from Vietnam. Ven. Pen Pon would be the abbot of Wat Chenchea Trae for many years, until his death. He recalled that many monks ordained at that time but only two from Samrong District, which is a significant distance from Trang.

9. Interview with Kaev Nin August 8, 2003, and Sept. 6, 2006.

10. Harris writes about Paen Sen but does not discuss his involvement in ordinations (2007, 179–80).

11. According to Chan Sang the Thammayut ordinations were performed at Wat Khan Long in Trang District; I am not certain if this represents the same wat and group of monks described by Kaev Nin.

12. He doesn't remember last names, but could give me the following first names: Mon (the younger monk), Chut, Phiromy, Noeum, and Nuel.

13. See Marston 2002. Ven. Diep died in October 2011.
14. I wrote about Ngun Son in Marston 2006.
15. Interview with Sao Sareth, Sept. 12, 2006.
16. Ven. Diep recalls only seven monks going.
17. Personal communication, Luis Gomez, October 2006.
18. Presumably associated with the Asian Buddhist Council for Peace (ABCP), with its headquarters in Ulan Bator. An ABCP delegation visited Cambodia in April 1979 and a Cambodian delegation attended an ABCP conference in June (Harris 2006).
19. Ven. Thien Tam, one of the Vietnamese monks who participated in the ceremony, told me that the two figures responsible for this ceremony were Chea Sim and Matt Ly. Interview, June 28, 2010.
20. Buu Chon's name was given on a radio broadcast at the time. The participation of Buu Chon and Gioi Nghiem is mentioned in a short account of Theravada Buddhism in Vietnam by Binh Anson. On a visit to Bu Quang Temple in 2006, the abbot listed for me the four monks from that temple who had been involved in the ceremony: Buu Chon, Gioi Nghiem, Sieu Viet, and Thien Tam. A Cambodian press agency report in French states that "the ceremonies took place under the chairmanship of venerables Thita Silo, Kolalo, and Kosla Chetto" (SWB 1979). We should probably assume that these are a journalists' attempts to record Pali names of the sort given to monks at their ordinations, which a Theravada monk might tend to use on a formal occasion. They do not tell us very much.
21. Do Trung Hieu doesn't mention that they were Khmer Krom, but this is clear from their names, from the interview with Prak Ing, and later my interview with one of the monks in Rach Gia.
22. Thien Tam told me in 2008 that Buu Chon had been resident at Chraoy Chongvar Temple when he was in Cambodia. This is not inconsistent with him studying at Wat Lanka, since he could have taken the boat across the river to study.
23. Interviews with Ven. Thien Tam on June 8, 2008, and June 28, 2010. I note however that Prak Ing told me specifically that Sieu Viet was not Ta Choeuy.
24. His short biography is available at http://www.budsas.org/ebud/milinda/ml-00.htm.
25. Do Trung Hieu and Ohashi both give his name as Danh Âm, a more Khmer-sounding name. According to Oudom Danh, a Khmer Krom man living in the United States who was once a monk in the area, Ngô Van Âm, while definitely a Theravada monk in Rach Gia, was the son of a high-ranking Vietnamese communist leader and a Sino-Khmer mother, thus somewhat ambiguously Khmer.
26. These names were given to me by Ven. Danh Dinh in an interview on June 15 at Chua Roch Soi Temple in Rach Gia, who identified the four Khmer Krom

monks in a picture of the ordination ceremony. These names are consistent with those given in Do Trung Hieu except for the case of Ngô Van Âm. Ohashi spells the last name Danh Diêm and gives the name of a fifth monk, Danh Ôn.

27. Interview with Pen Sovan, July 2, 2010. On the other hand, Gotesman (2002, 73) says that Tep Vong was "a forty-nine-year-old former refugee in Vietnam, who served as a founding member of the Front and, later, as vice president of the National Assembly." The phrase "a founding member of the Front" is slightly ambiguous, since it seems to imply that he was present when the Front was founded on November 27, 1978, in Vietnam, but could refer to the Front government founded in Phnom Penh in July 1979. According to Harris (2005, 192), Kaet Vay was a member as well, although the account by Do Trung Hieu of how he came to join the group of monks being ordained leads me to question this. (I note as well that Ohashi [2008] says that, according to a Khmer monk in Tra Vinh Province, Vietnam, Tep Vong went to his temple soon after liberation and requested robes but was refused. I am wary of this statement, since the monk interviewed did not actually meet Tep Vong, and the story raises more questions than it answers. Pen Sovan was clearly indicating that Tep Vong had been in Cambodia the whole time—but is it possible to reconcile his story of meeting Tep Vong in June with the other accounts that place him as a refugee in Vietnam?)

28. Interviews with Prak Ing, July 26, 2003, and March 19, 2007. Samdech Loh Lay, when asked the same question said he was sure that Noun Nget, Et Sum, and Prak Dith had ordained with Nel Mony. He was uncertain about Kaen Von and did not mention Din Sarun.

29. Interview with Suos Mao, June 16, and 19, 2010.

30. Interview with Thien Tam, June 8, 2008.

31. I also interviewed one of the monks ordained, Samdech Noun Nget, but found his account sufficiently inconsistent with others that I have used details from it only with great care.

32. The Do Trung Hieu account says Kampong Cham, but he is consistently described elsewhere as coming from Kampong Thom. Suos Mao, who claimed to have accompanied him, also said they did not fly but went by road.

33. The oral version in circulation in Kampong Thom, as reported to me by persons at his former *wat*, is that like Nel Mony he kept the robes on his person and wore them at night.

34. Thien Tam and the monk at Rach Gia also reported that the death was due to liver problems.

35. The website states: "The death of His Holiness Buu Chan was a doubtful question. He was reportedly involved in an automobile accident when he was on his way to a pilgrimage in Phnom Penh, Kampuchea. He died when he was brought to a hospital. No one knows what really happened to him." Nel Mony, who obviously has his own ax to grind, also mentioned the death and hinted at foul play.

36. Prak Ing states the Sieu Viet was preceptor. Gioi Nghiem, a more senior monk, seems like the more logical choice, and Prak Ing's statement may simply be an indication that names were never made clear and subsequent documents were few. Since Prak Ing and others make a point of saying that the monk they knew as Ta Choeuy was not the preceptor, then if he was Sieu Viet, that would itself confirm that Sieu Viet could not have been the preceptor.

37. Government memoranda in 1982 and 1986 decry the problem of monks with illegal ordinations, an indication that the problem persisted (especially with reference to younger monks). Government memorandum dated Oct. 1, 1982, signed by Chea Sim, "*Sarachar stey bi kar reapcham brah buddhasasna ekbhap samaggibhab aoy pan parisoddh hmat cat.*" Government memorandum dated June 3, 1986, signed by Min Khin, "*Secktey naenam stey bi kar anuvattn gol nayopay camboh buddhasasna.*"

38. Ibid., 1986 document.

39. Early in 2006, Tep Vong was elevated to a position above *both* of the orders, at which time Noun Nget, the other remaining monk from the September 1979 ordination, became the Mahanikay patriarch.

40. Interview with Buu Kri, March 15, 2007.

41. Chan Sang told me he left the monkhood in 1985, but Rin told me that Chan Sang had left the monkhood in 1983 or 1984.

References

Binh Anson. 1999. "Theravada Buddhism in Vietnam." http://phatgiaonguyenthuy.com.

Bizot, François. 1988. *Les traditions de la* pabbajjā *en Asie du Sud-Est*. Göttingen: Vendenhoeck & Ruprecht.

Blackburn, Anne M. 2003. "Localizing Lineage: Importing Higher Ordination in Theravadin South and Southeast Asia." In *Constituting Communities: Theravada Buddhism and the Religious Cultures of South and Southeast Asia*, edited by John Clifford Holt, Jacob N. Kinnard, Jonathan S. Walters, 131–49. Albany, NY: SUNY Press.

Bourdeaux, Pascal. 2007. "Du temps où le vénérable Hô Tông se nommait Lê Văn Giang: Etude de la fondation du bouddhisme theravada vietnamien à travers quelques éléments de biographie (période 1883–1940)." Unpublished ms.

Gombrich, Richard. 1988. *Theravada Buddhism: A Social History from Ancient Benares to Modern Colombo*. London and New York: Routledge.

Gottesman, Evan. 2002. *Cambodia After the Khmer Rouge: Inside the Politics of Nation Building*. New Haven: Yale University Press.

Harris, Ian. 2005. *Cambodian Buddhism: History and Practice*. Honolulu: University of Hawaii Press.

———. 2006. "Entrepreneurism and Charisma: Two Modes of Doing Business in Post-Pol Pot Cambodian Buddhism." In *Expressions of Cambodia: The Politics of Tradition, Identity and Change*, edited by Leakthina Chau-Pech Ollier and Tim Winter, 167–80. London, New York: Routledge.

———.2007. *Buddhism under Pol Pot*. Phnom Penh: Documentation Center of Cambodia.

Keyes, Charles. 1986. "Ambiguous Gender: Male Initiation in a Buddhist Society." In *Religion and Gender: Essays in the Complexity of Symbols*, edited by Carolyn Bynum, Stevan Harrell, and Paula Richman, 66–96. Boston: Beacon Press.

———. 1994. "Communist Revolution and the Buddhist Past in Cambodia." In *Asian Visions of Authority*, edited by Charles F. Keyes, Laurel Kendall, and Helen Hardacre, 43–73. Honolulu: University of Hawaii Press.

Lê Húu Dan. 1995. *Tai lieu soi sáng su that*. Fremont, CA: Lê Húu Dan.

Lefferts, H. Leedom Jr. 1994 "Clothing the Serpent: Transformations of the Naak in Thai-Lao Theravada Buddhism." In *The Transformative Power of Cloth in Southeast Asia*, edited by Lynne Milgram and Penny Van Esterik. Canadian Council for Southeast Asian Studies, The Museum for Textiles.

Löschmann, Heike. 1989. *Die Rolle des Buddhismus in der Gesellschaftlichen Entwickllung der Volksrepublic Kampuchea nach der Befreiung vom Pol-Pot-Rebime 1979 bis Mitte der achtiziger Jahre*. PhD diss., Humboldt-Universität.

Marston, John. 2002, "La reconstrucción de budismo 'antiguo' de Camboya." *Estudios de Asia y África* 37 (2): 271–303.

———. 2006. "Death, Memory, and Building: The Non-Cremation of a Cambodian Monk." *Journal of Southeast Asian Studies* 37 (3):491–505.

———. 2011. "Introduction." In *Anthropology and Community in Cambodia: Reflections on the Work of May Ebihara*, edited by John Marston, 5–20. Melbourne: Monash University Press.

———. 2013. "El restablecimiento del monacato camboyano."*Estudios de Asia y África* 150 XLVIII (1), Enero–Abril.

de Nike, Howard J., John Quiglye, and Kenneth J. Robinson, eds. 2000. *Genocide in Cambodia: Documents from the Trial of Pol Pot and Ieng Sary*. Philadelphia: University of Pennsylvania Press.

Ohashi Hisatoshi, 2008. "Diffusion of Vietnamese Theravada and Its Re-Import into Cambodia." In *Khmer People in Southern Vietnam: Their Society and Culture*, edited by Hisatoshi Ohashi and Naomitsu Mikami, 3–32. Tokyo: Keio University Press.

Ovensen, Jan, Ing-Britt Trankell, and Joakim Öjendal. 1996. *When Every Household Is an Island: Social Organization and Power Structures in Rural Cambodia*. Uppsala: Uppsala Research Reports in Cultural Anthropology.

Nguyen Quoc Viet and Nguyen Dai Tuong. 2006? "Religions in Communist Vietnam." Available at http://www.danchu.net/ArticlesChinhLuan/ CollectionVN/NguyenQuocViet001.htm.

Quinn, Kenneth. 1976. "Political Change in Wartime: The Khmer Krahom Revolution in Southern Cambodia, 1970–1974." *Naval War College Review*, Spring: 3–31.

Rappaport, Roy A. 1999. *Ritual and Religion in the Making of Humanity*. Cambridge University Press.

Rhys Davids, T. W., and Hermann Oldenberg, trans. 1881. *Vinaya Texts*, Part 1. Delhi: Motilal Banardsidass.

Scott, James C. 1998. *Seeing Like a State: How Certain Schemes to Improve the Human Condition Have Failed*. New Haven and London: Yale University Press.

Sou Ketya, Hean Sokhom, and Hun Thirith. 2005. *The Ordination of Buddhist Monks in Cambodia: Past and Present*. Phnom Penh: Center for Advanced Study.

Summary of World Broadcasts. 1979. "Vietnamese Buddhists in Cambodia." FE/6255/A3/7, Sept. 21; "Reordination of Buddhist Monks" and "Vietnamese Buddhist Delegation in Cambodia," FE/6231/A3/6-7, Sept. 28.

Swearer, Donald K. 1995. *The Buddhist World of Southeast Asia*. Albany, NY: SUNY Press.

Taylor, Keith W. 1992. "The Early Kingdoms." In *The Cambridge History of Southeast Asia*, 137–82. Cambridge: Cambridge University Press.

Thanissaro Bikkhu. 2002. *The Buddhist Monastic Code II: Vol. II, The Khandhaka Rules Translated and Explained*. Valley Center, CA: Metta Forest Monastery.

Van Gennep, Arnold. 1964. *The Rites of Passage*, translated by Monika B. Vizdon and Gabrielle L. Caffee. Chicago: University of Chicago Press.

Vickery, Michael. 1986. *Kampuchea: Politics, Economics and Society*. London: Frances Pinter; Boulder: Lynne Rienner.

Wells, Kenneth Elmer. 1939. *Thai Buddhism: Its Rites and Activities*. Bangkok: The Bangkok Times Press.

Zucker, Eve. 2007. "Memory and (Re) Making Moral Order in the Aftermath of Violence in a Highland Khmer Village in Cambodia. PhD diss., London School of Economics.

THE GRASSROOTS NEGOTIATION OF MODERNITY

ALTERITY TO MODERNITY:
Village-Based Self-Sufficient Farm Production in Northeastern Thailand

Ratana Tosakul

Introduction

The opening of the 10th International Conference on Thai Studies by Her Royal Highness Princess Maha Chakri Sirindhorn of Thailand, at Thammasat University, January 9, 2008, was followed by three keynote speeches: one by Charles F. Keyes entitled "The Village Economy: Capitalist and Sufficiency Based: A Northeastern Thai Case." It was a significant reminder that rural farmers in northeastern Thailand (locally known as Isan) do act according to their Buddhist moral principles despite their enthusiastic embrace of capitalism.

Keyes traced the changes in Thailand over the past forty years. He said that Thai villagers have left behind what has been called the "sufficiency economy" to undeniably embrace the global capitalist system, but their economic decisions, aspirations, and life choices remain significantly tempered by Buddhist teachings based on moderation and self-reliance. Keyes's reminder of the economic world of rural villagers in Thailand provides a good framework for the ways I develop my arguments in this chapter. Commercialization of agriculture has profoundly penetrated rural areas of Thailand since the 1960s, when the first national economic development plan was drafted (Ratana 1997).

By the 1980s, a call emerged for sustainable development through "sufficiency" farming techniques as a development alternative to modernizing rural agriculture in Thai society, the initiative primarily of some NGOs and village leaders, many of them from northeastern Thailand. The sufficiency economy approach has, however, been modified and developed by Thai elites for political and economic reasons.

In this chapter, I investigate the cultural logic of economic action by farmers in Isan who have opted to embrace the sufficiency approach. I chose to focus on the case of a farmers' group in Isan named the In-Plaeng Network, located in Ban Bua village of Sakon Nakhon Province. In-Plaeng literally means the creation of the god Indra. This case was selected because it is well known locally and internationally in NGO and academic circles as well as by some concerned Thai state agencies. In-Plaeng has been regarded as a successful translation of the concept of sufficiency economy into practice.

Data for this paper is primarily based on documentary and field surveys. In 2005, I carried out anthropological fieldwork with Ban Bua villagers. In addition, supplementary information was drawn from an August 2007 interview with Bamrung Kayotha, one of the most famous farmer leaders from northeastern Thailand and a consultant to the Assembly of the Poor at the national level. Bamrung is a farmer from Kalasin Province in Isan who has practiced organic farming according to the philosophy of the sufficiency economy over the past twenty years.

Specifically, I will discuss how villagers of Ban Bua, who constitute the majority of the members of the In-Plaeng Network, understand and regard the sufficiency economy approach and what their economic rationality has been in relation to it. I argue that the sufficiency economy approach as understood and practiced by villagers in Isan does not entirely negate capitalism, as the general public in Thailand might have thought. Although the approach proposed by some local NGOs and some farmer leaders, particularly from Isan, starting in the 1980s, could be regarded as a critique of Thai state-led capitalist development policies, the sufficiency economy approach, surprisingly, does exist within the framework of capitalism.

Conceptualizing the Economic Rationality of Farmers

To understand the local interpretations of Thailand's sufficiency economy and how local people put it into practice, we must take into consideration their cultural references (Keyes 1983). Theoretical works of Ricoeur (1971) and Keyes (1983; 1991) are useful for understanding folk interpretations of economic rationality. Ricouer (1971) suggests that villagers acquire primary understandings of their world from the cultural "texts" available to them, in the broadest sense of the word. These "texts" are structured to make coherent statements about aspects of the world in which they live; they become fixed through villagers' memories as well as in actual written texts and other forms of cultural inscription (such as rituals or folk arts) so that such "texts" transcend the time and place in which they were created.

Keyes (1983) suggests that one of the primary traditional cultural sources for explaining the economic rationality of Thai-Lao villagers in Isan is their practical morality, which is rooted in the Buddhist worldview. Keyes (1983) further argues that villagers in Isan seek to advance their family interests not only with reference to their Buddhist culture but also the conditions of the wider socio-political-economic setting that constrain their lives.

Also, in agreement with Keyes, I have argued elsewhere (Ratana 1997) that in the process of the modernization of Thailand, beginning at the turn of the nineteenth century, the village culture of Isan has been significantly influenced by "new texts" deriving from their interaction with state-led rural agricultural development policies, their out-migration experiences both within the country and internationally, their participation in the expansion of the global capitalistic market economy, and the promotion of nationalism in the school system and the mass media. In addition, some villagers construct their notions of economic rationality from interactions with other social groups, such as non-governmental organizations (NGOs), other villagers' groups, and academics.

Village-Based Sufficiency Economy Approach

By the 1980s, local and international NGOs working primarily in the field of integrated rural development to promote the well-being of rural communities in Isan and elsewhere in Thailand began to play a significant role in critiquing the state-led capitalist development approach. They perceived that such a heavily market-driven approach could undermine the well-being of rural communities at large. They argued that commercialization of farm production for export was not a feasible strategy for poor farmers, especially for small farmers in Thailand. This was due to unfavorable market price mechanisms, which did not favor the rural agricultural farming sector. Small farmers fell victim to exploitation via market price mechanisms. Also, commercialized farming depended heavily on the use of chemical substances that were harmful to humans and the natural environment. These NGOs and some village leaders initiated the idea of sufficiency farm production for rural poor farm households as a development alternative to improve their disadvantaged position in the wider market economy.

The idea of sufficiency farming was initially introduced by European international NGOs, which were major financial donors to several local Thai NGOs between the 1980s and 1990s. These local NGOs were later also exposed to ideas and practices of some Japanese NGOs and farmer movements focused on organic farming, alternative markets, and sustainable development.

The essence of sufficiency farming, as practiced by villagers in Isan, is integrated organic farming, growing diversified food crops in combination with animal husbandry, instead of mono-crop agriculture, such as cassava and sugarcane plantations, as is often seen in capitalist farming in Thailand. The diverse selection of crops grown and animals raised in integrated organic farming depends first on the farm family's consumption needs and is not driven by market motivations as in capitalism. Whatever is left over from home consumption can then be sold in the market. Also, the use of decomposed fertilizer and herbs for agricultural production is strongly promoted.

It was in the late 1980s that a network for alternative agriculture was formally established among local NGOs and farmer's organizations in

Thailand, and later in 1998, the Sustainable Agriculture Foundation (Thailand) was set up to act as a coordinating body for promoting sustainable agriculture in rural development as an alternative to capitalist farm production (Anusorn 2003) The local movement for sustainable development in Thailand also originated in the broad "anti-neoliberalism" feelings of some local NGOs and farmer leaders, particularly from Isan. Nonetheless, individuals and groups in the larger overall movement cannot be seen as homogeneous. They each manage their own economic activities relating to sufficiency farming independently. Some are quite different from others in their approach in terms of their definitions, ideas, and practices. Generally, all do share a common orientation against globalization (Bell 2008), and a common belief system, based on Buddhist principles, emphasizing moderation, self-reliance, hard work, patience, and self-restraint in the face of material temptations and desires (Keyes 1983).

According to a database for groups involved in sufficiency economy activities in Thailand organized by Pipat Yodphruttikan in 2006, there are 626 groups currently involved in activities relating to the sufficiency economy throughout Thailand, primarily at the grassroots level. Of these, 448 are classified as having minimal involvement, 126 as actively engaged in both philosophy and action, and 12 considered model farmers (Pipat 2006, 7). The distribution of the total 626 groups by regions is as follows: central plains: 140; west: 9; east: 11; north: 51; northeast: 259; and south: 156 (Pipat 2006, 5). Economic activities relating to the sufficiency economy can be classified as follows: 25 groups in royal development projects; 64 groups as farmer models; 117 groups as community models, 4 groups as private businesses; 339 groups as community enterprises; 43 groups as saving groups; and 34 groups classified as "others" (for example, local knowledge masters) (Pipat 2006, 6). Albeit small in number, the movement indicates a significant historical moment in Thailand where grassroots movement began to emerge, calling for sustainable development in agriculture and providing a development alternative to Thai modernity. The In-Plaeng Network is an exemplar of the grassroots movement, which I turn to in the following section.

Learning from Experiences of Farmers in the In-Plaeng Network

The majority of members of the In-Plaeng Network are from Ban Bua, whose population is primarily of the Ka-loeng ethnic minority, a Mon-Khmer speaking group. Their ancestors migrated across the Mekong River from Kammuan Province of Laos to reside in Thailand in the distant past. Similar to most rural populations in Thailand, villagers of Ban Bua strive to pursue the economic interests of their families.

Ban Bua is a rain-fed agricultural community that has been increasingly integrated into the global market economy. This integration was particularly evident by the 1960s. Thus, I will focus on the economic transformation of Ban Bua from the 1960s onwards.

The majority of villagers in Ban Bua are small agricultural producers. They grow both glutinous and non-glutinous rice for home consumption and for sale domestically and internationally. Several older villagers (sixty years old and above) told me that, since childhood, they have also relied on the rich natural products of the forest and other resources of the Phu Phan mountain area for the survival of their families.

Life in the past was frequently recalled by older villagers of Ban Bua as one of hardship, self-sufficiency, abundance of forest and land, and high levels of cooperation among kin and neighbors, both within and between village communities. Similar to Ban Nong Tuen, where Keyes has conducted anthropological fieldwork since 1963, and other communities in Isan, changes in Ban Bua (and processes of modernity) were the result of the greater incorporation of the northeast into Thai national systems and the integration of the region with domestic and international capitalist production and consumption following reforms implemented during and after the reign of King Chulalongkorn at the turn of the nineteenth century (Keyes 1967; Ratana 1997).

In 1961, the government, led by General Sarit Thanarat, initiated the first national economic development plan, emphasizing national economic growth through the modernization and industrialization of the country. Also, the government aimed to suppress communist ideology and subversive movements related to it in the rural countryside, especially in the northeast. Thus, the government created a special development plan for the northeast in 1962 in order to gain villagers' loyalty (Ratana 1997). During the 1950s and 1960s the Phu Phan mountain area was classified as a significant stronghold of communist insurgents. and therefore a very politically sensitive area. Accordingly, infrastructural development was introduced into the area, such as road connections between communities and the capital of Sakon Nakhon Province. Since the 1960s, road improvement and other state-sponsored infrastructure developments have contributed to local people's material conveniences, facilitated the expansion of the market economy, and enabled military operations.

Like villagers elsewhere, the majority of Ban Bua villagers have strived to pursue the economic interests of their families through a number of strategies. In general, they respond rationally to economic incentives and opportunities available to them (Popkin 1979) within the political economic structural constraints, and with reference to a practical morality based on Buddhist worldview as their primary source of cultural reference for their economic actions (Keyes 1983). They have made every possible effort to improve the economic interests of their families, which can be said to be far beyond the level of economic subsistence. These farmers do not live close to the margin of subsistence, nor can we say they have little scope for profit maximization (as Scott 1976 characterized peasants in Southeast Asia in general). Farmers from Ban Bua are quite fortunate in that they have access to the rich forest products and other natural resources of the Phu Phan mountain area and various rivers and streams in the area. Yet, they have tried in every possible way to advance the well-being of their families.

Similar to what has occurred in other communities, villagers in Ban Bua have expanded rice landholdings. Between 1988 and 2005 the average rice landholding increased from 11.25 rai (1.8 hectares) to 21 rai (3.36 hectares) per household. Since the mid 1960s, most villagers have adopted new high-yield varieties of rice associated with the use of chemical fertilizers. Their average rice production increased from 250kg per rai (0.16 hectare) in 1988 to 315kg per rai in 2005. They produce rice for both export and home consumption.

In 1966, based upon the recommendation of agricultural extension officials in Thailand and the expansion of the global market, the majority of villagers began jute production, converting parts of the forestland around Phu Phan mountain into cultivatable farmland. Two years later, when the price of jute went down, many switched to cassava. Again, the price of cassava fluctuated greatly. By the early 1970s, almost every household had fallen into a cycle of debt. They were in need of cash to buy chemical fertilizers and pay for the hired labor needed for rice and cassava production. Thus, many took loans from the Bank of Agriculture and Cooperatives (BAAC) and from private moneylenders in the area that charged high interest rates. When the European market stopped purchasing Thai cassava products, most farmers of Ban Bua and elsewhere in Isan went bankrupt. Based upon the recommendation of agricultural extension officials, they shifted to growing cashew nuts. Unfortunately, most farmers could not pursue their economic interests effectively no matter how hard they tried, as the cashew trees did not bear fruit for six years.

By the end of the 1970s, Ban Bua villagers had an average of 40,000 baht (US$1,176) debt per household. Despite the range of farming activities, there was not enough farm employment for everyone in the community due to a population increase and land limitations, since another state agency, the Forestry Department, now prohibited land encroachment into the forested area of Phu Phan mountain. Some families set up small convenience stores in the village whereas others invested in other small-scale enterprises, such as stalls for selling local food and desserts. About one-third of the community (mostly males) migrated to work at the various kinds of jobs available in the urban industrial zones in Bangkok and other major cities, domestically and abroad. Some village women migrated to work in factories, the service industry, or as maids to wealthy Bangkok families. A few, as a strategy for poverty eradication, chose to marry Western men and migrated to reside with their husbands overseas (Ratana 2005). Through out-migration, villagers became aware of their relative poverty compared with those living modern urban lifestyles in Bangkok, and a perception arose of their economic and cultural inferiority. This is a historical and cultural legacy of what has been called the "internal colonialism" (Anderson 1978) of Bangkok's power over the regional peripheries throughout the country since the reign of King Chulalongkorn (Keyes 1967; Ratana 1997).

Thus, I argue here that villagers of Ban Bua are in many ways similar to villagers in other communities in Isan and elsewhere in Thailand. They are rational farmers who seek to advance the economic interests of their families in every possible way, based on the economic opportunities available to them. The idea of the sufficiency economy, introduced to them in the late 1980s, has been another economic option, offering them hope that it could help improve their economic position within the capitalist system.

Reinventing Traditions for Protecting Rural Economy

Since 1988, the villagers of Ban Bua have been interacting with academics and local NGOs. They have thus been exposed to another new cultural source for constructing their local interpretations of the sufficiency economy. In 1988, representatives from the NGO Village Foundation and academics from Sakon Nakhon Rajabhat Institute chose Ban Bua as a field site for a research project focused on the Kaleong culture and its transformation to modernity. Thawatchai Kunwong, a young graduate volunteer, was employed as a research assistant. He was sent to live in the community and developed a close rapport with villagers. He finally decided to become an "insider" of the community by settling down there for good. While living in the community, Thawatchai has been a catalyst in stimulating villagers to review and reflect on what has happened to their way of living economically and their natural environment following the commercialization of agriculture since the 1960s.

Also, in 1990, another NGO, the Association for Rural Development of the Northeast, came to support the work of Thawatchai and the villagers by providing training in organizational skills and sustainable development techniques. Through intensive discussion and field visits to different integrated demonstration farms throughout Thailand between 1988 and 1989, some village leaders became aware of their disadvantaged position in the market economy. They realized that small farmers were in a position neither to negotiate with traders at different levels nor to regulate capitalistic market price mechanisms that had never favored small agricultural producers. Also, they were made aware of the destruction of the Phu Phan mountain forests as a result of the commercialization of agricultural production.

The idea of revitalizing their traditional community culture, emphasizing villagers' cooperation and mutual sharing as well as practicing the sufficiency economy, were thus stimulated in discussions and field trips. Finally, thirteen villagers began to organize themselves into a group called Klum Kong Thun Phan Kla Mai Phuen Ban, which literally means "local plant-breeding promotion fund." They aimed at preserving the Phu Phan forest's natural environment through re-forestation with its original plant species. The group's name was later changed to In-Plaeng in 1992, by a group of visitors to the village. These thirteen farmers began to put the idea of sufficient integrated organic farming into practice. They made food production their first priority rather than, as previously, monoculture cash crops. One of the group leaders explained his idea of sufficiency economy, as follows:

> I understand that the idea of sufficiency economy means to live moderately and in harmony with the natural environment. The market economy caused small farmers to fall into a vulnerable position, as we experienced previously. Sufficiency economy is giving first priority to our food production and to all that we need to consume in our daily lives. Whatever is left over could be sold in the market. We need to create food security for our families first through sufficiency farm production. We also need to protect our natural environment that gives us sources of food and other necessities in life. In the past, sufficiency economy was predominant in the community culture. Our forefathers used to live this way. Social changes have led us into the global market economy of contemporary times. We do not object to industries and modernity. But we need to rethink and combine the good aspects of our traditions with those of the modern world. I think we need to strengthen our capacity in order to have some self-protection against outside harmful influences.

The aim of the In-Plaeng Network has been to promote self-reliance, human security, and sustainable development by local communities. The philosophy of the sufficiency economy of the In-Plaeng Network highlights moderation, self-reliance, community cooperation, and sharing between farmers.

Buddhist Morality and Economic Action of Farmers

I agree with Keyes (1983) that villagers in northeastern Thailand acquire their primary notions of their world from the social, political, and economic contexts within which they live, and from their religious beliefs. Buddhist philosophy puts a great emphasis on individual action, responsibility, and its consequences. Under the law of karma, each person is responsible for his or her own deeds. Thus, the economic success of a person and a family is understood as the individual's responsibility as determined by karma (Tambiah 1970; Kirsch 1982; and Keyes 1983; 1993). If one wants to achieve economic success, one should follow the Buddhist path and be hard working, moderate, self-reliant, simple, economical, patient, humble, and restrain oneself from temptations and desire (Keyes 1983; 1991).

The In-Plaeng Network committee members see sufficiency farming philosophy as largely influenced by Buddhist principles emphasizing moderation, hard work, patience, and self-reliance. Also, to live one's life according to the Buddhist philosophy, one should refrain from material temptations.

The case of a male villager, whom I call Serm, illustrates this point well. Serm and his wife are poor farmers with two sons. His family has been part of the In-Plaeng Network since 1994. Similar to many others in Ban Bua, he faced market price fluctuations for all the cash crops his family produced between the 1960s and 1970s. In the end, his family had debts totaling 30,000 baht (US$ 882). After joining the In-Plaeng Network, the family stopped growing a cash crop monoculture. Instead, they planted diverse food crops for home consumption and sale. Still, they have continued to grow rice for export. In other words, the family did not stop producing rice for export even when they chose to engage in sufficiency economy practices.

Also, they have replaced the use of chemical fertilizers and insecticides with decomposed fertilizer. Today, there are over three hundred species of plants on their farm. These products are for home consumption and for sale. Food crop diversification also helps revitalize soil fertility. The family has enough food for home consumption. Their average annual sale of farm products is about 60,000–70,000 baht (US$1,765–2,059), which is more than enough for the family, as most of their food is available from their farm. Also, they have been able to save some money earned from sufficiency integrated farming and other income sources, such as the sale of paddy and remittances from sons who migrated to work in Bangkok. Serm and his wife used some parts of the saving to purchase an additional 32 *rai* (5.12 hectare) of farmland. In addition, they have been able to pay off the debts generated by past cash crop production. Serm and his wife have also restrained themselves from material temptations and desire. They live moderately. His wife is responsible and hardworking, with what Thai call "a cool heart," and patience. Serm and his wife think that knowledge, moderation, self-reliance, hard work, frugality, and perseverance are important factors contributing to his family's economic success.

Rational Farmers

Keyes (1983) is right when he notes that villagers in Isan are rational farmers who seek to advance the economic interests of their families in every possible way based on the economic opportunities available to them, despite national political economic constraints they have encountered. The majority of Ban Bua villagers confirm this point.

All the members of the In-Plaeng Network have had at least one member of their families migrate to work locally or internationally. Serm's family is a vivid example. While he and his wife have engaged in integrated organic farming and in rice production for export, their sons have migrated to work in the industrial service sector in Bangkok. Their sons send money home on occasion, which has contributed significantly to the family's economic interests.

Another example is Mali's family, who joined the In-Plaeng Network in 1995. Her family is considered a "middle farm family." Similar to all other In-Plaeng Network members in Ban Bua, the family has engaged in diverse economic activities. Mali works at her grocery store in the village, from which the family derives its main source of income. Her husband works as a janitor at a village primary school. In his free time, he works as a carpenter, making or repairing home furniture. Both Mali and her husband help with the work of their integrated organic farm. Similar to all other members of the network, the family fell into debt following market price fluctuations for cassava. They decided to adopt the sufficiency farm approach to reduce farm investment expenses caused by expensive chemical fertilizer and pesticides. Also, they thought that by working in integrated organic farming, the family would be able to reduce their expenses, since food would be available on their farm. Further, they could reduce medical costs because they would have better-quality farm products for home consumption. They would be healthier, as they would not expose themselves to chemical substances. When asked if the family wanted to withdraw from the market economy and entirely embrace the sufficiency economy, they expressed the opinion that it would be impossible to survive. The income generated from this type of farm is not enough to sustain the family all year round. It only helps reduce some food, medical, and farm investment expenses. They need to combine the various economic activities available to them to advance the well-being of their family.

 I have now come to realize that I was mistaken in initially thinking that the sufficiency economy as understood and practiced by the villagers of Ban Bua works entirely against neo-liberalism. It is now clear to me that these families comprise flexible farmers seeking to pursue the interests of their families in every possible way that is available to them. They do not object to industry and modernity. They simply want to reduce or minimize economic risks while enthusiastically participating in the expansion of the global market economy through the adoption of the sufficiency economy approach. In my view, the approach applied by these villagers has been implemented logically within the framework of capitalism. Through the sufficiency economy approach, farmers have reduced the investment costs of their farms, such as those of fertilizer, food for home consumption, and medical expenses.

Another Advocacy Perspective by a Prominent Farmer Leader

In August 2007, I had a chance to talk to Mr. Bamrung Kayotha, a well-known Isan farmer leader, at his farm residence in Kalasin Province. I was impressed by the peaceful, shady, and cool atmosphere of his organic farm. His house is located by a big pond full of fish. On his farm, there are a variety of plants, trees, and home-grown vegetables, as well as pigs and poultry. He and his wife produce food chiefly for home consumption and for sale in the local market. They hardly buy any food. They also state that their family will not encounter food shortages for at least a few years. They believe they have enough food supplies. Bamrung further reiterates his belief that his organic farm is a vivid exemplar of a farm family in Isan putting the philosophy of Thailand's sufficiency economy into practice in the past decade.

Similar to many farmers in Ban Bua who have adopted sufficiency economy practices, Bamrung twenty years ago used to go bankrupt because he depended chiefly on mono cash crop production, such as cassava. Nonetheless, his family had no debt, because they had non-farm production. After training in Japan in organic farming, he returned home and began to put it into practice, mainly for home consumption and for local sale. Still, the family retains some plots of farmland for rice cultivation for export and home consumption.

Bamrung is obviously in favor of the sufficiency farm approach, which his family has practiced over the past twenty years. He believes that this idea can help address the four basic human needs: for food, clothes, shelter, and medicine. If farmers could produce at least 80 percent of what they need to consume and use in their everyday lives, this would be the best guarantee of basic security.

Nonetheless, Bamrung feels that farm production based on the concept of the sufficiency economy alone is not enough to help farmers survive. There should be alternative markets for producers and consumers of organic products. This would redress the problem of unfavorable market prices that are biased against the agricultural sector. The state should step in to help organize this. Organic farming production does not aim at profit maximization as in capitalistic farm production. For him, organic farming aspires to enhance peaceful coexistence between humans and nature. Building environmental awareness in the public to help protect the natural environment is a must. Also, this type of farm production stresses the farmers' sufficiency economy. It aims to provide security for both farmers and consumers by promoting a system in which producers receive a fair share of the economic distribution and consumers pay a reasonable market price. Thus, direct sale from producers to consumers is a major component of the alternative market. Also, he believes that the alternative market has to be combined with an alternative way of living, which should correspond to the philosophy of the sufficiency economy, highlighting moderation, self-reliance, simplicity, perseverance, moral values, and knowledge, as well as health and environmental concerns.

In addition, Bamrung mentioned that the philosophy of sufficiency economy would benefit farmers best if it was accompanied by policy support and advocacy to make farmers' problems known to the state and to the public. Farmers in Isan and elsewhere need to catch up with the current political economic issues, and be informed on both the implications of various policies and how they impact local communities. Organizing farmers to defend their political and economic interests is necessary to establish a proper platform for farmers (especially small farmers) to negotiate with other concerned parties, such as state policy-makers and businessmen.

Finally, Bamrung believes that in pursuing their economic interests based on the philosophy of sufficiency economy, farmers need to have allies from different organizations to support their work and to exchange knowledge, skills, and information for updating their organic farming movements, as well as other related activities.

At this point, I do agree with Bamrung that the approach may work to guarantee food security for farmers, at least at a certain level. In the case of Bamrung's family, after twenty years of applying the approach, they are not wealthy. They live moderately. I wonder how his family would support the higher education of their only child and what they would do if a family member became ill and needed special medical care in hospital. I also agree with the critique of the sufficiency economy approach by Walker (2008). Visiting Bamrung's farm convinced me that the approach places all responsibility for poverty eradication on the farmers themselves. This has made it possible for the government to avoid, or play a low profile in, addressing any redistribution of resources or income to the rural population of Thailand. Also, I feel that it is possible for Bamrung's family to pursue the sufficiency economy approach because his family currently has no debt. They love what they have been doing on the farm. They do not have many dependents. They are hard-working, self-reliant, and live moderately.

The Sufficiency Economy Is Not Applicable to All

The In-Plaeng Network originally began with thirteen pilot farm demonstrators. Today, the network has extended to cover four provinces in Isan, including Sakon Nakhon, Kalasin, Mukdahan, and Udon Thani. Members comprise of 890 communities in eighty-four sub-districts of twenty-two districts (Ratana et al 2005).

Surprisingly, only a handful of farmers in each community are members of the In-Plaeng Network. In Ban Bua itself, about one-third the total farm families have applied the sufficiency economy concept. The majority of villagers are still pursuing the economic interests of their families in various ways, as already mentioned. Many villagers who have not yet put the concept into practice mentioned that they do not have enough farmland to plant diversified crops. Others said that they do not have enough labor to help work on the farm. Also, they think it takes time to reap the benefits from an integrated sufficiency farm. They do not have enough financial resources for their families' everyday use and are in need of cash for different family activities, such as paying for their children's education fees, medical bills, house construction, and other contingencies. They like the idea, but it is not appropriate for them to put into action at the moment. Landless peasants think that this philosophy is not for them, as they have no farmland.

More Criticism of the Sufficiency Economy Approach

Following the economic crisis of Thailand in mid-1997, His Majesty King Bhumibol of Thailand initiated a policy that modified the sufficiency economy approach and applied it to all sectors and levels of Thai society as the main national development and administrative approach. It was espoused by the military coup-installed government led by General Surayudh Chulanont as a path to modernize Thailand between 2006 and 2007.

While sufficiency farming techniques have been acknowledged by a small number of villagers, some local NGOs, some Thai academics and other Thai elites, as well as some foreign academics, have, critically, raised the important issue of the practical implementation of the philosophy. Two panel sessions on sufficiency economy held January 9, 2008, at the 10th International Conference on Thai Studies in Bangkok covered many critical issues. I think it is fair to say that the sessions provided for an open and honest critical discussion.

Several critics in the sessions argued that there was no clear support for the system, and no clear-cut policies for putting the theory into practice at different levels: from the village level, to regional and national levels. Also, Thailand has based its national political economy for centuries largely on the development of capitalism for modernization; one wonders how feasible the sufficiency economy approach can be in this context. This is exactly why farmers in Ban Bua view the approach with confusion, given ambiguous state policies and practices for rural and agricultural development. Furthermore, academics in the sessions developed the idea that the promotion of the principle was a political maneuver of the coup-installed government led by General Surayudh Chulanont and Thailand's elite.

One critic, Andrew Walker of the Australian National University's Research School of Pacific and Asian Studies, expressed the view that the sufficiency economy had become an ideological tool through which the ruling elites could avoid the responsibility of addressing any serious income or resource redistribution to the rural poor, who form the vast majority of the country's total population. Another critic, Peter Bell, from the State University of New York at Purchase, disagreed with the recommendation of the United Nations Development Programme (UNDP) that other countries apply the approach, which he thought was irrelevant. He argued that it was not grounded in a coherent and viable economic theory, concluding that the approach simply represented a sharp critique of Thai state-led capitalist development policies. The sufficiency economy concept expresses a sentiment of anti-globalization that gained weight in the context of the 1997 financial crisis.

The sufficiency economy approach is currently being supported vocally by relevant government departments in technical advice to villagers. But the majority of villagers in Thailand are poor and in debt. Since it takes a while to reap the benefits from an integrated organic farm, how would it be possible for them to take care of their families and repay debts while waiting for the economic benefits associated with the approach. Not many Thai villagers are like Serm's family in Ban Bua, whose sons are able to support them, especially at an initial stage of their integrated farm production. Similarly, in the case of Bamrung, he had income from non-farm production in order to start his organic farming. Also, the ways concerned government departments have introduced the sufficiency economy approach is relatively weak when it comes to providing proper financial support (especially for those farmers who have high levels of debt) or to facilitating other infrastructural arrangements, such as providing proper technical assistance, promoting alternative market outlets, and finding ways of maintaining reasonable prices for necessary farm inputs, such as decomposed fertilizer.

In addition, since the sufficiency economy does not aim at profit maximization, income generated from sufficiency farming is generally not sufficient for proper social welfare for farm household members, or, for example, higher education for their children, and it will be necessary for the state to develop necessary policies and implement structural changes to make this philosophy feasible in practice.

Epilogue

Much like Keyes (2008), I have come to the conclusion that the villagers of Ban Bua and elsewhere in Thailand strive to pursue the economic interests of their families. They seek every possible means to advance their economic position. Villagers have unequivocally embraced the global market economy, but their economic actions and decisions are influenced by Buddhist teachings of moderation, hard work, and self-reliance. Although they are at a somewhat disadvantaged position within the capitalist system, they do not deny industry and modernity. But they seek to have a development alternative that warrants their economic risks as well as possible. The sufficiency economy approach seems to provide them with such a solution. It is evident that the sufficiency economy practices do not stand in opposition to commodity capitalist circuits. These practices are not for all, but in fact are only fully accessible to farmers with sufficient land, credit, and additional non-farm income resources.

References

Anand Panyarachun. 2006. "The Wisdom of the Middle Path." *International Herald Tribune*, May 25.

Anderson, Benedict R. 1978. "Studies of the Thai State: The State of Thai Studies." In *The Study of Thailand: Analyses of Knowledge, Approaches and the Prospects in Anthropology, Art History, Economics, History, and Political Science*, edited by Eliezer B. Ayal, 193–252. Athens, Ohio: Ohio University Center for International Studies, Southeast Asian Program.

Anusorn Unno (2003) *Sustainable Agriculture Movement in Thai Society*. Bangkok: Sustainable Agriculture Foundation (Thailand).

Chayan Rajchagool, Soren Ivarsson, Voravith Charoenlert, and Yukti Mukdawijitra. 2008. "Further Reflections on Sufficiency Economy," a panel discussion, 10th International Conference on Thai Studies, January 9, 2008, Thammasat University, Bangkok, Thailand.

The Committee for Sufficiency Economy Mobilization, National Economic and Social Development Board, NESDB-Thailand. 1999.

Keyes, Charles F. 1967. *Isan: Regionalism in Northeastern Thailand*. Data Paper No. 65, Southeast Asia Program, Ithaca: Cornell University Press.

———. 1983. "Economic Action and Buddhist Morality in a Thai Village." *Journal of Asian Studies* XLII (4): 851–68.

———. 1991. "Buddhist Detachment and Worldly Gain: The Economic Ethic of Northeastern Thai Villagers." In *Collected Essays in Honor of Professor Saneh*

Chammarik, edited by Chaiwat Satha-anand. Special Issue of *Journal of Political Science Thammasat University* 16 (1–2): 271–98.

———. 1993. "Buddhist Economics and Buddhist Fundamentalism in Thailand." In *Fundamentalism in Burma and the State: Remaking Politics, Economics and Militance*, edited by Martin E. Marty and R. Scott Appleby, 367–409. Chicago: University of Chicago Press.

———. 2008. "The Village Economy: Capitalist and Sufficiency-based-A Northeastern Thai Case " Keynote address, 10th International Conference on Thai Studies, January 9, 2008, Thammasat University, Bangkok, Thailand.

Kirsch, Thomas A. 1982. "Buddhism, Sex Roles and the Thai Economy." In *Women of Southeast Asia*, edited by Penny Van Esterik, 16–41. DeKalb, IL: Center for Southeast Asian Studies, Northern Illinois University, Occasional paper 9.

Pattana Kitiarsa. 1992. "Peasant Modifications in Managing a Farmers' Association: A Case Study of the Northeast Peasant Economy." MA thesis, Ateneo deManila University.

Plambech, Sine. 2007. "Managing Migration: Risks and Remittances among Migrant Thai Women." MA thesis, Institute of Social Anthropology, Lund University, Sweden.

Pipat Yodphruttikan. 2006. *Database on Community Groups Applying Sufficiency Economy in their Daily Lives*. Thai Pat Institute, Rural Reconstruction Foundation under Royal Patronage.

Popkin, Samuel L. 1979. *The Rational Peasant: The Political Economy of Rural Society in Vietnam*. Berkeley: University of California Press.

Prapas Pintoptang. 1998. *Kan mueang bon thong thanon: 99 wan samatcha khon chon* [Politics on the Street: 99 Days of the Assembly of the Poor]. Bangkok: Kerk University. Data Paper 14.

Ratana Boonmathya. 1997. "Contested Concepts of Development in Rural Northeastern Thailand." PhD thesis, Department of Anthropology, University of Washington.

Ratana Tosakul (Boonmathya). 2005. "Cross-Border Marriage: Experiences of Village Women from Northeastern Thailand with Western Men" Amsterdam: Institute of International for Asian Studies and University of Amsterdam. Forthcoming.

Ratana Tosakul, Chantana Benjasup, Parinyaporn Promduang, Supa Vittaporn, Surachai Chummee, Suvipha Praireephinat. 2005. *Doen thi la kao, kin khao thi la kham: Phum panya nai kan chatkan khwam ru khong chumchon* [One step walk, one step bite: local knowledge management]. Khon Kaen: Learning Promotion for Happy Community Project supported by Thailand Health Promotion Foundation and managed by National Research Fund of Thailand.

Ricoeur, Paul. 1971. "The Model of the Text: Meaningful Action Considered as a Text." *Social Research* 38 (3): 529–62.

Scott, James C. 1976. *The Moral Economy of the Peasant: Rebellion and Subsistence in Southeast Asia*. New Haven: Yale University.

Tambiah, Stanley J. 1970. *Buddhism and the Spirit Cults in North-East Thailand*. Cambridge: Cambridge University Press.

UNDP. 2007. Thailand Human Development Report 2007: Sufficiency Economy and Human Development. Bangkok: UNDP.

Walker, Andrew, Danny Unger, Jim Glassman, and Peter F. Bell. 2008. "Sufficiency Economy." Panel discussion, 10th International Conference on Thai Studies, January 9, 2008, Thammasat University, Bangkok, Thailand.

CHRISTIANITY, MODERNITY, AND CREATIVITY:
The Construction of a Lahu Baptist Identity

Judith M. S. Pine

A middle-aged man sits on a small pile of flat stones. He wears comfortable walking shoes, dark slacks, a white T-shirt, and a straw hat. On his left wrist we see a wristwatch. His right hand points to the ground on his right side, indicating another pile of stones. Below this black and white photograph is a caption that identifies the stones as the site of a temple belonging to A Sha Fu Cu, a nineteenth-century Lahu religious and political leader (2000, 14). The man is Rev. Yawnasan, a leader in the Lahu Baptist community in Thailand, and the photo is one illustration in an article describing a trip to Yunnan Province, China, published in the *Htai-lim Li Sha Tan*, a news magazine published by the Thailand Lahu Baptist Convention. Rev. Yawnasan's movement across national and ideological borders is made possible by his affiliation with a religious tradition brought to Southeast Asia by missionaries who also crossed borders and sent home messages. The message he sends in this photograph emphasizes a modern Lahu identity that connects to its past not through myth but rather through archeological remains. The construction of this Lahu modernity is the subject of much of my research, and the theme of this chapter.

It was Keyes, writing with Tanabe in *Cultural Crisis and Social Memory* (Tanabe 2002), who introduced me to Simmel's (1990) description of modernity as involving a rupture between past and present, resulting in a struggle between the desire to return to the values of the past and the desire for an abstract rationality associated with a forward gaze. Some schools of anthropology have over the past twenty-five years questioned the existence of this rupture, seeing it as an artifact of those doing the describing rather than an experience of those described (Fabian 1983). This anthropological tendency insists upon the "coevalness" (to use Fabian's term) of the "modern" and the "traditional," and focuses attention upon the creativity with which those who are not dominant meet the challenges of cultural contact. The dichotomy remains deeply problematic, creating as it does false images of homogeneity at either end. In this, it suggests a striking relationship to the concept of hybridity, which, as Ewing (2006, 267) points out, may both "posit and constitute homogenous collective identities" joined in bicultural individuals. Modernity, as a position, a sort of cognitive space, seems an inadequate or at least incomplete metaphor for the bundle of concepts that are indexed by the term. Spitulnik (1998, 63), noting that "modernity does not mean the same thing in all places and in all contexts," describes modernity as "a cultural construct which holds that people can move towards a better life and a more 'evolved' society, through the acquisition of certain kinds of knowledge, goods, technologies, and lifestyle habits." The concept of modernity I am using here—one certainly influenced by Keyes—is one of meaningful, contextualized practice. That is, modernity is something one does. The context of this practice may include, and in the Lahu case I would argue does include, a sense of cognitive geography in which there is a gaping chasm between the modern and the not modern.

In Rev. Yawnasan's photograph, I argue, we find a bridge of creativity that allows at least some people to be both modern and Lahu within the context of multiple heterogeneous identities, central among them Lahu-ness, Protestantism, and modernity itself. This bridge seems to incorporate the rupture that Simmel describes, not by spanning it but by using it to distinguish a particular sort of past about which modern, scientific claims, associated with ethnic and religious identity, may then be made. The values of the past, viewed through a nostalgic modern lens, are seen as the foundation for the modernity from which they are viewed, an act of creativity which demonstrates the continued agency of people on the periphery in the face of a globalizing modernity intent on homogenizing the "other." In this chapter, speaking from the specific case of Lahu Baptists in Thailand, I will discuss some key aspects of modern Lahu Baptist identity as it is practiced in present-day Thailand, situating this identity within the Lahu Baptist history that forms it, and exploring the tensions that develop not simply within a modern identity, but in a context of a modern Thai state, within which modernity is a significant and compelling idea and multiple modern identities may be available.

Lahu Christianity

Rev. Yawnasan exemplifies Lahu Protestantism, both in this text and in his own text. Certainly a central object of his trip and the article he wrote was the conversion of Lahu animists to Protestant Christianity. One aspect of the creativity that I am exploring here lies in the way Lahu believers have explicitly incorporated Christian missionaries and conversion to Christianity into a pre-missionary Lahu worldview, what I will call a pre-modern proto-Christian past. Lahu mass conversion to Baptist Christianity becomes part of a narrative of Lahu Christianity understood as a very modern, steady forward progress that pre-dates the arrival of missionaries, and creates a Lahu Baptist identity which is seen, from the inside, as both Protestant and authentically Lahu. This narrative is described in the words of one Lahu man, "We Lahu already knew God, we only needed to learn about Jesus." The idea of a pre-missionary proto-Christian past is, I contend, a central element of Lahu Protestant modernity.

Keane (2002) argues that "the project of becoming self-consciously 'modern' can resemble that of religious conversion," in that both are transformative rejections of what are seen as earlier errors. Keane further asserts that late nineteenth- and early twentieth-century Protestant missionaries often found themselves either intentionally or accidentally on the side of science, "disenchanting some part of the world" (Keane 2002, 67). Protestantism, as Keane indicates, is a forward-looking tradition that historically "helped define and identified itself with a new era" (ibid., 68). Despite the more evangelical bent of some of their number, the

Protestant missionaries who proselytized Lahu in Burma and Thailand were arguably this sort of self-consciously modern Protestant.

Missionaries in Southeast Asia found themselves working primarily with the upland "tribal" peoples, having had much less success among the dominant lowland Buddhist peoples, a phenomenon that Keyes (1996) has discussed in detail. The fact that they were working with people on the periphery, what Tsing (1993) calls "people from out of the way places," must certainly have increased the sense among these missionaries that they were bringing not just salvation but civilization to their converts. Encountering Christian missionaries in late nineteenth and early twentieth centuries,[1] Lahu and other upland peoples, were more likely to convert to Christianity than were the lowland Buddhists dominant in the region, and it has been argued that access to a modern identity is a key element of this conversion (Kammerer 1990).

William Young, the most dramatically successful of the Baptist missionaries, began working with Lahu in 1903, keenly aware of the fact that dreams and prophecy appeared to have predicted his arrival (Walker 2003, 573–5). He made good use of these portents, baptizing hundreds of converts, very likely with the idea that he was receiving divine assistance. Kataoka (1998) points out that some view Young's work as exemplifying opportunistic behavior by missionaries, but a more generous interpretation can be made. Just as early settlers in North America saw a divine hand in the depopulation of the land by disease, missionaries in the uplands of Thailand, Burma, and China required no irony to read the prophecies of a return of a golden or white book as the hand of the divine "preparing the field for harvest." This harvest included the provision of key components of modernity, especially modern education. On the ground, the harvest took the form of hundreds of conversions. Indeed, Young reported 1,046 baptisms in 1904–5 and 4,419 baptisms in 1905–6, figures which led to concern among his colleagues and even to a formal investigation conducted by Dr. A. H. Henderson and Rev. C. H. Heptonstall, themselves experienced missionaries in the area (1963, 411).

One significant part of Young's work was the liberal distribution of pamphlets in Shan to Lahu "seekers." While some Lahu may have read Shan, it is likely that these books had more meaning as icons or fetishes of civilization and power, arguably icons of modernity. In the late nineteenth century, A Sha Fu Cu, whose temple ruins are shown in Rev. Yawnasan's photograph, reportedly told his followers to expect a white man with a golden book who would lead them to triumph. A Sha Fu Cu was, according to the historical record, an able messianic Mahayana Buddhist leader who mobilized Lahu followers in Yunnan and built several important temples. There is no evidence that A Sha Fu Cu had any connection with Christianity in his lifetime, although Christian missionaries were becoming active in the region. Baptist Lahu draw a clear connection, however, and use this connection to construct a distinctively Lahu past which can easily coexist with a very modern Lahu present.

Young's mission did not create a new modern narrative for Lahu converts. Instead, Young became part of an existing Lahu narrative, taking a familiar place within Lahu culture. Through much of their history, the Lahu seem to have been involved in violent resistance against lowland authority, often led by messianic "priest-chiefs." In fact, the Lahu achieved a reputation for violent resistance against the Chinese empire during the eighteenth and nineteenth centuries (Walker 2003, 227–29). The men began their careers as *paw hku* (traditional Lahu priests), went on to claim special supernatural powers, institute religious revival, and finally enter the world of politics (Walker 1974). Fitting well into this pattern were Christian missionaries such as the charismatic Young (whose family[2] continues to play a role in northern Thailand) with their offer of eternal life, perhaps imperfectly understood, and their call for adherence to moral rules similar to those of previous revivals.

Protestant missionaries have had a complex relationship with the state in the region. For the purpose of this paper I will concentrate on the kingdoms of Siam and Lanna, and the nation-state of Thailand, which encompasses both.[3] Protestant missionaries in Bangkok in the early nineteenth century met with initial resistance from Phra Nangklao (King Rama III) (1824–1851), and there was little successful missionary activity during his reign, although the first Baptist mission was founded in Bangkok in 1833 (Swanson 1984, 4). With the ascension of King Mongkut (Rama IV) (1851–1868), who gained insights into Western ways of thinking and was stimulated to reflect on the nature and essence of Buddhism by conversations with missionaries (Keyes 1987, 41), Protestant missionaries found themselves in a less difficult position.

In 1855, the government of King Mongkut signed the Bowring Treaty opening Thailand up to international trade and initiating the process that led to Siam's transformation into a modern nation-state (Keyes 1987, 44). Shortly thereafter, in 1858 Rev. Daniel McGilvary arrived in Bangkok to be sent, with other missionaries, to open the first mission station outside of Bangkok, in Phetburi (Swanson 1984, 5). It may be that the relative lack of success in achieving converts led missionaries to view expansion into Lan Na, and especially Chiang Mai. Certainly, Dr. Dan Beach Bradley, who had begun mission work in Siam during the reign of Phra Nangklao, was deeply interested in the north and cultivated a relationship with the Chao Muang Kawilarot of Chiang Mai. This relationship was made possible by the unique circumstance of missionaries in Siam. As Wyatt notes, "Whereas Christian missionaries elsewhere in Asia during this period had access for the most part only to the lower classes or ethnic minorities, in Siam they reached young men of the elite" (1984, 177).

Chiang Mai, along with the other major principalities of the north of what is now Thailand, was from the beginning of the nineteenth century a tributary of Siam. The Chao Muang (Lord of the Principality) of Chiang Mai was foremost of the northern Chao Muang, and was also referred to as *Chao Chiwit* (Lord of Life) (Walker 1992 [1988], 20). In 1860, when McGilvary married Bradley's daughter, the couple sent a piece of wedding cake to Chao Muang Kawilarot, who happened to be in Bangkok at the time. They received the Chao Muang as a visitor the following day. In 1863–64 McGilvary led a survey trip to Lampang, Lamphun, and Chiang Mai, where they met with high officials who assured them they were welcome. However, in September of 1869 the Chao Muang reportedly ordered the arrest and subsequent execution of two Christian converts (Swanson 1984, 14–15), telling McGilvary "he considered that leaving the religion of the country was rebellion against him, and he would treat it as such" (Hughes 1989, 6). Chao Muang Kawilarot died in 1870, however. Chao Phraya Suriyawong, regent to King Chulalongkorn (Rama V) (1868–1910), took this opportunity to name Chao Intanon as Chao Kawilarot's successor, passing over the logical heir in favor of a candidate "more sympathetic to Bangkok's policies" (Wyatt 1984, 194). These policies seem to have included tolerance of missionary activities in the north. When conflict between the northern government and the missionaries arose again in 1878, they appealed to King Chulalongkorn directly. His response was to direct local authority to draft an edict using whatever wording they liked. This edict, issued October 8, 1878, asserted that "a person may choose any religion he or she desires" and that "any person may become a Christian without hindrance and that Christians had the right to observe the Sabbath" (Swanson 1984, 28).

While McGilvary and his fellow Presbyterians were developing relationships with the Siamese state and its principle northern tributary, American Baptist missionaries were working in Burma with upland people including the Lahu. Although McGilvary encountered Lahu in what is now northern Thailand as early as 1886 (McGilvary 1912, 333–37) he does not report success in conversion, and it is likely that he would have been uncomfortable with the mass conversions that Young achieved a few decades later.

A Sha Fu Cu and the Proto-Christian Past

As I have noted elsewhere (Pine 1999), A Sha Fu Cu, a mid-nineteenth-century messianic leader who in China is associated with the Buddhist tradition, is seen by Christian Lahu as foretelling the coming of Christianity (see also Walker 2000, 733). The Protestant Christianity that lays claim to A Sha Fu Cu is that modern form to which Keane refers, a rational and modern religious ideology that looks to science, here archeology, for information about the past. Thus, Paul Lewis, working with his wife Elaine as a Baptist missionary in the latter half of the twentieth century with the Lahu and Akha, is able to make the argument that it was more important to translate the New Testament than to translate the Old Testament, as the Lahu already had their own body of myths (Lewis 1981). This rational perspective must, however, encompass an acceptance of prophecy as rational in order to connect A Sha Fu Cu to modern Lahu Baptists. Since this claim provides a historical link to a pre-missionary proto-Christian past, it is an important and necessary one.

The link drawn between the Lahu prophet and Lahu modernity is also made apparent when Rev. Yawnasan tells us that "*A Sha Fu Cu pa cheh ta kui ven hta chi beu Heh pa hkaw k'o, 'Shin Mi Cheun' teh meh ve yo*" ["The location of A Sha Fu Cu's temple is called 'Shin Mi Cheun' (Ximeng Shan?) in the Chinese language"] (Yawnasan 2000, 14, my translation). Placing the temple within the cognitive universe of the Chinese, with whom the Lahu have interacted for centuries, provides yet another tie to civilization/modernity, and an important one. Within Thailand, Lahu people often find themselves without citizenship or legitimate claim to land, as is illustrated for ethnic minorities more generally in other chapters in this book. Nishimoto (1998) provides an insightful look into the sense of loss that is prevalent among those who are thus disenfranchised by the Thai state. By presenting this name as the Chinese-language name of the place, Rev. Yawnasan seems to challenge the legitimacy of the name while at the same time placing the ruins within modern, nation-state oriented time and space.

In a mimeographed booklet with the English-language title "Lahu Baptist Chronicle," published in Pang Wai, Burma, in 1976, S. Yohan writes, "of our Lahu Search for God/G'ui sha," describing the role of A Sha Fu Cu as a prophet of the coming of Christian missionaries. Yohan introduces the A Sha Fu Cu story by asserting that, "We Lahu people were eager to worship God/G'ui sha, but had not had the opportunity to seek him yet in Tibet, where people worshiped spirits. It came to pass, however, that a village priest emerged who taught the right path to God, and built a great temple to God" (Yohan 1976). A key element of this right path, as reported by Harold Young (n.d., 126), son of William Marcus Young, took the form of teachings and prophecies that "prepared the people in a most amazing way for the coming of the Christian gospel." The bridge that Rev. Yawnasan illustrates in his photograph was built by Baptist Lahu upon the foundation of this "amazing preparation."

Ethnic Identity, Borders, and Nations

The Baptist Lahu with whom I conduct my research (particularly the elite) are not "pre-modern" but rather are fully modern people, people with history who view the past through a nostalgic lens and face generally forward in linear time. They are also distinctively Lahu, a distinctive identity that is almost entirely discursive. That is to say, Lahu people are Lahu because they say they are Lahu, generally in a dialect that is associated with the Lahu language. Anthony Walker, the foremost ethnographer of the Lahu, argues that they are "a collectivity of human beings who, despite their lack of common social, political or economic institutions, share a feeling of 'Lahu-ness' which goes beyond their common language (albeit with considerable variation between the major dialects) to embrace the idea of a shared past" (2003, 52–53). The discursive nature of Lahu identity does not separate them from others in the region, as Keyes (2002) makes clear in his discussion of the history of ethnic identity in Asia. The lack of any formal Lahu political presence in Thailand, at least at the national level, and the absence of any international Lahu political entity, contributes to the visibility, among the Lahu, of the discursive construction of identity that is likely to be found in any ethnic community (and perhaps any human community). That is to say, the act of constituting identity through discourse is not unique to Lahu, but it is more visible in the absence of other means through which shared identity is often constructed.

The largest population of Lahu can be found in China, in which the Lahu Autonomous County of Lancang is governed by ethnic Lahu. In Burma/Myanmar, a significant Lahu presence of some two hundred thousand has included a Lahu MP (currently in exile), as well as a Lahu army engaged in resistance against the central government. The Lahu in Thailand are only perhaps eighty thousand strong and have no significant political presence at a national level. One does not readily conceive of the Lahu as playing a role in what we commonly perceive as the Thai state. There is no transnational political entity to which all or many Lahu belong, but the sense of shared Lahu-ness, like Lahu people themselves, crosses national borders.

The feeling of Lahu-ness that characterizes Lahu identity does not seem to require much maintenance in rural Lahu villages, where monolingual Lahu speakers may be found and where Lahu language is in daily use. Daily dress is not all that different from neighbors of other ethnic groups and tends to reflect the requirements of agricultural work as well as the habits of dominant groups to a great extent. When my husband and I asked friends to help us identify the Lahu women in a series of slides depicting the transplanting of paddy rice, one man joked that his wife, in her conical hat, tubular skirt, and men's shirt, looked just like *khon* Isan, a northeastern Thai woman.

The Lahu do have a variety of costumes associated with ethnic subgroups, varying also according to religious affiliation. These costumes may be worn on special occasions, especially New Year's and New Rice festivals. For the Lahu people I knew, traditional dress was seen as special occasion attire, and dressing in traditional garb does not connect one to a pre-modern Lahu past but rather includes one in a modern Lahu present. In such circumstances, the "oppressive authenticity" described by Sissons (2005), which prescribes a dramatic distinction between the modern and the "authentic" traditional, is not generally experienced by rural Lahu.

One case that illustrates this occurred on the day a number of young Lahu women in my village were asked to dress in traditional costume for a group of Japanese visitors. The girls came out to pose in their traditional costumes, but in at least one case wearing Hello Kitty sandals. The photographers insisted that this inauthentic footwear be removed before photos were taken, and the girls spent several minutes finding a pair of unadorned sandals. Here, I want to point out particularly that from the perspective of villagers, Hello Kitty sandals are Lahu footwear, because Lahu people wear them. When, during later New Year's and New Rice celebrations, villagers once again donned traditional clothing, a wide variety of footwear could be observed.

Lahu in Thailand

The village in which I did my fieldwork lies on the Mae Nam Kok, or Kok River. It is a relatively large village of some two hundred Lahu people in the Thai province of Chiang Mai, near the border of Myanmar/Burma. Lahu lived in the region north of the Mae Kok "since at least 1900, probably since 1875" (Hanks 1965), and Lahu is spoken not only in upland villages, but also by northern Thai shopkeepers in the nearby city of Fang.

In the late twentieth century, Hickey notes that:

> Frequently, a Lahu village recognizes the seniority in its area of one particularly (sic) headman not necessarily its own. This "area" may comprise no more than two or three villages or more than a hundred. When a village moves into a new area, it tends to conform to the existing power structure both in the hills and in the neighboring lowlands. Today, as in the past, influential [Lahu] hill "chiefs" have received recognition not only from their hill neighbors but also from valley leaders, such as Shan princes, Chinese mandarins, or modern district officials of China, Burma, Laos or Thailand (1978, 231).

The recognition of influential Lahu leaders continues into the twenty-first century. Generally, such leaders are perceived by lowland authorities as being thoroughly modern individuals and skilled in building ties that cross ethnic and political boundaries.

The physical border between Thailand and Burma could be crossed with relative physical ease, although not without real danger, allowing the passage of people and goods. On one occasion, a pair of Lahu women attending seminary in Kengtung, Burma, passed through our village on a fundraising tour, teaching a small group to sing "Jesus Loves Me" in English and collecting a few baht before moving on to the next Thai Lahu Baptist village. My neighbor in the village was an avid collector of cassette tapes of Lahu Baptist choirs, recorded in Burma and sold by traveling merchants who walked into the village carrying their wares. On a visit to my field-site village in August 2007, I was given a VCD of Lahu karaoke produced in Burma. When the producers of a UNESCO AIDS and prostitution education project in the form of a radio soap opera brought together a test audience of young Lahu women from Burma, China, and Thailand, the women suggested an improved soundtrack and recommended specific Lahu songwriters and singers. These musicians were brought to Thailand from Burma to compose and record songs for the soap opera, which was broadcast or distributed on cassettes throughout the Lahu speaking world. The songs composed for the radio program were then distributed on CDs throughout the Greater Mekong Sub-region. The heteroglossic discourses that work to construct both authentic and modern Lahu individuals and communities take place within this context of porous borders.

The School, Modernity, and Creative Tension

The provision of formal education was a central goal of the Protestant missionary effort from the beginning (Antisdel 1931), and providing access to formal education continues to be one of the central efforts of Christian organizations such as the Thailand Lahu Baptist Convention. These organizations do not run schools of their own, but rather offer Lahu children opportunities to attend Thai state schools. Thai modernity is available to Christian Lahu through this education and through the media, which permeates even remote upland villages. Access to education in Thai cities, and thus to good education, is available to Christian children who are sent to dormitories run by religious organizations. The focus of efforts must, necessarily, be on a mastery of the subjects taught in the Thai school, where, as Keyes (1991) points out, children are shaped into members of a Thai polity. Despite the fact that Theravada Buddhism is a component of the curriculum, Lahu Baptists willingly send their children to school, perhaps viewing the religious education received in the dormitories as a balance to the conflicting religious ideology offered in the school. Certainly there is no other element of the school's project which conflicts with the desires of the Lahu Baptists I know.

The Baptist Lahu with whom I work are committed to providing their children with good, modern Thai education. At least one family who was not able to send their children to dormitories in the cities of Chiang Mai or Fang used a small tractor to transport children down to a nearby Buddhist non-Lahu village whose school was seen to be superior to the small elementary school in the village in which I lived, and the official village headman took a rental house in the city of Fang so that his children could attend an urban school while living with his parents. The Thai modernity that Lahu children have access to in the school is not a Lahu identity. Provision of education through a variety of institutions, including the Public Welfare Department, missionary organizations, the Border Patrol Police, and the Ministry of Education, was integral to Thai government policy regarding upland peoples such as the Lahu in the latter half of the twentieth century. Hickey (1978, 29) describes the Royal Thai Government's July 6, 1976, policy statement and outline of program for hill people as being justified in terms of problems, these problems being "population pressure," lower standard of living, opium addiction, and ecological damage due to swidden cultivation. The text of this policy included the following, as quoted by Hickey:

> Since Thailand's hill people are minority groups who can mix with the Thai people peacefully, it is appropriate to use the "integration policy" as a guide in operations. This policy seeks to generate a sense of belonging and loyalty to the Thai nation through giving tribes people (sic) full rights to practice their own religions and cultures as they like (30).

Here, a state policy of integration is proposed in contrast to assimilation, and there is clearly some disagreement about the possibility of Lahu being both Lahu and Thai. In the 1970s, both integration and assimilation policies were being put into place by different agencies (Hickey 1978, 35). The problems associated with upland peoples—overpopulation, lower living standards, opium addiction, and environmental damage—drove a wide variety of policies (Manndorff 1966) that have had an impact on Lahu in Thailand, but none is so central to modern identity as the school. Lahu children in Thai schools have access to a very different modern identity, one that may prove difficult to integrate into a Lahu identity.

Rural Lahu children learn to be Thai (or perhaps Thai-Lahu) in the same way rural northeastern Thai children learn to be Thai, in what Keyes (1991) so memorably termed the "proposed world of the school," a microcosmic version of the Thai state within which space and time are ordered, and children learn their place within this system. In my field site, the school taught Lahu children that their place within the system was on the periphery. Teachers arrived on Monday late in the day and left early on Fridays. The raising of the flag and singing of the national anthem were haphazard at best. In other Lahu villages, school practices were more uniform, more like those in urban schools, but teachers generally still left the village over the weekend, and interaction between teachers and villagers was relatively restricted. The teachers, in their role as ethnic Thai in the microcosm of the state, seemed to me to place Lahu children just outside a modern Thai identity. This mixed blessing leaves space for the potential development of a modern Lahu identity. In Baptist villages, Sunday school,[4] where Lahu literacy is taught, forms a counterbalance to the Thai school to some extent. Early missionaries clearly understood the role of education as a modernizing activity, as illustrated by the Ca Law Li series of children's books, in which Ca Law and his family learn habits of "proper," modern diet and hygiene, as well as agricultural practices such as composting.[5]

Urban Lahu children attending state schools with Thai and *khon muang* (northern Thai) classmates have less space within which to develop a modern Lahu identity, while the parents of these children are the modern Lahu who shape that identity entering the twenty-first century. The tension between modernity and Lahu-ness engendered in the Thai school may be overcome (perhaps) by modern Lahu publications, if literacy in Lahu becomes an urban skill. Sunday school at the Lahu Baptist church in Chiang Mai is conducted in Thai and Lahu, however, and on those occasions when I have visited, the Thai orthography was used to write out both Lahu and Thai for students to read. The peripheral economic position of Lahu has made keeping Lahu-language publications in circulation difficult. Other media may, in the long run, become the locus for the formation of a modern Lahu identity which crosses both international and urban/rural borders. The popularity of the UNESCO-sponsored radio soap opera and its accompanying CD demonstrates the potential for an international Lahu media presence that could form a counterbalance to the modernizing projects of states and the transformative power of urban schools. I am currently engaged in research exploring the circulation of Lahu-language karaoke and film, which may be seen to form an important element of the ongoing construction of Lahu modernity.

Conclusion

The modern Lahu identity, which, I argue, is illustrated in the photograph of Rev. Yawnasan, does not preclude a high degree of integration into the Thai polity. The fact that this particular Lahu modernity is firmly connected to a Lahu Baptist identity seems to create a unified Lahu modernity which is not a hybrid identity connecting modern (Thai) individuals who are also traditional (Lahu) individuals. A Lahu Baptist Thai individual is not balancing between two or more separate and distinct identities. Any effort to disentangle the various elements of such an identity make abundantly clear the amorphous nature of each of what might have been imagined to be its component parts. Just as ethnic identity is a practice, as Keyes (1981) so cogently points out, the practice of modern Lahu-ness is inherently active, not the realization of a state of being but rather a continuous process for which individuals and groups take up and make use of a variety of tools. The archeology to which Rev. Yawnasan refers is an example of such a tool.

The development and maintenance of a discourse constructing a modern Lahu identity gains support and energy from the tension between its elements, creating a relationship between ethnicity and modernity within which each supports the other, while neither takes a dominant position. This tension generates and is generated by narratives like Rev. Yawnasan's. The interplay of this tension with that created by the state narratives of identity, within which Lahu people find themselves, adds further complication to the process, so that modern Lahu identity must be created within a variety of national and international discourses.

Educated, modern Lahu individuals travel as tourists across national, cultural, ideological, and linguistic borders to gaze nostalgically at the archeological ruins associated with a pre-missionary proto-Christian past constructed through the writing of a (Protestant) Lahu history. Mobility and nostalgia are brought back to Lahu Baptist villages, and the farmers who live in those villages, through the photograph and the story in the Li Sha Tan, offering modernity to those who cannot (yet) move as freely through the world. The nineteenth-century missionary encounter, itself self-consciously modern and intentionally modernizing, brought with it a future of access to technologies of communication and transportation with which twenty-first century Lahu may be both modern and Lahu.

Notes

1. Swanson (1984) reports contact between Presbyterian missionaries and Lahu in the Chiang Rai region as early as 1886, and notes that in 1892 Dr. Daniel McGilvary, a founding member of the Presbyterian mission in what then was referred to as Laos, along with his colleague, Dr. James W. McKean, baptized thirteen Lahu in 1892.

2. Five generations of the Young family have served as missionaries in Southeast Asia and China.

3. One illustration of the complexity of ethnicity, nation, and conversion is the report of the first Siamese convert to Baptist Protestant Christianity, a conversion credited to Ann Hazeltine Judson in Rangoon in 1819 (Swanson 1984, 3).

4. Lahu literacy is taught in Sunday school, but not every Christian village has an active Sunday school program.

5. The underlying assumptions inherent in these topical choices is a topic to which I hope to return in future writing.

References

Antisdel, C. B. 1931. "1824–1853: Roman Catholic and American Baptist Mission Schools." *Journal of the Burma Research Society* XXI (I): 1–13.

Du, Shan Shan. 1999. "'Chopsticks Only Work in Pairs': Gender Unity and Gender Equality among the Lahu of Southwest China." PhD diss., University of Illinois at Urbana-Champaign.

——— . 2000. "'Husband and Wife Do it Together': Sex/Gender Allocation of Labor among the Qhawqhat Lahu of Lancang, Southwest China." *American Anthropologist* 102 (3): 520–37.

Ewing, Katherine Pratt. 2006. "Between Cinema and Social Work: Diasporic Turkish Women and the (Dis)Pleasures of Hybridity." *Cultural Anthropology* 21 (2): 265–94.

Fabian, Johannes. 1983. *Time and the Other: How Anthropology Makes Its Object*. New York: Columbia University.

Hanks, Lucien. 1965. "The Lahu Shi Hopoe: The Birth of a New Culture?" In *Ethnographic Notes on Northern Thailand*, edited by L. M. Hanks, Jane R. Hanks, and Lauriston Sharp, 72–83. Ithaca: Cornell University Dept. of Asian Studies.

Hickey, Gerald, and Jesse Wright. 1978. *The Hill People of Northern Thailand: Social and Economic Development*. Thailand: USAID/Thailand.

Hughes, Philip J. 1989. *Proclamation and Response: A Study of the History of the Christian Faith in Northern Thailand*. Chiang Mai: Payap University Archives.

Kammerer, Cornelia Ann. 1990. "Customs and Christian Conversion among Akha Highlanders of Burma and Thailand." *American Ethnologist* 17 (2): 277 (15).

Kataoka, Tatsuki. 1998. "On the Notion of 'the Lost Book' in the Early Mass Conversion to Christianity among the Lahu in Upper Burma." *Journal of Asian and African Studies (Ajia Afurika Gengo Bunka Kenkyu)* (56): 141–65.

Keane, Webb. 2002. "Sincerity, 'Modernity,' and the Protestants." *Cultural Anthropology* 17 (1): 65–92.

Keyes, Charles F. 1976. "Towards a New Formulation of the Concept of Ethnic Group." *Ethnicity* 3: 202–13.

———. 1981. "Dialectics of Ethnic Change." In *Ethnic Change*, edited by Charles F. Keyes, 4–30. Seattle: University of Washington Press.

———. 1987. *Thailand, Buddhist Kingdom as Modern Nation-state*. Boulder, CO: Westview Press.

———. 1991. "The Proposed World of the School: The Villagers' Entry into a Bureaucratic State System." In *Reshaping Local Worlds*, edited by Charles F. Keyes, 89–130. New Haven: Yale University Press.

———. 1993. "Why the Thai Are Not Christians: Buddhist and Christian Conversion in Thailand." In *Conversion to Christianity: Historical and Anthropological Perspectives on a Great Transformation*, edited by R. W. Hefner, 259–83. Berkeley: University of California Press.

———. 1996. "Being Protestant Christians in Southeast Asian Worlds." *Journal of Southeast Asian Studies* 27 (2): 280–92.

———. 2002. "'The Peoples of Asia': Science and Politics in the Classification of Ethnic Groups in Thailand, China, and Vietnam." *Journal of Asian Studies* 61 (4): 1163–203.

Lewis, Paul, and Elaine Lewis. 1981. Oral History Interview, Tape 1-8. Chiang Mai: Manuscript Division, Payap University.

———. 1984. *Peoples of the Golden Triangle: Six Tribes in Thailand*. London: Thames and Hudson Ltd.

Manndorff, Hans. 1966. "The Hill Tribe Program of the Public Welfare Department, Ministry of Interior, Thailand: Research and Socio-Economic Development."

In *Southeast Asian Tribes, Minorities and Nations,* vol. 2, edited by P. Kunstadter, 525–52. Princeton, NJ: Princeton University Press.

McGilvary, Daniel. 1912. *A Half Century among the Siamese and the Lao.* New York: Fleming H. Revell Company.

Nishimoto, Yoichi. 1998. "Northern Thai Christian Lahu Narratives of Inferiority: A Study of Social Experience." MA thesis, Chiang Mai University.

Pine, Judith M. S. 1999. "Lahu Writing/Writing Lahu: Literacy and the Possession of Writing." In *Globalization and the Asian Economic Crisis: Indigenous Responses, Coping Strategies, and Governance Reform in Southeast Asia,* 176–85. Vancouver, BC: Institute of Asian Research, University of British Columbia.

Simmel, Georg. 1990. *The Philosophy of Money.* T.B.a.D.F., translated by Kaethe Mengelberg. New York: Routledge.

Sissons, Jeffrey. 2005. *First Peoples: Indigenous Cultures and Their Futures.* London: Reaktion.

Sowards, Rev. Saw Aung Din, and Rev. E. E. Sowards. 1963. "Work Among Lahus, Was, Akhas." In *Burma Baptist Chronicle,* G.S.a.E., edited by Sowards, 407–19. Rangoon: Board of Publications, Burma Baptist Convention.

Spitulnik, Debra. 1998. "Mediated Modernities: Encounters with the Electronic In Zambia." *Visual Anthropology Review* 14 (2): 63–84.

Swanson, Herbert R. 1984. *Khrittachak Muang Nua: A Study of Northern Thai Church History.* Bangkok: Chuan Printing Press Ltd. Part.

Tanabe, Shigeharu, and Charles Keyes, eds. 2002. *Cultural Crisis and Social Memory: Modernity and Identity in Thailand and Laos.* Honolulu: University of Hawaii Press.

Tsing, Anna Lowenhaupt. 1993. *In the Realm of the Diamond Queen: Marginality in an Out-of-the-Way Place.* Princeton, NJ: Princeton University Press.

Walker, Anthony R. 1974. "Messianic Movements among the Lahu of the Yunnan-Indonchina Borderlands." *Southeast Asia* 3 (2): 699–712.

———. 2003. *Merit and the Millenium: Routine and Crisis in the Ritual Lives of the Lahu People.* New Delhi: Hindustan Publishing Corporation.

———. (1988) 1992. "Exorcising Jaw and Meh Spirits: Three Lahu Nyi (Red Lahu) Ritual Texts." In *The Highland Heritage,* edited by A. Walker, 339–82. Singapore: Suvarnabhumi Books.

Wyatt, David K. 1984. *Thailand: A Short History.* Chiang Mai: Silkworm Books.

Yawnasan, Rev. 2000. "Nga aw pon mvuh mi aw suh te pe." In *Htai-lim li sha tan* (*Htai-Lim News*), 13–16.

Yohan, Sala. 1976. *La hu Hkri ya aw mo Ra sa van Aw lawn (1901–1976)* (Concerning the history of the Christian Lahu). Pangwai: Lahu Baptist Church.

Young, Harold. n.d.. *To the Mountain Tops: A Sojourn among the Lahu of Asia.*

CONTESTED CITIZENSHIP:
Cards, Colors, and the Culture of Identification

Pinkaew Laungaramsri

Introduction

On Friday September 8, 2005, more than eight hundred villagers from border communities of Tha Ton Subdistrict, Mae Ai District, Chiang Mai Province gathered before the Administration Court building in Chiang Mai as they listened to the reading of a verdict that ruled that a Mae Ai district office order to remove the name of 1,243 villagers from the household registration was unlawful. The court verdict came as a result of many years of local effort by villagers to regain their citizenship after it was revoked by the district office in February 2002. For Mae Ai district officials, the rationale for such revocation was based on their belief that these people were not "Thai." This is simply because these people have never been permanent residents, as they constantly cross the border between Thailand and Burma. Some of them have even obtained the "pink card," the identification card for a displaced person with Burmese nationality. Local people, however, argued that they once had the Thai ID card before moving out of the villages due to political turbulence between the Burmese army and the ethnic insurgency in that area in 1971. Since they lost their Thai ID cards, their subsequent acquisition of the "pink card" was because of fear of deportation. District- and local-level disputes went on for several years with no progress, as all the relevant documents stored at the district office that could have been used for verification were destroyed in a 1976 fire. As a result, the Tha Ton villagers had no choice but to file a lawsuit against the Local Authority Department, and it was successful.

The politics of identification cards in the Mae Ai case is representative of the unsettling relationship between state and subjects in the border area. Over the past three decades, cards have become the strategic tool used by the state to differentiate the Thai from the non-Thai "other." Issuance and revocation of cards for border-crossing people have become common state practices. At the same time, amendments of the Nationality Act are enacted now and again, changing the legal definition of a Thai citizen. As more colors have been assigned to new identification cards, and confusion about them increasingly complicates the interaction between the state and the people, widespread card disputes and scandals have proliferated.

In tracing the genealogy of the scientific modes of classification of ethnic differences used by the modern nation-state in Asia, Keyes (2000) maintains that the political application of such science has not only resulted in the production of hierarchical order but also the fixing of national and thus ethnic boundaries. These ethnological projects of classification undertaken in various countries of Asia, though based on flawed assumptions, have served as a powerful tool in differentiating between the national and the ethnic "other." I would argue further that the ways ethnic classifications become operational in a society, as both tools of the state and a sign of its capacity, depend on an effective methodology. As Scott (1998, 2–3) suggests, the modern state's project to appropriate, control, and manipulate the cultural diversity of its inhabitants is carried out through tools of simplification and legibility, by "rationalizing and standardizing what was a social hieroglyph into a legible and administratively more convenient format" (2–3). In the case of Thailand, I maintain that a methodological tool that has powerfully rendered ethnic diversity legible is the system of identification cards, which serves a dual function of national embrace and disembrace. A product of the Cold War era, such a system is not merely a means by which the state controls populations but also is constitutive of the sovereign nation-state itself. By tracing the history of the identification card system and shifting ideas of citizenship, this paper explores the changing relations between the state and its subjects. Inconsistent functions and meanings of cards assigned to different groups of people reflect the state's unstable notions of citizenship and its anxiety towards mobility. Who counts as "members" and as "different," and where and when difference may legitimately be represented, are historically contingent. In the case of Thailand, the inherent instability in both the meaning and the limits of citizenship identity and difference is well illustrated at the border, whereas shifting card practices reveal the constant negotiation between forces of normalization and differentiation, and of national security and economic liberalization. As the state's attempt to define people is often incomplete, the deployment of the state's methods of identification among the people so designated always implies tension and contestation. Reappropriation and reinterpretation of identification cards has been a strategic means of negotiation by the people classified as the non-Thai "other." It is in this context that the notion of citizenship is often problematic, while the project of classifying and defining peoples will thus forever remain, as Keyes (2002, 1194) argues, "work in progress."

The Embracing Citizenship

When the idea of citizenship was first introduced in Thailand in the early twentieth century, it was not really clear what it meant. Since the reign of King Chulalongkorn, colonial expansion has made it inevitable for the Siamese elite to rethink the once diverse ethnic conglomeration of Siam as a homogenous Thai nation, employing a European ideology of race. The creation of Thai nationality was carried out in the form David Streckfuss calls "reverse-Orientalism"—the transformation of the "other" into Thai as a form of resistance against European colonialism. The materialization of "Thai nationality" was carried out by the subsequent King Vajiravudh (Rama VI). Interestingly, what concerned him was not how to define citizenship but rather how to turn the non-Thai subject into a Thai citizen. The Naturalization Act was then implemented in

1911, prior to the first Nationality Act in 1913. As Saichol (2005) notes, competing Chinese nationalism, widespread among overseas Chinese in Siam, was alarming, and one way to suppress the increasing mobilization and politicization of Chinese nationalist sentiment was through assimilation. The significant requirement of official naturalization was that those eligible to be citizens had to prove they had had at least five years residency in the kingdom. At the same time, offspring of those with approved citizenship were automatically eligible to become citizens.

In the reign of King Rama VI, assimilation through legal naturalization served as a means to orient the people who the king defined as "born as Thai, being Chinese as vocation, registered as English" (Saichol, ibid.) and to transform them into Thai in soul and spirit. Legal naturalization was a characteristic strategy of "Thai-ization" (*kan klai pen Thai*) and a state attempt at monopolization of the Thai nationalism. In keeping with the trajectory of transforming the multi-ethnic kingdom into an exclusive nation-state, the newly modern Thai state has continued to define Thai nationality by cultural qualities associated with the three elements of Thai language, Buddhism, and loyalty to the king. However, such effort at the homogenization of Thai national identity did not receive much support by the Chinese, who constantly challenged the hegemonic notion of the Thai nation and thus rendered the project of assimilation problematic.

Despite the widespread propagation of Thai nationalism, Thailand's 1911 Nationalization Act and 1913 Nationality Act did not define citizenship, nor its rights and obligations. If citizenship means "full membership in the community" (Marshall 1950), the nature of the legal bond between the members and their Thai community, and an elaboration of what a legal status of membership means is absent from the text. In the early period, citizenship was a somewhat ambiguous notion of incorporation that did not yet enter the realm of administrative apparatus. Although a naturalization certificate was issued, it was not a national identification document and was not used by the state as a means for identity control. The state's attempt to regulate movement across national boundaries was also in its infancy. The unsettling notion of a means of embracing citizenship, with loosely regulatory mechanisms, thus allowed for the possibility of interpretation and negotiation. As a result, for non-Thai, particularly Chinese, to be Thai or not to be Thai remained a political and cultural choice that could be maneuverable. However, such possibility became increasingly difficult with the development of a state identification card system in the middle of the twentieth century.

Culture of Identification and the Proprietary Citizenship

Since 1932, in the post–absolute monarchy era, official thinking about citizenship has undergone a significant shift. Under the regime of Phibun Songkram, the Thai race (*chonchat Thai*) had been emphasized as the significant trait of Thai nationality. The emphasis on Thai race as the basis of nationalism served multiple purposes—to undermine the previous idea of Thai-ness centered around the allegiance to the monarchy, to exclude the Chinese from the political sphere, and to provide a protective ring against communist expansion (Saichol 2005; Keyes 2002). At the same time, the dream of a unified Thai nationality extended across national boundaries, culminating in a short-lived pan-Thai movement (see Keyes 2002, Crosby 1945). It was also in the reign of Phibun Songkram that "Thai" was turned into an official identity, making people's identities and nationality within the boundary of the nation-state. In 1939, Siam was renamed Thailand, the country that defined "Thai" as its culture, citizenship, and territory. In 1943, the regime launched a first experimental identification card, authorized by the Identification Card Act. This card applied to Thai who resided in Pranakhon (Bangkok) and Thon Buri Provinces.

The invention of Thai identity cards used in conjunction with the household registration document represents a new method of the Thai state authority to circumscribe, register, regiment, and observe people within their jurisdictions. The identification card as a form of state power was necessary not only because of the bureaucratic control it entailed, but also because it implied the establishment of citizenship by binding body, identity, and citizenship together. It is worth noting that state inscription on population is by no means a recently modern project. In pre-modern Siam, the most effective control of corvee labor was carried out through methods of body marking, the tattooing of the wrist of a *phrai luang* (commoner who worked for the king), identifying the name of city and master.

Unlike tattooing and other pre-modern forms of registration, the purpose of modern state inscription through an identification card is not for labor control but to ensure the national loyalty of the subject of the state. The card has also brought with it the notion of proprietary citizenship that allows the state to maintain direct, continual, and specific contact between its ruling bureaucracy and its citizenry. However, one enduring problem the state faced in constructing a system of official identification was how to articulate identity to a person/body in a consistent and reliable way. As body and identity has never been in permanent or fixed connection, the task of describing identity accurately and consistently was a major challenge to the state. Thorough technologies must then be designed to facilitate the identification process. Binding identity to the body was thus done by technologies that included photographs, signatures, and fingerprints, and by the use of legal practices, for example, the requirement to carry identification cards at all time.

The state's notion of proprietary citizenship through the enforcement of identification cards has not only served to fix identity and loyalty as subject to one nation-state, but has also been used as a powerful tool to discipline stubborn/bad subjects. In the history of suppression tactics, identification card inspection has been employed as a state's means of surveillance and punishment against popular demonstrations and political movements. The historical construction of official Thai identity epitomizes the state's attempt to establish a form of ownership over individual citizens, reflected in different technologies of identification. Proprietary citizenship has been exercised through the making of a permanent, indelible identity which is lasting, unchangeable, always recognizable and provable. Identification cards as a function of state capacity to create documentary evidence and bureaucratic records have enabled the state to recognize specific individuals. Official Thai identity acquires its meaning and power not only through the system of classification but also through the active interactions with the state machinery which constantly monitors, regulates, and guides personal conduct, thus legitimizing the state's intimate bond with its citizen.

Cards, Colors, and the Contingent Citizenship

Although citizenship is commonly regarded as a matter of the relations between individuals and the state to which they belong, it is also one of the markers used by states in their attempt to regulate the movement of people across borders. Citizenship at the border is often historically volatile, reflecting the state's changing view towards border and mobility. In its transformation towards the modern nation-state, government of people gave way to government of territory, so the need for clearly bounded divisions of ownership and control correspondingly increased, with the border becoming a state weapon (Wilson and Donnan 1998, 8–9). Nevertheless, the effective control of territory also depends on the way in which identity can be effectively regulated.

Despite the fact that immigration has always been central to the process of nation building, the historical connection between route and root (Clifford 1997) as basis of societal formation has often been written out of the collective memories of the modern nation-state. Fluid boundaries have been suppressed by territoriality as one of the first conditions of the state's existence, and the *sine qua non* of its borders (Wilson and Donnan 1998). As Castles and Davidson (2000) note, the regulation of immigration is only a recent phenomenon, dating from the late nineteenth century, while state policies to integrate immigrants or regulate "community relations" date only from the 1960s. Yet, assimilation and differential exclusion have been made natural and inevitable processes of what Castles and Davidson (ibid.) call the controllability of difference.

Whereas borders represent spatial and temporal records of the relationship between people and state, such records often include the state's anxiety towards mobility across national boundaries. Contingent citizenship is therefore a product of shifting state-ethnic relations at and across borders as mediated by diverse ideological and political economic forces at different periods of time. Such forces, which oscillate between inclusion and exclusion, have been played out both symbolically and concretely, constituting a "politics of presence" as "an embodied enactment of toleration or intolerance" (Yuval-Davis and Werbner 1999, 4). In the case of Thailand, the politics of presence is well illustrated in the complex yet arbitrary systems of identification cards at the border.

The borders of Thailand, post–World War II, can be characterized by a tension between national security ideology and forces of economic integration. Between 1965 and 1985, borders became highly politicized, with a migration influx of refugees, displaced people, and political asylum seekers. On the Thai-Burmese border, the Thai state indirectly supported the armed forces of the ethnic minorities that were fighting the government of Burma as a kind of "buffer state" (Caouette, Archavanitkul, and Pyne 2000). The security policy of this period was designed in order to prevent spread of communism from nearby countries (ibid.). It was in this period that the so-called "colored cards" (*bat si*) were designed as a means of securing the borders through certifying individual identity and controlling movement across the border. Most of these diverse identification card programs were poorly planned and lacked consistent rationales (e.g., the definition of an immigrant can vary, depending on date of entry into Thailand, ethnic identity, and political history), resulting in confusion rather than effective measures of control. Throughout the two decades of "colored cards" and registration of people classified as non-Thai others, the implementation of differential exclusion has often been in a state of flux. For example, some cards might be eliminated, leaving the card-holders with no future, while other cards were upgraded to a Thai identification card. After 1989, with the waning of the Cold War era, borders acquired new meaning as a gateway to economic integration. New types of cards were invented for "alien labor" (*raeng ngan tang dao*), as a means to both regulate the flow of cross-border immigrants and reap benefits from new economic resources. While controversy regarding alien identity cards has escalated and the demand for Thai identification cards among hill people and migrant workers has intensified, ID card scams have become widespread, adding further chaos to the colored card scheme.

Table 1. Chronology of Implementation of Identification Cards and Coins for Non-Thai Citizens in Thailand

Year	ID category	Status	Use and issues
1967	Vietnamese Refugee ID Cards White card with blue border	Children of Vietnamese refugees who entered Thailand between 1945 and 1946 were eligible for Thai citizenship. Vietnamese refugees who have not acquired Thai citizenship must ask permission from governors before traveling out of province of residence. Issued by Police Department	Batch 1 issued: 24/08/1967 expired: 23/08/1973 Batch 2 issued: 02/08/1980 expired: 01/08/1982 Batch 3 extended expiry date of batch 2 to 03/12/1988 Batch 4 issued: 19/07/1990 expired: 18/07/1995 Batch 5 expired: 26/08/1997
1969–1970	Hill Tribe Coins	No longer in use Issued by Department of Administration	Used as verification of settlement in Thai kingdom between 1969 and 1970. Widespread selling of coins and difficulty in establishing proof of ownership
1970	Former Kuo Min Tang Soldier ID Cards White card	Cabinet Resolution on 06/10/1970 assigned immigrant status to former KMT soldiers. Cabinet Resolution on 30/05/1978 allowed legal naturalization of former KMT soldiers for their contribution to the Thai nation in fighting communists. Cabinet Resolution on 12/06/1984 allowed children of former KMT soldiers to acquire Thai citizenship. Those who have not yet acquired Thai citizenship must ask permission from governors before traveling out of province of residence.	Three batches of cards have been issued.

Year	ID category	Status	Use and issues
1976	Immigrants with Thai race from Ko Kong, Cambodia Green card	Issued to former Thai citizens and their children whose citizenship was removed when Ko Kong was returned to Cambodia.	Three batches were issued between 1976 and 1989
1977	Illegal immigrants with Thai race from Cambodia White card with red border	No official status has yet been assigned.	Immigrants with Thai race from Cambodia who entered Thailand after 15/11/1977. Thai government has used this date to separate legal from illegal immigrants from Cambodia. Most of this group resides in Trat Province.
1978	Displaced Person with Burmese Nationality ID Cards Pink card	Cabinet Resolution on 29/08/2000 assigned alien status to pink card holders. Children of this group born between 24/12/1972 and 25/02/1976 were eligible for Thai citizenship.	Three batches were issued between 1976 and 1993 for ethnic groups from Burma who entered Thailand before 9/03/1976
1984	Haw Chinese Immigrant ID Cards Yellow card	Cabinet Resolution on 21/06/1984 assigned the status of legal immigrants to those who entered Thailand between 1950 and 1961. Children of Haw Chinese immigrants whose citizenship was removed are eligible to regain their citizenship.	Four batches were issued. This card is applied to former soldiers of KMT and their families who entered Thailand between 1950 and 1961 and could not return to their home country for political reasons. These immigrants resided mainly in Chiang Mai, Chiang Rai, and Mae Hong Son Provinces.
1987	Nepalese Immigrant ID Cards Green card	Formerly classified as Displaced Person with Burmese Nationality. Cabinet Resolution on 29/08/2000 assigned the status of legal immigrant, and children who were born between 24/12/1972 and 25/02/1992 were eligible for Thai citizenship.	Entered into Thailand at Thong Pha Phum, Kanchanaburi Province.

Year	ID category	Status	Use and issues
1988	Independent Haw Chinese ID Cards	Cabinet Resolution on 27/12/1988 assigned temporary residential status.	Entered Thailand between 1962 and 1978.
	Orange card	Cabinet Resolution on 29/08/2000 assigned legal immigrant status for those who entered the country before 3/10/1985, and illegal status for those who entered afterwards.	This card applies to relatives of former soldiers of KMT who migrated into Thailand between 1962 and 1978.
		Children who were born between 14/12/1972 and 25/02/1992 are eligible for Thai citizenship.	
1989–1990	Former Malayu Communist ID Cards Green Card	Cabinet Resolution on 30/10/1990 assigned legal status and granted citizenship to children who were born in Thailand.	
1990–1991	Highlander ID Cards Blue card	Approved by Cabinet Resolution on 05/06/1999. Highlanders are classified into two types: (1) nine groups of hill tribes (2) non-hill tribes, e.g., Shan, Mon, Burmese, etc. Legal status is granted to those who entered Thailand before 03/10/1985 and are eligible for Thai citizenship. Children of those who entered before 3/10/1985 and born between 14/12/1972 and 25/02/1985 are also eligible for Thai citizenship.	Surveyed and registered by district and Dept. of Administration.
1991	Malbri ID Cards Blue card	Classified as "highlanders," considered as indigenous people of Phrae and Nan Provinces. Entitled to Thai citizenship.	

Year	ID category	Status	Use and issues
1991	Displaced person with Thai race and Burmese nationality Yellow card with blue border	Thai who resided on the borders between Siam and Burma before boundary demarcation in the reign of King Rama V and refused to move across the border afterwards. Political tension between SLORC and ethnic insurgency along the borders resulted in the movements of these Thai into Prachuap Khiri Khan, Chumphon, Ranong, and Tak Provinces. Cabinet Resolution approved the naturalization of people who entered Thailand before 10/03/1976.	First batch used the same card as displaced persons with Burmese nationality, but added a stamp stating "with Thai race."
1991	Lao Immigrant ID Cards Blue card	Lao who moved to live with relatives in Nong Khai, Ubon Ratchathani, Loei, Nakhon Phanom, Mukdahan, Uttaradit, Chiang Rai, and Nan Provinces (not in refugee camps). No official status has been assigned. Children are not eligible for Thai citizenship. Issued according to policies by the National Security Council and the Second Regional Army	First batch used the Highlander ID Cards (crossing out "Highlander" and adding "Laotian Immigrant"), due to limited budget).
1994	Thai Lue ID Cards Orange card	Considered as Thai race originally resided in Sipsongpanna, Yunnan, China. Cabinet Resolution on 17/03/1992 assigned legal immigrant status. Children born in Thailand are eligible for Thai citizenship.	Two batches were issued. Formerly classified in the same group as displaced persons with Burmese nationality (pink or blue card).
1996	Hill tribe outside Residential Area ID Cards (Hmong refugees in Tham Kabok, Sara Buri Province)	Deported to third countries	Two batches were issued. Population: 14,602

Year	ID category	Status	Use and issues
1999	Highlander's Survey Cards Green card with red border	Issued according to the Master Plan for Development of Communities, Environment and Opium Control. Started in Tak Province in 1998. Cabinet Resolution on 29/08/2000 required that card-holders verify their status within one year.	Surveyed and registered in order to determined appropriate statuses according to nationality law.
1992–2004	Alien Labor Cards	Cabinet Resolution on 17/03/1992 allowed temporary residency for illegal migrant workers in four commercial provinces: Chiang Rai, Tak, Kanchanaburi, and Ranong. Workers must have work permits. Cabinet Resolution on 25/06/1996 extended residency for illegal migrant workers for two years. This applied to workers of Burmese, Cambodian, and Lao nationalities who work in eleven industries in forty-three provinces. Workers must register and acquire work permits. Subsequent cabinet resolutions extended periods of stay for these workers every year.	Nine batches (nine extensions) were issued between 1992 and 2004
2007	Highland ID Cards Pink card: electronic with thirteen digits and a magnetic stripe		First batch started in 2007. They replace the former highland ID cards (for hill tribes and non-hill tribes)

Source: Adapted from Darunee Paisanpanichkul 2005

Since 1967 there have been at least seventeen different kinds of ID cards imposed on the different groups of immigrants who entered Thailand at different times and with different reasons. The system of identity designation by cards is rather chaotic, inconsistent, and arbitrary. While different deadlines of entry into Thailand have been set to differentiate Thai from non-Thai citizens, types of immigrants were unevenly categorized, using random criteria of ethnicity, political ideology, or elevation. Discursive policies regarding border and border crossing have also been present. At a time of political pressure shaped by an ideology of national security, the attitude towards immigrants was restrictive, resulting in an assertion of clear separation of members of different categories from "others": "us" from "them." However, in periods of economic liberalism and national prosperity, policy often entails permissive approaches towards population movement and political rhetoric about the importance of open borders. Immigration policies today are still characterized by the shifting motivations of the state, between limiting its obligation toward immigrants and ensuring the availability of the human resources the immigrants supply to the Thai economy. As a result, restrictions on temporary residency and alien labor ID cards have become more extensive every year, with increasing fees required by state agencies.

Contested Citizenship and the Everyday Practice of ID Cards

Writing from a feminist perspective, Yuval-Davis and Werbner (1999) look at citizenship as contested terrain. The degree to which the political agency of subjects determines or is determined by unsettling collective forces is key to the everyday politics of citizenship. As they argue, rather than simply being an imposed political construct of identity, citizenship as a subjectivity is "deeply dialogical, encapsulating specific, historically, inflected, cultural, and social assumptions about similarity and difference" (3). Negotiating citizenship has brought about different cultures of identification in which the relationships between state and citizen and the non-citizen "other" are reinterpreted.

The everyday use of identification cards by Thai and non-Thai citizens challenges claims to authority in determining who belongs to the nation-state and who does not, as a central component of sovereignty. Throughout the history of citizenship-making, wherever identification cards have been invented and implemented as the state attempts to classify subjects residing within or attempting to enter state territories by controlling their mobility and demanding total allegiance, such attempts have also been contested by local people. Various practices ranging from discarding/returning the cards (*khuen bat prachachon*), burning the cards (*phao bat prachachon*), or refusing to apply for identification cards have become symbolic protests against the hegemonic idea of what it means to be "Thai." For over three decades, as the state has attempted increasingly to enforce the ID card system, the cards have been turned into a battlefield by marginal groups in negotiating their position with the nation-state. The performative character of cards has become a subversive tool of local critique against a government that is often indifferent or weak in taking care of poor and marginal communities. Two examples of grassroots political practice of ID cards are illustrated below.

> Three hundred farmers from the People's Network in 4 Regions have decided to call off their demonstration after camping in front of the government house since 12 March 2007. The demonstration did not receive any clear answer from the government regarding the way to solve their debt problems. The group which included elderly and children showed their disappointment pertaining to the Cabinet Resolution on 27 March which did not issue any measurement relating to their problem. It was clear that the government was not only unresponsive but also indifferent to local demand. The group has then planned to march to meet the members of the National Legislative Assembly before walking on foot to Lao PDR in order to set up a Center of Stateless People and will ask for a permission to reside there. Before entering into Lao PDR, the group will return their ID cards to the Thai government at the immigration office at the border. (*Daily News,* March 28, 2007)

> If (the government) passes this (National Security) Act, there will be two states ruling the country. The constitution will be meaningless... (We) will have to fight forcefully... particularly, the Human Right Commission and academics must join together in resigning (from the National Legislative Assemby)... We must stage a symbolic protest. If (the Council for National Security) refuses to stop, (we) must turn down the 2007 Constitution, though it has improved on the one in 1997. For the people, they must join together in the burning of identification cards as a strategic means to reject the power of the dictatorship.
>
> Pipob Thongchai, member of the Committee for the Campaign for Democracy, August 2007

If citizenship is a product of the creation of the modern nation-state, one of the great paradoxes of such construction is that the process of control and constraint also constitutes a moment of emancipation. Like all hegemonic discourses, modern citizenship has never been absolute. While the identification card is fundamental to proprietary citizenship, it has been reappropriated and used as a dialogical tool by people in expanding participatory politics that call for a righteous state. It is within this terrain that autonomy and the right to be different are pitched against the regulating forces of the state identification system and its demand for definite national belonging. Like state formation itself, constructing citizenship has been not only a problematic and unfinished process of defining boundaries and identities but also a project of reworking social and political practices.

One interesting arena of local reworking of citizenship is at the border. As a counter-construction of citizenship (Cheater 1999), border crossing and multiple identities practiced by both individuals and families undermine the rhetoric of unified solidarity and singular national identity. In his study of ethnic minorities at the Thai and Malaysian borders, Horstmann (2002) notes that dual citizenship and the holding of multiple identification cards constitute an important strategy employed by the "trapped minorities" in response to the state's rigid boundary surveillance and citizenship policy. Multiple citizenship rights have been acquired by these minorities through various means, including the registration of children's birth at a location across the border, marriage, making use of kinship relations or inventing them, and applying for naturalization. Horstmann argues that the adoption of dual citizenship not only reflects the plurality of local social life, but has played a long historical role in relations between the social worlds of Thai and Malay communities cutting across national identities (ibid.). Border populations therefore use the documents of the state to their personal advantage, producing their identity cards to facilitate border crossings.

Similar practices are also found among members of border communities and immigrants along the border between Thailand and Burma, where identities are fixed by different kinds of colored identification cards. Adoption by Thai citizens of children of immigrant parents from Burma whose legal status remains uncertain is a fast-lane strategy to guarantee permanent citizenship for the youth. Through this adoption strategy, young children will also be able to have access to a better education, as they are entitled to Thai citizenship. As different kinds of identification cards for immigrants are issued every year in different provinces and with different purposes, with no clear information about which cards will promote a more promising status, acquisition of multiple colored cards has been a speculative strategy among individual migrants. In my interview with a family in Piang Luang village, a border community between the Shan State in Burma and Wiang Haeng District in Thailand's Chiang Mai Province, four members of the same family, including father, mother, and two children, have obtained three different kinds of identification cards. While residing in Chiang Rai Province, the father had a yellow card (Haw Chinese Immigrant ID Card), the status to which he is entitled as a son of a former KMT soldier. After marrying his wife who lives in Wiang Haeng District, he has not abandoned the yellow card but is now applying for a pink card (new electronic Highlander ID Card). According to him, the yellow card does not have any future. His wife has had a pink card since she moved into Thailand. The two children, however, have been adopted by two different Thai families and thus have different last names from their parents and from each other.

For ethnic minorities at the border and immigrants from Burma alike, colored identification cards have become assets with different kinds of value that have been accumulated and used to upgrade their status. The process of obtaining these cards is, of course, illegal and involves various scams. Some ethnic hill people who have been settled in Thailand for a longer time might work as brokers who travel to many villages in order to buy Thai ID cards from relatives of the deceased and sell them to new immigrants. Many Shan immigrants from Burma who have no card of their own make deals with friends in hill villages, adding their names to the house registration documents in order to obtain the ID card for highlanders. It is common that people who live at the border or in a refugee camp such as the one in Mae Sot District, Tak Province, might carry more than one card and use each of them for different purposes. ID cards are therefore not only the state instrument of control but are survival resources to be assessed, classified, and circulated according to a hierarchy of values that is usually predicated on the degree to which a given card can be turned into Thai citizenship and how much freedom of mobility it entails. Immigrants who have no cards are often considered as the poorest and most marginal, because if they are arrested they can be immediately deported back to their home countries. The alien labor card (a work permit for illegal immigrants) is considered valueless as it allows only limited freedom of mobility. A migrant worker with this card is prohibited from traveling outside the vicinity of the workplace. As a result, the person who holds an alien labor card will try to obtain a more valuable card, which allows more freedom of movement, such as a green card with red border, a pink card, or even a Thai nationality card. Negotiating mobility has thus been an integral part of redefining citizenship among immigrants and members of border communities in Thailand.

Conclusion

In this paper, I have tried to capture the shifting and conflicting constructions of citizenship and its complex apparatus of ID card systems. I have argued that the culture of identification in Thailand is characterized by its tension and contradiction, a product of the interplay between shifting official forms of domination and control, and minorities' experimentation and everyday practice.

The state's chaotic system of classification of nationality is often actively learned and reinterpreted in the local understanding of citizenship. While state differentiation between Thai nationals and alien "others" has long been integral to the process of nation building, such attempts have often been contested. Informal politics thus play a crucial role in shaping citizenship discourse among the Thai, as well as among non-Thai immigrants. Cards and colors, as a powerful technique of statecraft deployed to control mobility and fix the identity of border-crossing people, have often been employed by the non-Thai subjects as assets for circulation and tools for negotiation. The population of immigrants has been turned arbitrarily into an ambiguous ethnic category of non-Thai minorities; such transformation has often been in flux, resulting in diverse translations of everyday-life notions of citizenship. Contested citizenship constitutes, therefore, a reworking of national identification as something alive and exciting involving a multiplicity of actors struggling in an enlarged political sphere extending beyond the constrictions of legality. It is in this realm that the non-Thai "other" is allowed the possibility of being both subjectified and subject-making in the unstable state-ethnic relationship of modern Thai society.

References

Caouette, Theresa, Kritaya Archavanitkul, and Hnin Hnin Pyne. 2000. "Thai Government's Policies on Undocumented Migration from Burma." In *Sexuality, Reproductive Health, and Violence: Experiences of Migrants from Burma in Thailand*, Mahidol University: Institute for Population and Social Research.

Caplan, Jane, and John Torpey, eds. 2001. *Documenting Individual Identity: The Development of State Practices in the Modern World*. Princeton University Press.

Castles, Stephen, and Alastair Davidson. 2000. *Citizenship and Migration: Globalization and the Politics of Belonging*. Basingstoke: Macmillan.

Cheater, A. P. 1999. "Transcending the State? Gender and Borderline Constructions of Citizenship in Zimbabwe." In *Border Identities: Nation and State at International Frontier*. T. Wilson and H. Donnan, eds. Cambridge University Press.

Clifford, James. 1997. *Routes: Travel and Translation in the Late Twentieth Century*, Cambridge, MA; London: Harvard University Press.

Darunee Paisanpanitchakul. 2005. "Right to Identification Paper in Thai State." Unpublished MA Thesis, Thammasat University (in Thai).

Feeney, David. 1989. "The Decline of Property Rights in Man in Thailand 1800–1913." *The Journal of Economic History* 49 (2): 285–96.

Gates, Kelly. 2004. "The Past Perfect Promise of Facial Recognition Technology." *Occasional Paper*, ACDIS, June.

Horstmann, Alexander. 2002. "Dual Ethnic Minorities and Local Reworking of National Citizenship at the Thailand-Malaysian Border." Center for Border Studies, Queens University of Belfast.

Keyes, Charles. 2002. "'The Peoples of Asia'—Science and Politics in the Classification of Ethnic Groups in Thailand, China, and Vietnam." *The Journal of Asian Studies* 61 (4): 1163–203.

Krisana Kitiyadisai. 2007. "Smart ID Card in Thailand from a Buddhist Perspective." http://www.stc.arts.chula.ac.th/cyberethics/papers/Krisna-Smart%20 ID-buddhist.doc.

Marshall, T. H. 1950. *Citizenship and Social Class*. Cambridge: Cambridge University Press.

Matsuda, Matt K. 1996. *The Memory of the Modern*. New York: Oxford University Press.

Nitaya Onozawa. 2002. "The Labor Force in Thai Social History." www.tsukuba-b. ac.jp/library/kiyou/2002/3.

Pittayalonkorn, Prince. 1970. "Chat and Araya." *Pasompasan Series 3*, 141–42. Bangkok: Ruam San (in Thai).

Rabibhadana, Akin. 1970. *The Organization of Thai Society in the Early Bangkok Period 1782–1873*. Ithaca, NY: Cornell University Press.

Saichol Satayanurak. 2005. "The Mainstream Historical Thought about the Thai Nation." In *The Historical Thought about the Thai Nation and the Community Thought*, edited by Chattip Natsupa and Wanwipa Burutrattanapan. Bangkok: Sangsan (in Thai). http://goo.gl/J3rOrl.

⸻ "The Construction of Mainstream Thought on 'Thainess' and the 'Truth' Constructed by 'Thainess.'" Translated by Sarinee Achavanuntakul. www.Fringer. org.

Sankar, Pamela. 1992. *State Power and Record-Keeping: The History of Individualized Surveillance in the United States, 1790-1935*. PhD diss., University of Pennsylvania.

Scott, James C. 1998. *Seeing Like a State: How Certain Schemes to Improve the Human Condition Have Failed*. New Haven, CT: Yale University Press.

Torpey, John. 2000. *The Invention of the Passport: Surveillance, Citizenship and the State*. New York: Cambridge University Press.

Watner, Carl. 2004. "'Your Papers, Please!': The Origin and Evolution of Official Identity in the United States." *Voluntaryist*, Second Quarter.

Wilson, Thomas and Donnan Hastings. 1998. *Border Identities: Nation and State at International Frontiers*. Cambridge: Cambridge University Press.

Yuval-Davis, Nira. and Pnina Werbner, eds. 1999. *Women, Citizenship and Difference*. London and New York: Zed Books.

CROSSING BORDERS OF STATE AND NATION

NARRATING LEGITIMACY, NARRATING AGENCIES:

Citizenship Negotiations among Internationally Displaced Laotians in Northeastern Thailand

Suchada Thaweesit

Introduction

In the article based on his Association for Asian Studies presidential address, "The People of Asia: Science and Politics in Classification of Ethnic Groups in Thailand, China, and Vietnam," Charles F. Keyes stated, "In the modern world, nation-states have assumed preeminent roles not only in structuring the situation in which social relationships take place but more significantly in determining what differences are significant for the peoples living under their jurisdiction" (Keyes 2002, 1170). He went on to argue that although biology, linguistics, and ethnology have long been used to classify ethnic groups, these three factors are not the determinants of the differences among people. Instead, he maintained, ethnic identification is an outcome of the politics of nation building.

This argument not only helps us to understand the production of difference among people, but also the construction of "legitimate citizens" of the modern nation-state. Thus, the rise of the Thai modern nation-state not only led to the demarcation of the nation-state's border, but also to the notion of people's identity. Following Keyes, I argue that in Thailand, as elsewhere, people's nationality has been defined in order to distinguish "aliens" from citizens. As such, nationality, as a form of political instrument, has become the overriding determinant in defining a person and the person's civil rights within the nation-state's boundaries. I believe that the Thai nation-state's imagination of Thai-ness has adapted to social norms, legislation, and political patterns changing over time. Thus, the status of citizenship depends on the nation-state's politics as much as people's internalization of the nation-state's proclamation of who they are.

I also posit that, historically, imagined Thai-ness originated from the Thai ruling elite's reaction to their fears that the kingdom's territory was threatened by the expansion of French and British colonialism. To survive the colonial threat, the Thai nation-state began in 1899 to use the notion of Thai-ness to identify people living within its modern boundaries. Subsequently, the first Nationality Act, which laid the groundwork for legitimate citizenship for people living within these boundaries, was issued in 1913. However, the nationwide registration of residents as Thai citizens did not happen until the first census was conducted in 1956. At that time, the processes of imagining Thai-ness emphasized inclusion rather than exclusion, because it required people in the kingdom to identify themselves as Thai, regardless of whether their ethnic background was Lao, Khmer, Mon, Malay, etc. This principle underlines nationality policy as reflected in Thailand's Nationality Act.

Aihwa Ong's neo-liberalist perspective suggests that nowadays we have moved beyond the idea of citizenship as a protected status in a nation-state, a condition opposed to the condition of statelessness. Ong also optimistically states that "strict discriminations between citizens and non-citizens are dropped in favor of the pursuit of human capital," and that "the difference between having and not having citizenship is becoming blurred as the territorialization of entitlement is increasingly challenged by deterritorialized claims beyond the state" (Ong 2006, 499). As a matter of fact, if we apply this view in the Thai context, it would obscure how state powers affect the everyday life of immigrants and internationally displaced peoples. It would also overlook their day-to-day struggles within the state's regimes.

This chapter focuses on the struggles of internationally displaced Lao in the Isan region to be recognized by the Thai state as Thai citizens. It demonstrates that the Thai Nationality Act has continuously played a major role in identifying whether people are "citizens" or "others." The notion of citizenship, as defined by the Nationality Act, is based primarily on two considerations including descent (*jus sanguinis*) and place (*jus soli*). *Jus soli* can refer to either a place of birth or a place of residency. This act states that Thai nationality as well as citizenship can be acquired by birth registration or naturalization, meaning that either the person's mother or father, or both the father and the mother, must be a Thai citizen, or the person must be born or reside permanently in Thailand. However, the *jus soli* principle does not apply to the children of immigrants. Even though they may be born in Thailand, Thai nationality is not automatically conferred to them. This indicates that in Thailand application of the nationality law emphasizes *jus sanguinis* over *jus soli*.

It is important to make clear from the beginning exactly what the term "stateless" refers to in this chapter. The clarification is needed because there is a view that argues that "statelessness" and "stateless persons" do not actually exist. This view is based on the perception that in the modern era, states play preeminent roles in constituting and governing the lives of people who come to live under their jurisdiction. Even without citizenship, people are not free from state power and there is nowhere in the world where they can live beyond its reach. Therefore, the term "stateless" is at best only partially accurate, and at worst it obscures the fact that state power cannot be avoided. I find this qualification rhetorically appealing and theoretically valid. Nevertheless, it is more constructive and analytically useful to understand that through the exercise of its power (or the refusal to exercise certain powers), the state can arbitrarily deprive people of citizenship, thereby condemning them to statelessness and the marginal status that this entails.

I rely on Article 1 of the 1954 Convention on the Status of Stateless Persons in order to define the term "stateless" here. According to this convention, a stateless person is one who is not recognized as a national by any state under the operation of its law. It is important to note that there are two types of statelessness: *de jure* and *de facto*. *De jure* statelessness refers to the situation of persons to whom all countries refuse to confer citizen status, or deny them the right to reside within its territory. People of this group neither effectively establish citizenship nor residency in any state in the world. Truly stateless, most of them are regarded as "illegal immigrants" in the countries where they dwell. In Thailand, the category of "*de jure* stateless persons" refers to people who have no personal legal status in a civil registration system of Thailand or of any other countries due to a lack of proof or any documents to verify their nationality. Examples of this type of statelessness include undocumented displaced persons from Laos during the Cold War period, the subject of this research, and a group of people known as Rohingya.[1] The number of *de jure* stateless persons in Thailand has not been systematically calculated. In practice, they are often confused with or are combined with *de facto* stateless persons, undocumented persons, and migrant workers from neighboring countries.

De facto statelessness refers to people who possess a nationality, but their right to nationality is not recognized by the state in which they reside. It also refers to those who become refugees or displaced persons and their nationality is ineffective outside their homeland. Usually, the country where these people live becomes their "personal state," because it gives them the right to reside in the country but does not accept them as nationals. In Thailand, these people are referred to as "citizens without nationality," and are not referred to as stateless. This category includes hill tribes, refugees, and documented displaced aliens.

As of December 2004, the Thai government reported that the total number of stateless and nationality-less individuals in Thailand was approximately 2 to 2.5 million. The majority of them were ethnic minorities living in mountainous areas in the north, as well as populations living along the western corridor of the Thai-Burmese border. Currently, long-term illegal migrants and their children, refugees, displaced populations, and even undocumented Thai can be treated as stateless or nationality-less if their names do not appear in a household registration certificate.

According to the Universal Declaration of Human Rights, statelessness should not exist in any country, since everyone, it declares, is entitled to a nationality. Regardless of this declaration, most nation-states still apply citizenship or nationality laws to determine who is and is not a legal citizen. As a consequence, today we find multitudes of people around the world living in the limbo of statelessness. The effect of stateless or nationality-less status on people's lives is well documented in literature and on websites. Metaphorically, stateless persons are described as maintaining a "bare life," since they are not protected by laws and are therefore vulnerable to all forms of exploitation. When the nation-state in which stateless people permanently reside refuses to recognize them as citizens, they cannot secure the rights and securities due to a citizen, and it is thus difficult to better their lives and improve their prospects for the future.

Although many stateless and/or nationality-less people exist in Thailand, it is only recently that their stories have caught public and academic attention. The most well-known case, which brought the issue of statelessness forward, was the dispute over nationality and citizenship in Mae Ai District in Chiang Mai. In 2002, Mae Ai appeared in the media for the first time when the district chief revoked the Thai nationality of more than a thousand residents of Ban Rom Thai, a small border village. This village is situated very close to a small Burmese town across the border, and people in the towns on either side of the border are typically related by kinship and shared culture. District officials said that the villagers were non-Thai. Instead, they grouped them into the category of "displaced Burmese" ineligible for Thai citizenship. Moreover, they made the accusation that the people in this village acquired Thai nationality—and identity cards—through the bribery of corrupt local officials. Villagers' identity cards thus were nullified and their names were taken out of the household registration system. Subsequently, 1,243 Mae Ai residents were forced into a limbo of statelessness and were denied citizenship rights.

The villagers fought in the courts for three years to prove their Thai nationality. In September 2005, the Supreme Administrative Court announced their victory, and their Thai nationality, as well as their citizenship rights, was restored (Ekachai 2005). The story illustrates clearly that in the modern era the issues of identity cards and citizenship in a border zone, seen from an anthropological perspective as an "in-between space," become very crucial and problematic to the nation-state as well as to the people who live within it. The state's obsession with national security regularly affects the daily lives of people in the borderlands. On the one hand, the state can be seen to be applying citizenship and nationality regulations as a form of surveillance and population control in its territory, especially in the borderlands. On the other hand, it is possible to observe how the stateless in the borderlands—a group that may comprise ethnic minorities, hill tribes, refugees, displaced populations, and labor migrants—use their connections and local networks to encounter and negotiate with state powers and apparatuses of control and surveillance.

The Cold War-Displaced Lao in Isan

The northeast of Thailand, an area known as Isan, is a place in which thousands of displaced people who fled Laos during the Cold War have made their home. The political conflicts and wars in Laos between 1954 and 1975 uprooted many Lao from their homeland. The movement of Lao to Thailand began following the fall of the Royal Lao Government (RLG) in 1975. Initially, most displaced people were officers and soldiers who had sided with the RLG. They also included villagers who did not want to live under a communist regime that intervened in their daily activities. A second phase of migration to Thailand took place between 1977 and 1981. Many of these migrants were ordinary villagers escaping economic hardship caused by drought and by government reform of land and agricultural policies. A final phase of population displacement started in 1982 and continued to the late 1980s, this time due to both economic conditions and government mismanagement.

In all, more than 360,000 Lao fled the country between 1975 and 1992. This group included nearly all Western-educated Lao and upland minorities, especially the Hmong, who had supported the RLG and the United States' military effort in Laos. By the end of 1992, approximately 305,000 displaced Lao had been accepted as refugees and had permanently resettled in third countries, most commonly the United States and France. Forty thousand Lao—mostly Hmong—remained in Thai refugee camps. Twelve thousand of them were voluntarily repatriated to Laos under the supervision and assistance of the United Nations High Commission for Refugees (UNHCR). Even though international agreements mandated the resettlement or repatriation of all remaining displaced Lao in Thailand by the end of 1994, some twelve hundred of them, mainly Hmong, remain in Ban Na Pho camp, while more than thirteen thousand Lao, also mostly Hmong, reside in a Buddhist monastery in Phetchabun Province (Supang and Finch 1992).[2] Many of the internationally displaced Lao I interviewed cited war and the fall of RLG as the reason they fled the country. Several of them, especially those who were former soldiers, said that they were avoiding persecution, arrest, and being sent to reeducation camps. Some admitted that they were former members of armed resistance groups involved in attacks against the Lao government. Several displaced persons from Laos whom I met mentioned that they did not want to live in a country with which they were in political disagreement, in terms of ideology or measures of political control. One man told me that he and a team of around thirty men had been trained by the Thai military, which at the time played a role in supporting small groups of displaced Lao. The group was armed and sent back into Laos to gather military information. The military actions they undertook put them, their families, and Lao villagers who came into contact with them in danger. The only option for them afterwards was to help their families and these villagers to escape into Thailand in order to avoid persecution by the new government.

It is important to note that before and during my fieldwork there were several cases of displaced Lao in Isan shot dead by gunmen. News reports said that the men killed were suspected to be involved in insurgent activities of the Hmong leader Vang Pao or active leaders of other resistance groups. Some displaced Lao admitted that these murders made them fearful and anxious, but most people did not know much about the incidents. Many simply refused to comment.

In Isan, displaced Lao and their children comprise those who are stateless and nationality-less. A certain number of displaced Lao, both men and women, married local people and have mixed children. Due to the Thai government's fear of communist intrusion, local officials have been ordered not to register mixed Thai-Lao children, born from Lao fathers or mothers.[3] Also, many Thai who have formed a union with displaced Lao did not dare register their children, as this would mean revealing the illegal status of their marriage. As a result, many mixed Thai-Lao children have been documented as displaced Lao following the status of their father or mother, who is identified as a displaced person, although the children are, by some criteria, eligible for Thai nationality because one parent is a Thai citizen. Also, there are a number of mixed Thai-Lao children who have been mistakenly categorized as illegal economic migrants.

The Thai government has refused to define displaced people from Laos who entered Thailand illegally during the Cold War period as "refugees," but has preferred to consider them "Lao migrants." This terminology strictly applies only to those who entered Thailand between 1974 and 1975, during Laos' internal conflicts. The Thai government intended to allow them to stay non-permanently in the country and ordered that they live under the close monitoring and supervision of the Ministry of Interior. In 1990, displaced Lao who lived in eight provinces including Nong Khai, Ubon Ratchathani, Loei, Mukdahan, Phayao, Uttaradit, Chiang Rai, and Nan were documented in the house registration system for the first time.[4] The total number of officially documented displaced Lao remaining in Thailand was only 7,095 persons (Montri and Sathian 2004), whereas a number of them are treated as "economic migrants," otherwise undocumented persons, or stateless.

Undocumented people in Thailand are referred to as "persons with no personal legal status." This means that they have been living in Thailand for a long time, or since they were born, but have not been recorded in the national registration system. Currently, they have an identity card that is labeled "person without civil registration status." Children of displaced Lao who do not have documents to prove that their parents are documented displaced Lao, or if they are unable to prove that they were born in Thailand before February 26, 1992,[5] are often placed in this category. Undocumented people can be *de facto* stateless persons who may be entitled to Thai nationality if they can provide proof that they have been living in Thailand for more than ten years continuously.

It should be noted that the Thai government uses the term "Lao migrants" rather than "Lao refugees" to avoid any obligation to abide by the UN Convention Relating to the Status of Refugees. This is because the Thai government aimed to prevent large numbers of displaced people from entering the country. Regardless of whether they are documented or undocumented, displaced Lao are simultaneously deprived of citizenship rights by Lao PDR, where they were born, and also by Thailand, where they have subsequently settled.

Living Lives as "Suspended Citizens"

In January 2005, the Thai cabinet enacted a new resolution for a strategic plan to handle the status and rights problems of alien populations. The ultimate aim of the resolution was twofold: to build a more complete national population database and to enable stateless and nationality-less persons to become eligible for nationality. Some groups of people who were born in Thailand or have lived in the country continuously for more than ten years would be able to secure their fundamental rights as Thai citizens. According to this resolution, displaced Lao would be eligible for nationality. Yet, eligibility for citizenship was restricted to stateless persons who were documented as displaced Lao (*Lao opphayop*) in government records since 1990 and who held a displaced Lao identity card (*bat Lao opphayop*), which was a blue-colored card with a dark blue edge. Children of people who were not yet listed in the house registration database would not be eligible until they could prove their connection with their displaced parents.

This plan, however, has been carried out very slowly and carefully, and not unconditionally, because potential national security concerns are seen as much more important than human rights and human security. Therefore, the process of applying for Thai nationality for stateless Lao has been made excessively complicated and time-consuming. To start the process, local authorities need to be confident that applicants have records and identity numbers in the household registration database. Then, their eligibility for nationality is investigated. This step requires various supporting documents such as an identity card or a birth certificate, a school certificate, etc. In cases where applicants do not have reliable supporting documents, the authorities then require witnesses' affidavits, community hearings, or, in the case of stateless children, a DNA test. This procedure is put in place in order to verify people's status and their long-term connection with the Thai state. This process and the set of restrictions it entails have been set in place mainly because state authorities want to make sure that the plan will not enable illegal laborers and other new illegal immigrants to become eligible for Thai nationality.

The issue of applying for nationality is extremely complicated and difficult, even for documented displaced Lao. A young man who was incorrectly documented as a displaced Lao recounted that when his parents asked for information about applying for his nationality, a district officer suggested that he and his mother needed to take a DNA test to prove a biological tie. In this case, the mother holds Thai nationality while the father is undocumented Lao, even though in fact his father is the son of Lao parents who entered Thailand during Laos' civil war years. Making the long trip to Bangkok to take the test would have been very costly and a burden on the family. The young man thus decided not to continue to pursue nationality. Instead, he married a young Thai girl who lived in another village to ensure his future, hoping that he would be able to see his children registered as Thai nationals from birth.

In 1995, the Thai government announced a policy that aimed to register laborers from Burma, Laos, and Cambodia. Migrants from these countries are required to register in order to work in Thailand legally. Many undocumented Lao were asked to register as "migrant workers," including those who have had residency in Thailand for generations, and those with a Thai wife or husband, as well as documented displaced Lao from the war period. Village headmen told them that if they did not do so they would be charged as illegal migrants and subject to fines, arrest, and deportation. Therefore, a number of both undocumented and documented displaced Lao from 1974 and 1975 now hold TR38/1(*Tor Ror* 38/1), a document registering migrant workers. Many believed mistakenly that the document was a work permit that would allow them movement outside their restricted districts, so that they could travel to work in Bangkok or elsewhere in Thailand. This is unlike those with a displaced Lao identity card who are allowed only temporary stays in Thailand and are not allowed to work or travel outside the district in which they are registered.

The registration policy for migrant workers from neighboring countries has grouped together displaced Lao and illegal workers, resulting in complications that make it even more difficult to find solutions to problems of statelessness in Isan. The type of identity card and documents that people possess has become crucial for their future and for whether they can or cannot be granted permanent status and the rights given to citizens. Further, those who hold both a displaced Lao identity card and the TR38/1 for migrant workers are at risk because the computerized registration program will refuse their record and assign them to the category of illegal migrant worker.

Thus, even with this new strategy, stateless villagers in Isan still have a long way to go. One of the main problems these people face is the preoccupation with national security by state authorities at different levels. Most local officials with whom I discussed the issues have a bias against stateless Lao. In their view, they are classed as illegal aliens (*khon phit kotmai*) or non-Thai "others" (*mai chai khon Thai*). Many officials clearly expressed their concern that granting nationality to displaced Lao might affect the country's security. Some said that it might jeopardize the current good relationship between the Thai and Lao governments because the Lao government is afraid that some displaced Lao may be involved in anti-Lao government movements, drug trafficking, or other crimes. Another critical difficulty is that local officials do not know much about either the new strategic plan or the legislative procedure for approval of nationality. They also only have limited knowledge about Thailand's nationality laws. As a result, they do very little to advocate on behalf of displaced Lao. Many refused or were unwilling to deal with cases of stateless people who applied for citizenship. Several officials admitted that no one wanted to risk their career because "no one knows exactly who may or may not be eligible for Thai nationality; if we give a nationality to a problematic case we may get in trouble."

Displaced Lao with whom I worked are therefore "suspended citizens," because their lives are on hold awaiting rights that will possibly (and should) be conferred to them or their children. Despite the fact that new policies dealing with statelessness have been implemented, and despite the fact that some stateless Lao will thus finally be able to attain citizenship, their lives are currently still shaped by their difficult predicament. They are still treated by authorities as second-class citizens. The new Nationality Act states clearly in Section 19 that the Ministry of the Interior reserves the authority to revoke citizenship issued to non-Thai citizens if there is a suspicion that false information was provided when applying for citizenship, if there is any evidence of dual nationality, or if the naturalized person has committed any actions that are considered an insult to national security or contrary to public order and good morals. I frequently heard Thai authorities invoke these conditions when explaining the process of obtaining Thai citizenship to stateless villagers in order to ensure their compliance and loyalty to the Thai state.

In June 2007, officials from the Ministry of Interior held a conference with local officials and stateless Lao in a district in which I conducted fieldwork. This public conference aimed to inform the parties involved about measures to solve status and rights problems for displaced Lao. Nearly a thousand displaced and migrant Lao gathered at the district meeting hall to receive information. The officials presented information about rights, qualifications for applying for permanent status, and procedures for applying for citizenship. Much of this was communicated in difficult language filled with legal terminology, which made me suspicious of how many people present really understood the issues. None of the speakers addressed stateless persons' immediate concerns. Subsequently, when the meeting ended, one old displaced Lao man approached me and asked, "Will my son be permitted to travel to work in Bangkok? He finished school this year." Some other villagers showed me the documents and identity cards they had brought and asked, "Will this paper help me to become eligible for citizenship?" Hearing all these inquiries, I realized that the meeting was not helpful to them because it did not take into account concrete circumstances and everyday life struggles of stateless people.

The new strategic plan for solving status problems does not allow undocumented displaced Lao who missed the first registration in 1990 to apply for nationality, even though they entered Thailand in the period from 1974 to 1975. The displaced Lao who missed the 1990 registration include a group of people who lived in refugee camps but refused to be resettled in third countries, as well as displaced Lao who married Thai citizens and have been permanent residents of Thai border villages for more than a decade. My fieldwork indicates that documented and undocumented displaced Lao comprise the largest group of stateless people in Isan. Many never entered refugee camps; many others used to live in the camps but did not go to third countries. Many who escaped from camps to live with relatives in Thai villages subsequently married Thai villagers. Many migrated to live in Thailand prior to and after 1974–75 because they married local people and established families in Thai villages, thus living there throughout their adult lives. Many stateless people claimed that they entered Thailand between 1974 and 1975 but missed the registration process undertaken by the Ministry of Interior because the registration period was very short, lasting only one day. Many missed the registration because they had left their designated areas to work.

Nowadays, both documented and undocumented displaced Lao and their undocumented children in Isan live in a suspended state. As mentioned earlier, according to Thailand's various nationality acts, a person's nationality is first and foremost determined by the nationality of a one's parents, not by one's birthplace. Displaced populations from Laos are thus not entitled to Thai nationality automatically, despite the recent cabinet resolution attempts to acknowledge their right to Thai nationality. It is also common in Isan border areas to see members in one cross-border household assigned different categories according to Thailand's population classification system. For example, a father may be classified as a displaced person, the mother as a Thai citizen, and the son and daughter as illegal migrants. In my survey of 512 household samples of displaced Lao households in three districts in Ubon Ratchathani, more than thirteen hundred stateless and nationality-less persons were found. They include both adults and children. Most of them live in a limbo of statelessness. Their voices are unheard and their existence is unrecognized. I even heard one provincial authority declare that there was no such thing as stateless persons in Isan. Not surprisingly, little has been done to resolve statelessness in this region, compared to the case of the hill tribes in the north.

I would use the term "suspended citizens" to describe those awaiting the rights of nationality and other rights given to citizens. The majority of stateless villagers in Isan are poor and uneducated, and unable to take any steps to better their situation. They are not allowed to own land or houses, and they cannot apply for government loans or funds being offered at the village level. Without Thai identity cards, they are subject to the travel restrictions applied to displaced populations and migrant workers from neighboring countries. Stateless persons are afraid of being caught if they travel far from the villages where they usually live. If they risk travel and are caught by the police they will be asked to pay a heavy fine; if they do not have money to pay they will be put in confinement. This means that stateless persons are unable to travel in search of better incomes, which further aggravates their poverty.

As stateless/nationality-less persons, displaced Lao often see themselves as either "half human" or "not human" because their ability to enjoy basic rights is not endorsed by the state in which they live. Instead, they are kept in a weak and marginal position. The excerpts from interviews with stateless Lao presented here illustrate the difficulties and worries that stateless people in the northeast have expressed:

> "I don't know who I am. I'm neither a Lao nor a Thai."

> "I'm a person with no nation. Neither Thailand nor Laos counts me as a citizen. I don't know how to deal with my situation. I don't have any evidence to prove where I belong. I'm a person who has no genuine nation of my own."

> "I'm not a full human because I have no right to work, no right to earn money."

> "My children and I have no future here because we do not have Thai identity cards."

> "I have been living in Thailand for years. My children were born in Thailand, and they grew up in Thailand. I want to be a Thai and to live with my children here."

> "I wish my children to be granted Thai nationality even though I am not eligible for it."

> "I'm not an illegal migrant as my village folks often said. But I am afraid of being arrested and deported to Laos."

> "I have no family or relatives or even connections in Laos; how can I return to where I was born a long time ago? My home and my family are here."

The lack of a Thai identity card to present at hospitals prevents stateless people from gaining access to Thailand's universal coverage health-care scheme, which allows Thai citizens to visit doctors for a fee of approximately 30 baht (equivalent to approximately US$0.90). Stateless people in Thailand are also left unprotected by Thai labor laws. Employers regularly exploit them by taking advantage of their cheap labor and they often receive less than the legal minimum wage per day. They also are unable to register their marriage with a Thai citizen if they do not have any official documents to prove that they belong to any particular country. Recently, the law has begun allowing stateless people who want to pursue higher education to travel outside the province in which they reside, but they are required to obtain and renew permission at the provincial level every year until they graduate. However, because of poverty, few stateless children in Isan can afford any education higher than primary school. Furthermore, even though the Thai government does not bar stateless children from education, they are ineligible for government scholarships or loans.

Unlike stateless hill tribes in the north, stateless villagers in Isan are not united. They lack social networks and rely only on kinship ties and good relationships with Thai villagers. Because many in Isan are Lao culturally and linguistically, and their appearance is also Lao, it is difficult to distinguish stateless Lao from local villagers; thus they exist without eyes to see them or ears to hear them. The lack of knowledge about legal processes in claiming citizenship, coupled with an absence of collective awareness, has resulted in their inability to put pressure on the government to resolve their problems. In the villages, they have to keep their head down and voice nothing in order to assure officials that they will not cause any trouble or disrupt village order. There are few organizations working to better the lives of the stateless in Isan, compared to in the north.

Identity Politics: The Clashes of Naming

In this section, using data obtained from fieldwork, I attempt to understand the way in which *"khon* Lao," or stateless Lao from Laos, view themselves in terms of Thai-ness, Lao-ness and Isan-ness. In addition, I attempt to understand the complex identity of "*khon* Isan," or Isan people, through their views toward the displaced Lao who remain stateless in Thailand.

The Isan region extends from the Khorat Plateau to the west side of the Mekong River, the national boundary between Thailand and Laos. It is the largest and most populous region in Thailand, comprising almost one-third of Thailand's total area. The estimated population living in the nineteen provinces of the Isan region is around 20 million. The dominant ethnicity in Isan is Lao, meaning that most people share the same "descent" as ethnic Lao in Laos today. The number of ethnic Lao people in Isan is eight times greater than ethnic Lao currently residing within Laos.

Historically, Isan and Laos were considered a single region, in which people shared language, culture, and ethnicity. This territory came under the control of the Siamese state as a result of a series of treaties signed between the French and the Siamese during the period of French colonial presence in Indochina. Up to the present time, villagers on the both sides of Mekong River maintain traditional ties of livelihood, kinship, and common culture. In the past, intermarriages between people on both sides of the border were not an uncommon practice and Isan-Lao couples were not seen as problematic.

Perhaps the cultural intimacies and kin relations between Isan people and displaced Lao or Lao migrants made the circumstances of statelessness or nationality-lessness in Isan seem, for a time, unproblematic for the state, as well as for the stateless themselves, in comparison to the north. However, a changing social and economic landscape—the intrusion of modernity and state intervention at the village level, as well as a depletion of natural resources—has increased the concern about stateless Lao's right to citizenship, because the lack of Thai identity cards reduces them to the status of marginalized citizens whose freedom and rights to work, travel, obtain schooling, and own property are circumscribed by state mechanisms of surveillance and control.

In his pioneer work about *khon* Isan identity, Keyes proposed the term "Isan regionalism," explaining that "Isan" constitutes the collective identity awareness of people living in the northeast. He pointed out that Isan identity formation was shaped both by the larger political maneuverings of the modern Thai nation-state and by economic inequalities resulting from an imbalance in Thailand's development. People in Isan lived with poverty. As a result, the vast majority of them migrated temporarily to work in Bangkok or other parts of the country. Their inferior social and economic status in urban areas thus gave rise to feelings of regional collectivism (Keyes 1967, 36). They are keenly aware both of their Isan-ness and their Thai-ness. Although they are culturally Lao and feel close to the people living on the opposite side of the Mekong, they want to become part of a Thai nation-state and identify themselves as Thai in various circumstances.

Nowadays, people living in the northeast of Thailand are referred to by other Thai as "*khon* Isan," "Thai-Isan," "Lao-Isan," "Thai," or "Lao." Those in the northeast also refer to themselves with all the above names. The word choice depends on the situation, which may be associated with cultural-ethnic identity, social, or political intentions. Sometimes, the choice of term is not carefully made, but used simply because of familiarity. When northeasterners talk among themselves or among familiars they prefer to call themselves Lao, whereas when talking to persons from other regions they refer to themselves as *khon* Isan or *khon* Thai-Isan. However, Isan people with Lao ethnicity often confront the complexity of who they are. Are they Thai or Lao? And, are they Isan people?

The issue I address is the complex identity of Isan-ness and displaced Lao who become stateless in a community where, in fact, they are members culturally and ethnically, but not politically. I will use the views of Isan people towards stateless Lao living in the same villages and vice versa to understand this complex issue. Villagers in Isan always identify themselves as Thai and identify stateless villagers who come from Laos as Lao whenever they juxtapose Thai-ness to statelessness and nationality-lessness. I did not hear them use the term "Lao" for themselves or other Isan villagers (who are not stateless Lao) when they discussed the situation of stateless people with me or with one of my research assistants (whose is ethnic Lao from Isan). By classifying themselves as Thai, it is evident that they wanted to distinguish themselves and their fellow villagers from stateless Lao without legal status. They self-identify as Thai in this highly politicized situation.

However, they keenly realize that a majority of the Thai in Isan (Lao-Isan) and the Lao (Lao-Lao) are the same culturally and ethnically. Isan villagers often assert that "Lao and Thai are siblings; we came from the same ancestors and we need to help each other." One village headman stated that, "Many Lao from the opposite side of the river have come to live in our village for many years; they have become Thai now. They are good villagers, except they are not Thai citizens." Indeed, Isan people are aware of the ethnic and cultural roots they share with stateless Lao in their villages. They acknowledge that they are as much ethnically Lao as the stateless Lao are.

Still, a thirteen-year-old stateless girl in one district where I conducted my research bitterly complained, "I don't understand why my friends at my school called me '*I-Lao*,'[6] even though they speak the same language as me and as my younger sister." In particular circumstances, the Lao are associated with the status of outsider, as non-legal, inferior, stateless, and economically deprived people, a status that Isan people do not associate with themselves. Therefore, it is not surprising to hear that there are Lao-Isan parents who disapprove of marriage between stateless Lao and their sons or daughters. They do not feel disdainful of Lao ethnicity, but rather of the non-legal status of the stateless persons. Although Isan people are Lao culturally and ethnically, they prefer to be Thai in a political or legal sense because they can be part of the Thai nation-state, and considered more modern than those in the neighboring country on the opposite side of the river. In fact, no Lao-Isan people would want to exchange places with their more deprived relatives, either the Lao on the other side of the Mekong or the stateless Lao in the same villages as them.

None of the stateless villagers who participated in my research expressed the desire to return to Laos to claim citizenship. They want to live in Thailand and be granted Thai nationality. Contrary to Lao-Isan villagers, they still see themselves as Lao people, not Thai people. They don't see themselves as *khon* Isan either. One stateless villager told me, "I am a Lao-Lao person," meaning a Lao from Laos, not from Isan. However, these people are, in fact, not Lao in political and legal terms, but only in cultural and ethnic terms. Although they desire Thai citizenship, it does not mean they want to become Thai in ethnic terms. Rather, they want to become Thai citizens and have Thai citizen identity cards because they want the benefits of citizenship—to work and move freely in Thailand.

Stateless Lao villagers in Isan and their Thailand- or Laos-born children have no difficulty in saying who they are when asked, "Are you Thai or Lao?" If they trust you will not put them in jail, fine them, or deport them, they will simply tell you they are Lao. However, mixed stateless children of Thai and stateless Lao parents have difficulty answering the question. They often prefer to be thought of as Thai, not Lao, since they feel that being Lao is a marker of statelessness, or even of non-legal status in their own homeland.

Narrating Identities Narrating Agencies

Of the displaced Lao I interviewed, none has any verification that they are Lao citizens in the form of documents or relatives in Laos prepared to vouch for them. This is because many of these people uprooted their families from Laos under conditions of economic hardship in the context of war and communist reformation. Many left Laos at a very young age to join their families and never returned. It is highly likely that their civil records in Laos have also disappeared. If they wanted to return to Laos, they would have to subject themselves to an extremely difficult process to prove that they are former Lao citizens. No one I interviewed showed any willingness to go through this process—which would be very costly in economic terms, and also in terms of life security. The Lao government has never shown any intention to restore citizenship to the Lao refugees living in the limbo of statelessness in Thailand.

At the same time, the stateless people with whom I worked are not passive victims of the Thai state's technologies of power. The Thai state's practices of segregating non-Thai citizens has been resisted by displaced Lao in myriad ways. Many have their own ways of establishing or reworking citizenship and can better their difficult circumstances to different degrees. The following stories illustrate citizenship struggles among Lao refugees in Isan. By focusing on particular stories, I hope to demonstrate that displaced Lao living along Thailand's northeastern frontiers in Ubon Ratchathani actively, yet covertly, dare to break with the Thai state's technologies of power as they are imposed on their lives.

Many stateless refugees deliberately have their children marry daughters or sons of Thai villagers in order to gain access to resources and citizenship for their offspring. A numbers of them have their children use school certificates as travel passes to seek jobs in Bangkok as soon as they finish sixth grade at village schools. When they show the school certificates to the police, they usually let them go without asking any questions. Many leave the villages along with other Thai to find jobs, without waiting for permission from the governor. They know that if they travel in a group with Thai villagers they are unlikely to be noticed by the police.

Many families have their newborn child registered with Thai relatives, Thai friends, or even with a daughter married to a Thai man. Displaced Lao are not allowed to own land, houses, cars, or even motorcycles, and so some stateless families find the means of negotiating ownership of different kinds of property by registering them under the name of Thai relatives or village friends. To ensure that their stateless children will have a future in Thailand with their limited resources, they send them to Thai schools, or have their sons ordain as monks or their daughters become *mae chi* (Buddhist nuns), with the goal of allowing them to attain higher education. Furthermore, displaced Lao are keenly aware that demonstrating a strong connection to Thai-ness is the first step to attaining Thai citizenship. They therefore seek to attach Thai-ness to themselves by identifying with Thailand's major cultural symbols, including the Thai king, Buddhism, and the shared history between Isan and Lao people.

In one border district of Ubon Ratchathani Province, I heard a folk tale told by many displaced Lao. The tale involved the Mekong River, the people who live on the banks on either side, and the *naga* (or *phayanak*, mythical, sacred serpents) that are believed to live in the river. According to the tale, there is a belief that along the Mekong are several "Mekong gates" (*pratu khong*) that allow people to travel easily from Laos to Thailand. These are imagined gates believed to have been built by the river *naga*. Stateless Lao and Thai villagers believe that the gates will help relatives on opposite sides come to visit one another. One stateless villager, citing the story, told me that wherever we find significant numbers of Lao (Lao migrants in Thailand) we find a Mekong gate.

To bolster his claim, he mentioned other places such as Nong Khai and Nakhon Phanom, where large numbers of people from Laos have migrated permanently to Thailand. This district (where we conversed), he said, is one of the gates; therefore a lot of displaced Lao people have come to live there. Recounting the imagined gates invokes a strong tie between Lao and Isan people at the borderlands, at the same time it helps to legitimize migrations and make displaced Lao in the district seem part of Thai citizenry.

In another district of the same province where many displaced Lao have their homes, I heard a different story, but one with shared meanings with the tale from Khemarat. Displaced Lao there narrated a story of a prophecy about Vientiane. They recounted that the prophecy was written on a palm-leaf Buddhist manuscript and read widely among Lao monks for years before the fall of Royal Lao Government. The text read, "Lao brothers will fight each other. Vientiane will ultimately be destroyed. When Vientiane is gloomy and left neglected, you must go to find the *garuda* and live there." The *garuda* is a half-bird half-human creature often found in local sagas. It is believed to be an enemy of the *naga*. In reality, the *garuda* is the symbol of the Thai king as well as the Thai state.

One stateless villager, who was a former soldier of the Royal Lao Government, commented on this story when describing the numbers of Lao refugees in Thailand: "I never thought that this story would come true, but when we think back to Lao history, we see war occurred, Vientiane was seized by the communist regime, and many Lao fled to Thailand. I knew right away that this was our course, and when I came to live in Thailand I found the omnipresence of the *garuda*'s sign, which symbolizes the king. I therefore have no doubt why I am here." He implied that he had come to live under the protection of the Thai king and the Thai state. This story was confirmed to me by a Thai village abbot who claimed that he had read and heard it before Laos became a communist country. The abbot interpreted it for me, explaining that the person who wrote this tale must have been an astrologer and wrote this story when Vientiane was first built as the capital of Laos. This led me to another, related story told by stateless villagers. Most of those I interviewed tried to express to me that they loved the Thai king as much as Thai people do. They praised Thailand as an independent and democratic country that allowed more freedom to people than Laos. One man commented to me that, "Laos is a weak country. Brothers fought with one another. There is no freedom, and we are always dominated by other nations throughout our history."

In the villages, I observed that most displaced Lao behaved submissively when they presented themselves to local officials and to Thai villagers. They cooperated well with village headmen and participated in all the religious rituals held in the villages where they lived in order to win friendship and support from local people. Frequently, displaced Lao were described as good villagers who participated in all village activities. Many displaced Lao men became village guards and assisted border patrols in watching their villages and the borders. They were strict Buddhists who donated a great deal of what they earned to make religious merit.

In one small village where all the inhabitants were stateless Lao, I found that they had built their own Buddhist temple and a giant drum to demonstrate their strong connection with Buddhism. When I asked the head of the village about the purpose for this he replied, "To show that we are good people as well as good Buddhists who will not cause any trouble to Thai people and Thailand." It occurred to me that religious practices have been used by these people to emphasize their morality in order to gain trust and acceptance from Thai authorities and villagers.

Conclusion

The stories I have recounted here demonstrate that individuals and families who are stateless for prolonged periods of time do not simply yield to their situations. On the contrary, they often take it upon themselves to define and negotiate citizenship for themselves in order to resolve their statelessness to whatever extent they can. It is very important to state that negotiations and some success have been made because of the collaboration of local people.

I have illustrated how the Thai nation-state preserves the exclusive right to determine who should be granted citizenship. Even so, Lao refugee practices of self-identifying as members of the Thai nation-state indicate that the Thai nation-state's imagination of who is a citizen is increasingly problematic and limited. Lao refugees, marginalized as "stateless/nationality-less" by Thai citizenship legislation, have defined themselves as citizens in myriad ways, such as by cross-border marriage, the kinship system, child adoption, and purchasing citizenship. Many Lao refugees have attempted to gain access to Thai citizenship by associating themselves with the Thai nation-state's imagination of Thainess. This chapter points out that it is time for the Thai nation-state to refine its conception of citizenship by taking into consideration local histories and cross-border dynamics. Also, the Thai nation-state may need to rework its conception of Thai citizenry in order to incorporate the great diversity of people that exist within its territory.

Notes

This chapter is part of a research project entitled "Researching Lives of Stateless People along Thai-Lao and Thai-Cambodian Borders." The project was funded by the Rockefeller Foundation and was carried out from 2006 to 2008 through the Mekong Sub-region Social Research Center at Faculty of Liberal Arts, Ubon Ratchathani University.

1. This group refers to former Pakistanis who can be found both in Thailand and Myanmar.

2. After this chapter was written, there was international indignation, in 2009, when some forty-five hundred Hmong refugees in Phetchabun Province were forcibly returned to Laos.

3. The declaration of Revolutionary Party No. 337 (*Pho Wo* 337) in 1972 affected the legal status of children of displaced Lao. It stated that Thai nationals who had a parent that held alien status and came to live in Thailand without permission prior to December 14, 1972, automatically had their Thai nationality revoked. The declaration also restricted children of an alien parent who were born between December 1972 and February 1992 from claiming Thai nationality.

4. This registration had been undertaken under the supervision of the National Security Council and Royal Thai Military Force Region 2 according to the National Security Policy.

5. The third Nationality Act (1965) did not allow a person born in Thailand of alien parents to have a right to Thai nationality. This affected the children of displaced Laotians. Article 11 of the Nationality Act (second edition) BE 2535 (1992) stated that aliens born in Thailand were illegal immigrants unless there was an order under the Immigration Law that specified otherwise (Phunthip 2006). However, the Thai government attempted to integrate this group through the legislative system by granting legal status based on *jus soli* to the children of aliens who were born in Thailand. The current Nationality Act, enacted in 2008, is more progressive because it intended to more effectively reduce the number of people who encounter personal status problems or statelessness. It especially benefits people who were affected by the Declaration of the Revolutionary Party No. 337. According to Article 23 of this act, a person whose nationality was revoked by the Declaration of the Revolutionary Party No. 337, or a person who was born in Thailand but had not acquired Thai nationality as a result of the declaration, as well as his/her children, is able to reclaim Thai nationality by submitting proof to the district authorities.

6. A derogative term usually used to suggest the backwardness of Isan or Lao people

References

Keyes, Charles F. 2002. "The People of Asia: Science and Politics in the Classification of Ethnic Groups in Thailand, China, and Vietnam." *The Journal of Asian Studies* 61 (4): 1163–203.

Ong, Aihwa. 2006. "Mutation of Citizenship." *Theory, Culture and Society* 23 (2–3): 499–531.

Phunthip Kanchanacittra Saisoonthorn. 2006. "Development of Concept on Nationality and the Efforts to Reduce Statelessness in Thailand." *Refugee Survey Quarterly* 24 (3).

Supang Chantavanich and Philip Finch. 1992. *The Laos Returnees in the Voluntary Repatriation Program from Thailand*. Bangkok: Indochinese Refugee Information Center (IRIC), Institute of Asian Studies, Chulaongkorn University (Occasional Paper Series No./003).

Krom kanpokkhrong krasuang mahatthai. 2005 (2548). *Than khomun chon klumnoi thi yu nai khwam dulae khong krom kanpokkhrong suan kanthabian ratsadon samnak borihan kanthabian duan pruetsachikayon pho so 2548*. Krom kanpokkhrong Krungthep: Krasuang Mahatthai.

Montri Chongpunphon and Sathian Kokiattrakun. 2004 (2547). *Rabop than khomun prachakon nai prathet thai kong samnak borihan thabianrat krom kanpokkhrong krasuang mahatthai nai khon tangdao nai prathet thai khu klai bang? mi chamnuan thaorai? rabop thankhomun baep nai khu khamtop?* Kritaya Artchavanitkul, ed. Nakhon Pathom: Satabanwichai prachakon lae sangkhom. Mahidol University.

Ekachai Pinkaew. 2005 (2548). "Kanmueang rueang 'sanchat thai': Khwam khrumkhru khong phromdaen haeng rat lae phromdaen haeng manutsayachon korani panha sanchat khong chao Mae Ai amphoe Mae Ai changwat Chiang Mai." MA thesis, Thammasat University, Bangkok.

Thailand: The Observatory on Statelessness. NewsMekong.org. http://www.newsmekong.org/thailand.

TEMPORARY LIVES, ETERNAL DREAMS:
Experiences of Viet Labor Migrants in Savannakhet, Laos

Duong Bich Hanh

Introduction

Hien, thirty-four, and Minh, thirty, are from Ban, a village famous for *tuong*, a type of soy sauce, in Hung Yen Province, some nineteen kilometers outside of Hanoi. They married young and now have a ten-year-old son and a daughter of almost two. I met Minh in January 2007 at a small suburban market five kilometers out of Savannakhet town, in Laos, where she sat among many Lao sellers and some Viet sellers whose numbers had recently been increasing, selling tofu and soy milk to Lao buyers and a much larger number of Viet buyers, while her daughter crawled around happily on the gravelly ground behind her. Meanwhile, Hien was busy on a construction site on the other side of town, doing carpentry work on the houses of Laos' emerging middle class. Minh herself had not wanted to come to Savannakhet. "My husband was here and he wanted me to join him. He said if we work in two different places, it's harder to save money."

Ha, forty-six, from Phu Loc in Thua Thien Hue Province, sells fruit in Savannakhet's main market, a few kilometers from the smaller market where Minh sells tofu every day. Ha came to Savannakhet following her sister-in-law. She used to sell at An Cuu market in Hue, but business was not good: hardly anyone bought fruit. "People didn't want to spend the money. Here in Laos people don't care. They'll spend all the money they have today, and if tomorrow there's no money they'll eat sticky rice." Ha's husband sometimes joins her in Savannakhet for a period of a month or two, leaving behind a thirteen-year-old-son, who fixes bikes to earn money, and two daughters of eight and six to take care of themselves, while two older sons are working as apprentices for a motorbike repair shop in Ho Chi Minh City.

Thao, twenty, is also from Phu Loc. Her parents bought her a hairdressing salon in the central part of town for US$100 and forced her to move. After almost a year of taking classes and doing an apprenticeship at a hairdresser's in Hue, she came to Savannakhet in early 2006. The hairdressing salon is attached to her cousin's workshop, which produces ice cream and bread. Every day, she washes and cuts the hair of mostly Lao and Viet Kieu men, and helps out with ice cream production whenever she has free time. Not long after her arrival, she began a relationship with Duc, a young man who works in the bakery. His family is from Thao's neighboring community, and their parents have met in anticipation of a marriage to come. Both Thao and Duc talk about working in Savannakhet for a little longer, then returning to their *que* (home) to open their own bakery. Thao told me, "Even if it's poor, ugly and remote, it's still our *que*."

Ha, Thao, Minh, and Hien are among thousands of Vietnamese who for about the last decade and a half have been choosing Savannakhet as a home away from home. Most come from the central provinces of Vietnam, primarily Quang Tri and Thua Thien Hue. However, there are also over a hundred people who come from the same area as Hien and Minh, and are in fact related to the couple in one way or another. Most come to Savannakhet to seek economic opportunities, taking advantage of what they see as Lao people's lack of work ethic and tendency to spend money rather than save. This paper is about these sojourners: their concerns and fears, their aspirations and hopes, their lives and experiences, and their ultimate dreams of returning home one day for a better future. The data used for this paper was collected during fieldwork in Savannakhet in January and July 2007.

Viet Kieu Versus Viet Lieu

There are various estimates for the number of Viet residing and working in Laos, ranging from between thirty and forty thousand to fifty thousand. This population is often divided into two categories. One group consists of Vietnamese with Lao citizenship or permanent residency, often called Viet Kieu. Some families in this group have been settled in Laos for as long as four or five generations. The second group is formed by an increasing number of recent migrants from Vietnam, who often refer to themselves as Viet Lieu. These people hold Vietnamese passports or border passes and come to Laos under the visa exemption agreement between the two governments, allowing them to stay legally in Laos for thirty days at a time. However, most overstay their visa and, moreover, engage in employment and income-generating activities that their tourist status does not permit.

History of Viet Settlement in Laos

Over the course of Vietnamese history there have been many waves of emigration. The first recognized wave occurred during the Tu Duc reign (1847–83), when people fled the country to avoid a massacre (*binh Tay sat dao*). This was followed by another wave following the Ham Nghi reign (1884–85), after the failure of Can Vuong movement. Due to its geographical proximity, most migrants to Laos were from north-central and Red River Delta provinces.

At the end of the nineteenth century, the establishment by the French colonial government of French Indochina—including Tonkin, Annam, Cochin-China, Laos, and Cambodia—helped to facilitate mobility of residents among the regions. During this time, especially from 1899 onwards, migration of Viet into Laos became more notable. Some Viet were brought into Laos to work for the government administration. For most of the colonial period there were more Vietnamese employed in the administration than Lao, and in the 1940s, over half (12,400) of Vientiane's population (23,200) were Vietnamese working for the French. Other Vietnamese brought into the country work in mines and on plantations. Construction of major road networks linking areas of

Indochina during the early years of the twentieth century also brought into Laos large numbers of workers, many of them Viet.

Besides government administrators, miners, and plantation and road workers, there were also a number of other migrants who would be categorized as free or spontaneous migrants in current migration discourse. These migrants left their villages in search of adventure or economic opportunities, or to escape social problems, family crises, or famine. Crossing to Laos was considered an internal journey. Many, with great effort, crossed the border into Siam or went by sea to New Caledonia. In Laos, Viet migrants often lived in townships and became an important part of Lao urban life. In many townships the Viet became the majority, such as in Vientiane (43.0 percent), Thakek (85.0 percent), Savannakhet (72.4 percent), Pakse (62.0 percent), and Xieng Khoang (72.0 percent).

The Viet Kieu community in Savannakhet today

Mr. Sai, vice president of the Association of Vietnamese (*Hội người Việt Nam*) in Savannakhet, told me the story of his parents' move in the late 1930s, when they first settled in a village outside Savannakhet Town. When Lao residents of the town moved to Thailand in 1945, Mr Sai's parents moved in, and that was where he was born. "Until 1975," Mr. Sai said, "the Viet in Savannakhet were workers: builders, carpenters, seamstresses, mechanics. Some owned very small businesses, primarily selling food. Most other businesses were owned by the Chinese, who left the country soon after 1975 and had their businesses taken over by the Viet." Many Viet Kieu in Laos also left the country for Thailand, France, Australia, or the United States after having earlier moved to Laos. Now, over thirty years later, many of the twenty-eight hundred who remain in Savannakhet own houses on the side of the road that double as shops of different kinds. Eight Viet families own large companies or workshops.

Most Viet Kieu living in Savannakhet today were born in Laos, but only about 60 percent of them are Lao citizens. Mr. Sai gave me a brief overview of the Viet Kieu community in town in between filling in forms, affixing pictures, making photocopies, or giving stamps on applications that the association would later send to the Vietnamese consulate to apply for Vietnamese passports. While some Viet Kieu living in Laos have adopted Lao citizenship, many others only have permanent residency status, which allows them to live, work, and even run businesses in Laos, but does not entitle them to own property or study at institutions of higher education. The primary reasons for not adopting citizenship given by Mr. Sai and other Viet Kieu to whom I spoke were the complexity and cost of the application process (around US$500 to hire somebody to deal with all the paperwork), on the one hand, and the fact that Lao citizenship is not really necessary or useful, on the other. After all, there are always ways to get around restrictions. All Mr. Sai's property is registered under his son's name, who, by being adopted by a Lao family before the age of ten became a naturalized Lao, in anticipation of Mr. Sai's plan for his son to continue to higher education.

The Association of Vietnamese in Savannakhet operates four schools: a kindergarten in Seno, some thirty kilometers east of Savannakhet Town, two kindergartens in Lac Hong and Hoang Van, and a primary school called Thong Nhat "Reunion" in Savannakhet. The three schools in town have over five hundred students in total. Seven teachers are hired from Quang Tri (central Vietnam) every year to supplement a team of local teachers, most of whom are Viet Kieu. The education in Viet schools is bilingual, although more emphasis is placed on Vietnamese. Many Lao parents, primarily those who work for the government, send their kids to the Vietnamese kindergarten and primary school in the hope that later their children will continue their education in Vietnam. In classrooms, Lao children sit side-by-side with Vietnamese children, most of whom have Lao names and were born to mixed Lao-Viet couples. Chau, a twenty-five-year-old teacher in Lac Hong kindergarten, told me that most Viet Kieu of her generation have Lao partners, speak Lao, and celebrate Lao holidays as well as Vietnamese holidays. The term *luc xot* (lit., children of mixed parents) is used to refer both to children born to two Viet parents and children born to Lao-Viet parents. As Chau indicated, however, the former cases are more rare.

Recent Labor Migrants to Savannakhet

There are many similarities between the community of Viet Kieu in Savannakhet and the community of Viet who often refer to themselves as Viet Lieu. Both are of Vietnamese descent. Both come to Laos for economic purposes. What seems to be an essential characteristic of both groups is the nature of their visits to Laos. Most intend(ed) their stay to be no more than that: a stay. People in late colonial Vietnam and late socialist Vietnam alike planned their emigration in the expectation of return. What Andrew Hardy describes for migration in the early part of the twentieth century resonates with what is going on now in the late twentieth and early twenty-first centuries.

> Like those who traveled within the country, theirs was a strategy of temporary absence, usually aimed at improving a situation back in the village. They chose their destination for what it could offer in terms of fast economic gain: for the payment of a debt, achievement of an ambition, survival of famine. They chose it to escape from a social situation: the strictures of village society, a marriage of family convenience, a relationship turned to conflict. They chose it too out of that most youthful of values: "adventure." But when they left, they also meant one day to return . . . The journeys of these men and women were the latest comings and goings in a culture of migration that had nourished village life for centuries.

In a specific historical context, a "stay" for those Viet who came to Laos in the beginning of the twentieth century has become permanent. The Viet Lieu expect no such outcome, as long as the current situation continues (a topic that is further explored in the last section of the chapter). While the Viet Kieu community in Laos and its relations with the community of new Viet migrants deserves further research, my initial observations and conversations with members of both communities in Savannakhet indicate that there is very little contact between the two groups. It is fair to say that the relationship between the communities of Viet Kieu and Viet Lieu is almost nonexistent, except in some cases in which, through Viet Kieu contacts with their *que*, some Viet were brought from Quang Binh Province to work as helpers at restaurants owned by Viet Kieu families. Some Viet Kieu think Viet migrant men are violent people given to wife beating. Others show indifference at best. Hien is unhappy with such attitudes. "We are all migrants. We could have been in the same situation, but different histories have put us in different situations, and they treat us as if we were not equal."

Moving: Networks, Governments, and Brotherhood

The current phenomenon of Vietnamese coming to Laos to gain financial benefits can be seen as a result of many social dynamics at many levels and involving many people. This section of the paper analyzes three such social dynamics that help us understand the circumstances and conditions that allow the migration to take place. The first, of forming and utilizing social networks, is pertinent to many other forms of migration. While current migration practices blur the distinction between organized and free migration, in general the migration of Viet to Savannakhet I look at here can be classified as free migration. There is another type of organized migration that mobilizes Viet workers to go to work in Laos under contract with construction companies, but this is not my focus.

The social dynamic that makes the Viet migration to Savannakhet possible grows out of the special relationship that has formed and developed over a very long period of time between the Vietnamese and Lao governments. These "special and unique ties" can be seen to mute the illegal aspect of such cross-border migration and give it a character closer to that of internal migration. In many ways this was what happened in Viet migration to Laos in the 1930s, when the border between Vietnam and Laos was considered internal.

The third social dynamic involves Viet perception of Lao as being lazy, naive, and spendthrift, which, as I will show, has become almost an urban myth for the continuing waves of Viet migrants.

Social Networks

One of the earlier arrivals in Savannakhet was Dam, an animated and friendly man in his early fifties, who came as a carpenter in 1992 when there were still very few Viet in town. Pressured by his parents to leave his poverty-stricken home village in the Red River Delta province of Hai Duong, Dam joined his brother, brother-in-law, and a friend who had found some carpentry work in Dong Hoi, the capital town of Quang Binh Province.

> Based in Dong Hoi we got to know people traveling back and forth from Dong Ha (Quang Tri Province), so we ended up getting some work in Dong Ha. In Dong Ha I met a man who worked for a mine not far from here, and he said he could arrange the paperwork for me to come as well. So we got to the mine. The work there didn't work out, so we went further and got to Savannakhet. I went around to different carpentry workshops to look for work, and finally one took me in. I was so happy, I went back to the mine to pick up my belongings–just some clothes, bowls and chopsticks, pots and pans, and some dry fish, rice, and pumpkins I had brought from Vietnam–and got on my bike to get here. Every time I saw a patch of pumpkin vines on the side of the road, I would stop and gather some so I had some vegetables for my meal. All I needed to buy here was salt, pork lard, and fish sauce. Initially I was paid only 600 kip per day. It was hard. I wrote my wife, "Maybe I'll have to think about leaving this place, although I'm still so new to it that I don't even know every street yet." But slowly my pay went up, and I was so happy when it went up to 2,500 kip a day. Two years after I got here, the workshop I was working for, owned by some Viet Kieu, went out of business. So I started slowly to pick up my own work.

When I asked Dam whether in his most difficult moments he had ever thought of going back to Vietnam, he replied with a question: "No. How could I? We [he and his wife] had to sell our [Honda] Super Cub, our only valuable asset, to get enough money to arrange passports for the four of us. If I went back then, it would mean we had lost all we had for nothing." The consequence of such determination was a long separation between him and the family. In the first five years after Dam left home he made only two visits.

Fifteen years have passed since Dam's difficult days. He has also been involved in many business deals, from smuggling motorbikes from Thailand to Vietnam via Laos, to contracting trucks of clothes and half-hatched eggs from Vietnam for sale at Lao markets from tuk-tuks; from dealing precious stones, to smuggling precious wood (*tram*) out of the country, resulting in thirty-four days in jail and bail of almost US$1,000. All these business ventures failed or broke even at best, and Dam was fortunate to always have his carpentry job to fall back on. In 1997 his brother suggested that he bring his wife over because her life back home was too hard; she was working both in the field and at a factory producing tiles and bricks. Leaving their two sons behind with the parents-in-law, she came to join him, helping him in both carpentry and household work. Now, Dam and his wife live in a run-down house that they rent for 2,000 baht a month, together with their two sons, aged twenty-four and twenty-six, and twenty workers, many of them relatives, others residents of the same commune back in Hai Duong. Some of the houses next to theirs belong to his family members—two brothers, one sister, and one brother's son. Altogether they employ one hundred workers who are sent all over Laos to do carpentry work. Their clients are mostly Lao, and many of them are high officials or are related to high officials, including the former president Kaysone Phomvihane's family.

Dam's story highlights the importance of networks and personal contacts within destination areas. The network for people who come from Hai Duong or Hung Yen in the Red River Delta is especially essential because of its geographical location, which results in high(er) travel costs and little knowledge of the destination. Networks are especially important for job facilitation for both people who seek opportunities and people who seek employees. In many ways, networks have made the migration to Savannakhet much easier than it used to be. For most of the people I talked to, the jobs available in Savannakhet were what attracted them: they had no intention to come until they received a call from a potential employer, in most cases an acquaintance, or an acquaintance of an acquaintance.

Kien, twenty-five years old, got his job after a phone call from his brother, who had come to Laos a few months earlier to work with Hien. "I didn't think much. I just thought I'd never been to Laos before, so why not give it a try. It turned out to be so *chán* [boring, not satisfying or exciting] here. It's not easy to socialize with people, even with the Viet people. Viet here are different from the Viet in Vietnam." Having no girlfriend and earning just over one million kip a month, Kien doesn't know what his plan for the future is. "I'll just tag along here for a while and see how it goes." We both knew that it would not be hard for him to return to Vietnam—the investment needed for the move would be very small, both in financial and emotional terms.

The juxtaposition of the stories of Dam and Kien, despite their common dependence on the availability of social networks, indicates a great difference between the waves of migrants to Laos within the last decade and a half. For migrants of Dam's generation the move was expensive (it cost all his family had at the time), difficult (it took Dam a long time and a lot of money to figure out what was profitable and what was not), and it took him away from his family for an extended time (he was only able to visit his family once every two or three years). For migrants of Kien's generation the experience was very different. Kien, like many of his other friends and relatives, agreed to move to Laos without much thought of what would happen next. The move was easy and relatively inexpensive. It was only a matter of days before Kien could make the necessary travel arrangements, and travel expenses only amounted to a few hundred thousand dong. Nobody of Kien's generation plans or expects to stay away from their home for more than a year at a time, and in fact very few do. Those who visit home least frequently go back at least once a year at the time of Tet.

The study of internal migration within Vietnam, in particular the case of migration from the Red River Delta to the central highlands, has been revealing not merely for what it shows about migrants' experiences, but of broader processes in the region's transformation. Here, in the case of what can be considered transnational migration, the ease, low cost, and close contact with home that today's migrants enjoy can be attributed to a number of social and economic factors. This sort of migration has been made possible by previously established and continually broadening social networks. Migrants to Laos do not only use friends and relatives to reduce the burden of the high cost of the move; they use these relations to acquire jobs starting in the earliest stages of their migration. Another factor facilitating recent migration is the new fleets of transnational and, to some extent, national buses that link various locations of the two countries. Recent improvements in the living standards of a large part of the Vietnamese population have also made migration relatively less expensive: now few migrants come to Laos to avoid starvation in their homeland, as Dam did, but to accumulate savings. Travel documents have also become easier to obtain since the Vietnamese government relaxed its policy for issuing passports and the two states implemented a Vietnam-Lao visa exemption program.

Government Relations and Control

On the occasion of the thirtieth anniversary of the signing of the Friendship and Cooperation Treaty and the forty-fifth anniversary of the establishment of diplomatic relations between Vietnam and Laos, *Nhan Dan* (People's daily newspaper) wrote:

> Vietnam and Laos are two neighbors whose relations were formed and developed along their thousand-year history of national construction and defense. In the past seven decades particularly, the time-honored relations and loyalty between Vietnam and Laos, which were fostered by President Ho Chi Minh and President Kaysone Phomvihane, have been promoted by the two Parties, States and leaders, making it a priceless asset for the two nations and serving as a common development rule in their path toward prosperity and happiness.
>
> Vietnam and Laos' "special and unique ties" began as a joint struggle against colonial rule, and they continue to the present day. Vietnam so far has seventy-one approved investment projects in Laos, ranking third among countries investing in Laos: mainly in hydro-electricity, mining, transportation, and industrial crops. These investment projects have brought to Laos a great number of contractors, workers, and engineers who reside and work in Laos on a long-term basis, and to some extent

this group has been a catalyst for the waves of migrations discussed here. Fifteen years ago, Dam heard about the possibility of work in Laos through such a person. Eight years later Hien was introduced to Dam, who by then had been able to establish his own business after many struggles, through a Vietnamese irrigation engineer who had been traveling to Laos almost every month to supervise the work of his company. A year ago, when Hien himself was able to establish himself as a small contractor, he brought over Kien and almost a dozen workers from the home villages of both his father and mother. As networks grow, the number of current labor migrants to Laos in general, and to Savannakhet in particular, increases. With such constantly varying flows, it is hard to imagine that there could ever be any official figure for the number of Viet migrants there.

All migrants come into the country with their one-month visa exemption stamped on their border passes or passports. Although some go back to Vietnam on a monthly, or even weekly or daily basis, few leave the country within a month. Most stay at least a few months at a time, while some stay for as long as a year. The migrants not only violate the rule by overstaying their visa but also by their engagement in income-generating activities. The term "Lieu" that they often use to refer to themselves is an interesting reference to their illegal status. Their solution to the problem of illegality is simple. At most, a Vietnamese will only be requested to pay a fine when he or she crosses the border back to Vietnam. There is also a cheaper way: a smaller fine is paid to a certain office in Savannakhet. Nobody could tell me exactly what the office was: one said it was the police, while others said it was the office in charge of foreigners. All transactions go through an intermediary, and fees vary—a couple of hundred thousand could cover one person's stay for the whole year, and only a few months for another.

Until recently, the Lao government did little to control the influx of Viet migrants into the country. Every few months, an official from a *ban* (neighborhood, village) where Viet migrants stayed showed up with a notebook and pen to record the temporary residents and ask them to pay a fee, somewhere between 30,000 and 40,000 kip depending on the neighborhood. One such visit occurred when I visited Ha, the fruit seller in Savannakhet main market, whom I mentioned at the beginning of this chapter. In the same compound that Ha stayed, there was also a couple from Quang Tri and their two sons, aged five and seven, two women from Hue, and a few other Lao. While we were eating dinner, three men arrived and asked to see our passports. Names and passport numbers of all Vietnamese present (Ha and her husband who was visiting at the time, the Quang Tri couple, and myself) were recorded in the official's notebook. The two Hue women who had left for dinner before the officials arrived returned in the middle of the visit. Instead of coming in and submitting themselves to the authority, they turned around and waited until the men had left to come back. Everybody except me was asked to pay 30,000 kip. After the men left I was told that they were representatives from the *ban* and this was just one of their regular visits. The nature of such visits is not considered at all threatening, and by asking for a "contribution" to the *ban*'s budget, these visits in a way endorse and somewhat legalize the move of Viet labor migrants.

As I gathered from Viet migrants to Savannakhet, Lao (local) government control has recently become stricter. There have been attempts to send Viet migrants back to Vietnam from Pakse and Vientiane, and the Viet in Savannakhet suspected similar attempts would be made in Savannakhet in the near future. Nevertheless, nobody I spoke to seemed to be overly worried about it. Negotiating with Lao authorities has become an ordinary part of migrants' lives. People have different strategies to deal with the issue when it happens. People from border provinces can easily make a trip home and come back with a new stamp. People from more distant provinces are not always able to make such quick trips. Instead they make contact with people who are in a position to help. Hien was able to become friends with some staff of the office in charge of foreigners and believes such contacts can help him get his passport back if it gets confiscated during a raid.

I would argue that historical connections between Vietnam and Laos provide a context in which Vietnamese are likely to enter Laos initially, and the current relaxation in border controls (the availability of border passes and visa exemptions) helps to intensify the process, resulting in the increasing number of migrants today. But government-related conditions are not the only factors influencing migrant flows to Laos. As I have shown, economic and social networks—a common feature of migration in many parts of the world—also contribute to the process. The third factor is more unique to this study: what many Viet migrants consider the lack of a work ethic among Lao, and their habit of spending rather than saving.

Stereotyping the "Other"

Almost all Viet labor migrants to Laos, even those who come without pre-arranged work, find income-generating activities with ease. Most Viet men engage in construction and carpentry jobs, which often require a skill level that not many Lao men possess. Many construction projects in Savannakhet are taken up by Viet men like Dam, and to some extent, smaller contractors like Hien, who then hire other Viet migrants to work in their teams. A single such project can last from a few months to a year or two, depending on the availability of materials (especially wood, a material many Lao favor) and on the client's financial situation. Each contractor and his workers work on more than one site at the same time. Bigger contractors like Dam focus most of their time on making contacts and managing workers, while smaller contractors like Hien also spend their days sawing, hammering, planing, drinking tea, and smoking, like any of their team members.

Much of the work that Viet migrant women engage in does not require such substantial skills as that of men. When most women first come to Savannakhet they work as mobile traders selling cheap food and cheap clothes, because these businesses are flexible and do not need a great deal of capital. Some provide mobile pedicure and manicure services. Women who have been around longer usually manage to secure a place in a local market where they come regularly to sell plastic products, cheap jewelry and clothes, or fruit and other types of food. Some work as mobile vendors, selling boiled and half-hatched eggs or clothes, or providing nail-care services, while some, like Thao the hairdresser, or her cousin with the bakery, have more permanent working locations. Despite the ease of these kinds of work and the low start-up capital they require, Viet migrants do not face much competition from Lao women.

A common perception among Viet migrants in Savannakhet in regard to their Lao neighbors, especially Lao women, is that they are lazy. This comment was made over and over in my conversations with both Viet men and women, even those who did not live in Savannakhet and only came on periodic visits (such as drivers and guides of Vietnamese tour companies who meet their clients in Savannakhet to take them on four-day tours of central Vietnam). Lao women are often said to "only eat and gamble" (i.e., play cards), and "if they open a shop, they close at four to go home." Viet migrants tend not to be aware of or take into account the phenomenon of cross-border work-related migration from Laos to Thailand that has been going on for the last few decades. Perhaps perceptions of Lao laziness have been constructed partly to legitimate the move from Vietnam and the taking over of work that might very well be done by Lao.

The Lao are not only stereotyped as lazy. They are also said to be kind-hearted,—in many cases a quality to be taken advantage of. Any woman about to start doing business in the market knows that it will not be hard for her to find a Lao vendor who will happily share half of her space. This is hard to imagine in the more aggressive Vietnamese market environment, where one will be cursed at if she accidentally steps on somebody's turf. In an afternoon suburban market, Minh sits next to an old woman who suggests Minh call her "Mother" because "We sit next to each other every day," selling a few types of vegetable and fruit. They each pay 2,000 kip to the fee collector and loan each other plastic bags if either one of them uses up all her own. From time to time, Minh casually picks some loose longans from the Lao woman's stock to eat herself and offer to me, exchanging smiles and a couple of Lao words she has learned with the Lao woman, in between chatting with me or more noisily with Nga, a woman from Hai Duong who sells pork patties, about the Chinese movie they saw on TV the previous night.

As well as lazy and kind-hearted, Lao are also said be spendthrift, far more inclined to spend than save. Ha sells more fruit in the central market of Savannakhet than back in Hue, although here she also sits among many other fruit vendors, both Viet and Lao. Lao spending habits make it easier for Viet migrants to do business in Laos—another factor drawing Viet to Laos.

Viet perceptions of Lao, in many ways, resemble Viet perceptions of ethnic minority groups within Vietnam. This, I believe, is also a result of the close relationship between the Lao and Viet governments and their long-term brotherhood (*tinh anh em*). In this relationship, the Viet majority often assumes the role of *anh* (big brother/older brother), while the ethnic minorities, or in this case the Lao, take on the role of *em* (small/ younger brother). Official government discourse is to a great extent adopted by the public at large, and therefore many individual Viet look down upon ethnic minorities as naive, honest, backward, and lazy. What is more important for the discussion here is how this stereotype has been actively spread and utilized among the Viet labor migrants in Savannakhet in order to legitimize their presence in Laos.

Settling: Localizing Cross-Cultural Migration

As discussed above, Viet migration to Savannakhet bears characteristics of internal migration rather than transnational migration. This is especially true if we define transnational migrants, or trans-migrants, as, "those persons, who, having migrated from one nation-state to another, live their lives across borders, participating simultaneously in social relations that embed in more than one nation-state." The Viet migrants do cross borders, but given the processes discussed above, the political border they cross does not seem as significant as the cultural border. The movement of Viet to Laos entails encounters with people from a rather different culture. Aspects of this difference often mentioned by Viet migrants include eating habits ("Viet eat plain rice and Lao eat sticky rice") and worshiping practices ("They worship every five days while we only do it twice a month"). I call this type of migration cross-cultural, and this section of the paper examines how the establishment of locality has been used by Viet labor migrants to deal with such cross-cultural encounters.

On arrival in Savannakhet, people from Hai Duong and Hung Yen cluster together to form a specific locality. Most are Dam's neighbors, while others live in nearby streets. Kien shares a house with Hien's and his brother's families, sleeping on a bed in the house's main room. Other smaller Viet neighborhoods have also been formed throughout Savannakhet. Some Viet migrants share their living compounds with Lao workers who come from other provinces, but even so, little significant contact is made. During the daytime, the neighborhoods are quiet because everybody is at work, leaving behind only elderly people who are brought over to take care of small grandchildren. Clusters of Viet migrants often become lively again in the afternoon when people get back from their long and hard days at work, which can earn them anywhere between 50,000 and 100,000 kip. In the evening, people sit around watching Vietnamese TV programs received through the satellite devices some have installed. The houses of those who can afford such devices become gathering places for people of the neighborhood, with people spending time playing Chinese chess, talking, and watching popular programs into the night.

In many ways, the lives that Viet migrants live in Savannakhet resemble the lives they lived in their *que*. Most engage in the same type(s) of work they did back home, except for agricultural work that has become increasingly less important and less dependable for people in many rural parts of Vietnam. Outside work, Viet migrants there associate with people from their own *que*. Dam's wife insists on only accepting people of the same area (i.e., the north) in her husband's team, because "When you put people from different areas together, they fight." All Viet migrants cook and eat Vietnamese food. Even when people buy lunch at the market, they make sure to buy it from a Vietnamese vendor since the food tastes familiar. Although many said they like the Lao-style papaya salad and sticky rice, they rarely consume these dishes. When I showed up at Hien and Minh's place at lunchtime one day, they decided to go buy some pre-cooked food outside. Because the Vietnamese rice places only sell food together with rice, we went to a store owned by a Viet Kieu woman on the main road where over a dozen primarily Lao dishes were cooked and stored in big pots. That was the first time during her three years living in Savannakhet Minh bought anything from such a store, and it was also the first time she ate a Lao dish other than papaya salad.

The most popular eating place for single male workers who do not have their meals subsidized is a rice place owned and operated by a family from Quang Tri on a corner of a couple of main streets in the center of town. "*Com binh dan*" is painted in white on the store's big cupboard-cum-serving counter. Every day the store serves two main dishes, a type of vegetable and a soup, strictly central Vietnamese style (i.e., with lots of chili), and every customer is served all these dishes with a bowl of rice as soon as he sits down, for which he pays 6,000 kip. The restaurant is mostly frequented by men who work as construction workers for various contractors around town. They come on their own or in groups, chat quietly during their meals, and often leave as soon as their meals are finished. Sometimes they stay longer during dinner time to watch a soccer game on VTV.

Dam's street, Minh and Hien's alley, and the restaurant corner are just three of the many Viet concentrations that have been established all over Savannakhet over the last couple of decades. These places are where Viet who are far away from home interact, socialize, and recreate the life that they are familiar with. There is little effort made to learn about Lao things, except the little knowledge of Lao language that each Viet often picks up to facilitate their transactions with their jobs. Most interactions with Lao are strictly business-related. The Viet localities, however, have made the presence of Viet migrants in Savannakhet more visible than ever among the Lao residents there.

Despite the attempts of Viet migrants to congregate in their separate neighborhoods and maintain the lives with which they are familiar, in many ways their presence is also integrated with Lao social and economic life. Most Viet rent their houses from Lao. Some, like Minh and Hien, leave their children with a Lao woman everyday while they go to work. Although Minh occasionally complains about how lazy and, to some extent, backward Lao are, she acknowledges that her daughter's nanny is better than all the Viet nannies she has met. "She bathes her, feeds her. She can stay there for as long as we need to leave her. Every day when I pick her up, she's freshly clean and powdered." All Viet consume Lao fresh produce and admire how fresh and uncontaminated they are—"much better than what we have back home." The constant comparisons made by Viet of what goes on here with what goes on back home suggest that they are acutely aware of living a different life and are longing for the day when they can return.

Waiting to Return: Temporary Lives, Eternal Dreams

When Hien to came to Savannakhet in 2000, he joined a construction team of thirty people, stayed with them in the owner's house, ate their meals with them, and received his daily wage. Minh then stayed behind in Vietnam, worked their paddy fields, took care of their son, and did a range of other odd jobs including making tofu and selling it at a local market. As the synopsis above suggested, the main reason for Minh to come join her husband was to increase their capacity to accumulate savings for their future life, in particular to buy materials to construct a house within the next couple of years, and to pay for their children's education in a more distant future.

Saving in Savannakhet indeed seems to be easier than in Vietnam. Fierce competition with people characterized as "aggressive" everywhere in Vietnam, but especially in the big cities, was one of the main reasons for Viet migrants in Savannakhet to opt to work in Laos rather than in Hanoi, Da Nang, or Ho Chi Minh City. As I have already noted, work in Savannakhet is plentiful and Lao people are relatively easy-going. Moreover, the kip is strong (1 kip equals 1.6 dong at the time of writing), so savings accumulated during the months of working in Laos can be of a significantly higher value once converted to Vietnamese currency.

Migrants in Savannakhet also avoid the familial and communal obligations of life back home, such as contributing to weddings, funerals, and death anniversaries—all integral aspects of Vietnamese village life. Of course, visits are often required for special occasions concerning immediate family members, and in many cases these involve serious expenses. In 2004, Hien's father fell seriously ill, and, not long after Hien and Minh returned to Hung Yen, he died. After settling all the business for his mother, they came back to Savannakhet only to find out a few weeks later that their son had broken his leg. The couple went back home again and decided to stay on, since it did not seem to be worth it to spend all that money on traveling back and forth. They then had a daughter and remained in their village until late summer 2006, when both of them took the daughter back to Savannakhet with them, leaving the son behind under the care of his aging grandmother.

As this story shows, the advantages of living and working in Laos do not always come without cost. This was true for many of the other Viet migrants I met in Savannakhet. Most leave some members of their nuclear family behind. In fact, situations like that of Minh and Hien—where both husband and wife stay together in Laos—are rare. Most families cannot afford to do this, especially when they do not have other family members who can take care of their children back home. In most cases, one person works in Savannakhet while his or her spouse takes care of the children back home. Even for Minh and Hien the situation at home is getting harder, because "My mother-in-law is old and weak now; she won't be able to take care of our daughter. Our ten-year-old son is already enough for her. She also has many other grandchildren to take care of."

For many of the Viet migrants I met in Savannakhet, children and immediate family were something of a pressing concern. Everybody talks about taking opportunities when their children are still young (most have children in primary or early secondary years) and do not need their parents to be there to "educate" them. The money they save while living in Laos will be a good investment for their children's future, and when their children get to the age where they can easily be corrupted by bad influences in society (in late secondary or high school years), they will need to be home to protect them from these "social evils."

Another significant aspect of the temporary lives of Viet migrants concerns frugal living and eating arrangements. Just before the Tet festival, Hien and Minh moved to another house because Hien now no longer worked for his cousin but had become his own boss: he had his own contracts, he hired people for his own carpentry team, and people started calling him to offer him work. Their new house is in a muddy alley behind a noisy wood workshop. It looks temporary and especially small for six people: Minh, Hien, and their daughter, another couple from Hien's grandmother's home village, and Kien, the single worker I introduced above. The rent, however, is cheap, "only 700 baht a month, compared to 1,500 or 2,000 baht if you rent by the side of the road. If later we can hire more people, we'll move to a larger place." "You probably could only fit another person in here, I suppose," I said, looking around the small house with its two small bedrooms separated by a plank of wood for the two couples and a bed in the main area for Kien. A simple kitchen and bathroom stood behind the house, separated from the main living area by a brick wall. It turned out that I was wrong: Minh had everything planned in her mind and was waiting for the day when her husband's business prospered and they could hire more workers. "We'll just knock this wall over, move this room over there for the other couple, and put two more beds here. That'd be plenty for four workers. All we need is a small pathway to walk to the kitchen, and we can have our meals on these beds." Minh paused and then added, "I know it's hard. But we'll just have to live like this for a few years, saving up, and then we'll go home."

Everyday Minh gets up early to make soy milk and put it in the plastic bags, which she later takes around to different departments in the provincial hospital to sell to patients for 2,000 kip per bag. "The hospital is full of Viet sellers. The guards don't want us there. They try to kick us out, but we're persistent. We just go from one department to another, and they can't find us." After selling all the soy milk, Minh goes home to make more soy milk and also tofu to sell in the afternoon market. If one morning she cannot sell all the soy milk she has made, it can be turned into tofu, although tofu does not generate nearly as much as profit. Still, things are much more profitable here than back home. "For every kilogram of soy I can make a profit of 10,000 kip, while in Vietnam I could only earn 3,000 dong [about 2,000 kip] from it. I used to make tofu to sell too, but it was not easy. Competition is too fierce. Here, things are easier. Not too many people make soy milk and tofu to sell." Minh's soy milk customers are mostly Lao, but few Lao eat tofu. Luckily, there are a large enough number of Viet consumers who come to her market stall, most of whom are either mobile vendors or scrap-metal collectors who work in the vicinity of the market. Compared to other Lao who come to the market, they seem to be in a hurry, and their purchases are often much smaller. While Lao women tend to wander around with dozens of plastic bags dangling from their hands, most Viet know exactly what they want to buy, come to the market, shop, and leave quickly. A block of tofu for 1,500 kip bought from Minh and a small bundle of vegetables are enough for a meal for a Viet woman and her husband.

Ha also lives a very temporary life. She rents a tiny room containing a single bed with little room for anything else for 140,000 kip a month, and spends 10,000 kip on three meals a day: 3,000 for a bowl of congee when she gets up at dawn to go set up her fruit stall; 3,000 for a plate of rice with vegetables and a couple of pieces of unidentifiable meat sold by another Viet lady in the market; and a bowl of noodles at home at ten o'clock, after she comes back from her long day of selling at the main market during the day and at the night market in the evening. "Don't you get hungry when your lunch and dinner are so far apart?" I asked her naively. "No," she said, "I'm used to it." When I commented that life back in her home commune in Hue must have been a bit easier, she said, "No, it's not easier. But I don't mind hardship, as long as I can make some money for my children's schooling." Her older sons had to quit school to learn to repair motorbikes at a vocational school. Her two daughters are still studying in classes 4 and 8. "They study very well, each year they get *giay khen* [certificates of compliments] from the school." I noticed the pride in her eyes when she told me this, and was at least glad that she had her two daughters to remember during those long hard days of work in a foreign land.

Conclusion

In this chapter I have discussed the situations and experiences of recent Viet labor migrants to Savannakhet. I have shown how the experiences of Viet labor migrants in Savannakhet are shaped by national, local, and individual forces. In particular, I have described ways in which Viet experiences of mobility are informed by the relaxation of government controls and by Viet perceptions of Lao. For most Viet migrants, migration to Laos, or anywhere else for that matter, is an effective way of avoiding social obligations that at times can be cumbersome and costly. Moreover, migration to Laos has several significant unique benefits: work is plentiful, the kip is strong (at least in comparison with the dong), and Lao have the reputation of being not competitive and spending rather than saving.

As I have shown, the presence of Viet in Laos in general, and in Savannakhet in particular, is not new. However, I believe Lao at the local level have never experienced such frequent contact with Viet labor migrants in their land. Despite the fact that contact is made on a daily basis through transactions relating to the migrants' work, such as contact between a Viet seller and a Lao buyer in the market or on the street, or between a Viet construction worker or contractor and a Lao home owner, so far very little social interaction has been established as a result of this contact. Most Viet migrants who come to Savannakhet maintain a lifestyle removed from the political and social scene of the town in which they live. The only Lao event that Viet migrants talk about with excitement is a festival that is supposed to attract people from the whole region, and their excitement derives mainly from expectation of the opportunity to make the extra money that it presents.

All of the Viet migrants I met in Savannakhet talked of their plans of going home in the foreseeable future. Some plan to stay for a year or two, and some for longer. But nobody wishes to stay permanently, although such a stay is possible, especially for those with more money like Dam and his family. Other Viet in similar situations to Minh and Hien told me that they only worked and saved up to go home. Nobody expressed a wish to stay on in Laos, not that they would have been allowed to, legally; but I suspect they could have found a way if they wanted to. Everybody talks about going home as if the life they are living now is only a temporary one, a life that will eventually lead to a more permanent life, hopefully in the not too distant future, back home.

CROSS-BORDER HYPERGAMY AND GENDERED AGENCY:
Farang Husbands and Isan Wives on the Global Cultural Stage

Suriya Smutkupt and
Pattana Kitiarsa

Introduction

This chapter concerns a specific kind of mixed marriage in northeast Thailand (Isan) and its multiple and competing meanings (Abelmann and Kim 2005, 103). In the first decade of the new century, the issue of Isan village women marrying *farang* (Caucasian or Western) men and settling permanently in rural provinces throughout the poverty-stricken region sparked attention in the Thai media, in academic circles, and among government authorities. The questions we address here include: What theoretical tools can help us explain Thai-Isan and *farang* mixed marriage in comparison with cross-cultural or transnational marriages elsewhere? Why does the case of Thai-Isan women and *farang* men loom so large in the emerging global marriage market? What do these patterns of mixed marriage mean in the changing economy of global culture? We argue that mixed marriage between Thai-Isan women and *farang* men constitutes a cross-border project of gendered power relations and identity negotiations. It illustrates the notion of "gendered agency" (Constable 2005, 13) on the part of both the men and women. It involves delicate processes of negotiation by which men and women from different backgrounds can make sense strategically of their differences and the way each constructs "the other." While this construction of "the other" draws on "Orientalizing" and "Occidentalizing" discourses, in the last analysis neither Thai-Isan women nor *farang* men contract intimate relationships with pure or naive views of the world. Instead, their marriages can be characterized as contracts of mutual interest, whose longevity depends very much on how successful the relationship is and the extent to which they can come to terms with perceived and real differences.

We begin with a short summary of the history of mixed marriage in Thailand, a practice the state had effectively forbidden for centuries but began permitting among lower social strati as the country opened up to foreign trade, laying the groundwork for the phenomenon as it occurs now. Current practices are further rooted in the presence of US troops in Thailand during the Vietnam War, subsequent state encouragement of tourism, and an openness to the global economy. We go on to the core of the chapter: a close examination of the stories of the *farang* men and Thai women in these marriages and what their situation implies.

This chapter draws on ethnographic fieldwork in several villages across the provinces of Khon Kaen, Nakhon Ratchasima (also called Khorat), and Udon Thani, carried out on research trips in 2005, 2006, and early 2007. The subjects of our research were: (1) *farang* men formally married to Isan village women and settled in the region's rural villages or market towns, (2) the Isan wives of *farang* men, (3) the women's immediate relatives, and (4) village leaders. Suriya Smukupt, in particular, traveled extensively to conduct interviews and make field observations, ultimately interviewing fifty-nine persons (thirty-four of them *farang* men).

Our *farang* informants were predominantly European and American. All of them were seasoned travelers to Thailand and other Asian countries. Those we interviewed were from Austria, Belgium, England, France, Germany, Switzerland, Sweden, the Netherlands, and the United States.[1] They were mostly of relatively advanced age, with an average age of fifty-nine. The oldest informant was seventy-two and the youngest was thirty. They mostly had a high level of education; the majority had obtained bachelor degrees in fields such as engineering, business administration, organic chemistry, and computer science. Two held doctoral degrees (computer engineering and organic chemistry). Our Isan women informants were of rural family backgrounds, with low income and low education. Prior to their marriages to their *farang* husbands, they were among the waves of female workers from the Khorat high plateau entering the national, regional, and global industrial and post-industrial labor market (Mills 1999). Their average age was forty; the oldest was fifty-two; the youngest was twenty. Twelve out of seventeen Isan village women informants (70.58%) were divorcees with children; the remaining five had never been previously married. Many of those with children received no support from their Thai ex-husbands. The majority had finished only compulsory levels of education (four to six years) and there were only a few cases of high school and university graduates.

"Wives of *Farang*" as a Social Phenomenon

A survey by the National Economic and Social Development Board (NESDB 2004, 3) indicates that there are 19,594 Thai-Isan women who have married foreigners, and the vast majority of the husbands (87%) are of Western origin. These Thai-Isan women have continued to maintain close connections with their parents and with home villages by sending back remittances, making significant financial investments in property in their home areas, visiting their home villages on a regular basis, and conversing long-distance by telephone. Thai state authorities apparently view Thai-Isan wives and their *farang* husbands as a new source of foreign currency that can help boost the country's economy. Officials in many provinces have even sponsored public ceremonies of "soul-tying" (*baisi su khwan*) to welcome mixed-marriage couples to their provinces and, thus, formally acknowledge their contribution to the local economy and social life.[2]

As Thai-Isan/*farang* mixed marriage has established itself quickly as a social phenomenon, it has also resulted in notable scholarly attention. A five-month ethnographic study by Ratana Tosakul Boonmathya (2005), focusing on the experiences of the wives of *farang* (*phanraya farang*) in a village in Roi Et Province, shows how Thai-Isan women have retained a strong sense of belonging and connection to the locality of their original homes, no matter where they come to reside. She contends that the lived experience pertinent to the issue of cross-cultural marriage can be categorized together with that found in cases of transnational migration; she calls attention to the ways female gender, sexuality, and cultural identity are in open negotiation. Buaphan Phromphakphing and his colleagues from Khon Kaen University (2005) also examine cross-cultural marriage among Isan village women and its impact on the economy and culture of villages. They argue that cross-cultural marriage has improved the livelihood of the families left behind as well as notably altered villagers' attitudes: from being negative or indifferent towards black GIs and other American *farang* during the Indochinese War in the 1970s, to being more positive and accepting towards *farang* and other foreign husbands (i.e., from wealthy East Asian countries). In the past, women going out with *farang* were stigmatized as "rented wives" (*mia chao*) or casual prostitutes (Cohen 1982; 1986). Some other unpublished studies on the subject include Chaiphon Phonyiam (1999), Niphaphorn Yongkhampom (2004), Suphaporn Ngamwan (2005), and Suphawatthanakorn Wongthanawasu et al. (2005). These works also show how Isan villagers have come to appreciate their foreign in-laws' contribution to their immediate families and to the local economy.[3]

A close scrutiny of current Thai-language scholarship on Isan wife and *farang* husband relationships shows certain limitations. First, the abovementioned studies are usually one-sided stories. They represent views of Thai-Isan women or villagers and make the mixed marriage a somewhat local Thai event. The *farang* men's side of the story is relatively neglected. Second, we believe that defining mixed marriage solely as a "cross-cultural" marital/familial relationship is single-dimensional and problematic. In doing so, mixed marriage, as a Durkheimian social fact, is reduced theoretically and oversimplified ethnographically. Indeed, it is a multi-dimensional cultural phenomenon, involving such factors as race, gender, class, and nation of origin. The mixed marriages we consider could be defined as interracial or international as much as inter- or cross-cultural. It is in this sense important to widen our lens of investigation in order to take a fuller, more complete look at the phenomenon. Finally, these mixed marriages need to be conceptualized critically and grounded historically. Mixed marriage is part of a global cultural phenomenon resulting from what has been called "time-space compression," as it involves flows of people, capital, information, technology, and ideology. It fits well with the pattern scholars have called "global hypergamy" (Constable 2005), or "cross-border hypergamy" (Oxfeld 2005), in which women marry men with higher socioeconomic status and follow a path of upward social mobility.

A Short History of Mixed Marriage in Thailand

Historically, the bodies of Thai women have in certain contexts been subject to the state's strict control. For centuries, the phenomenon of mixed marriage of the sort we now find between *farang* men and Isan village women would have been unthinkable. Early contact between Siamese and *farang* was first recorded in the early sixteenth century in the kingdom of Ayutthaya. Portuguese, Dutch, and Spanish travelers, traders, and missionaries constituted the early populations of European men visiting and residing there between 1511 and 1597. The Dutch established a trading station in 1603, followed by the British in 1612. Besides European *farang*, there were also communities of Chinese, Japanese, Persian, Javanese, and the neighboring Mon and Malay residing and making a living in Ayutthaya. Mixed marriages between these foreign men and local women were inevitable because foreigners were not accompanied by spouses and had to spend some extended time abroad. The numbers of *farang* and foreigners of other nationalities and, consequently, the intensity of cross-cultural contacts, increased exponentially during the reign of King Narai (r. 1656–88), notably with the French embassies, and in the period following the founding of Bangkok as Siam's new capital in 1782 (Dararat 2006; Pattana 2010).

Mixed marriage, especially between *farang* men and Siamese women, was, however, from the official perspective, to be condemned. *Farang* men and most other foreigners were considered "non-Buddhist evils" (*mitcha thithi thang satsana*) (*Kotmai Tra Sam Duang,* vol. 4., 1962, 19). Siamese kings, since King Ekathotsarot in the mid-sixteenth century, strongly prohibited marriage between *farang* men and Siamese women on the grounds that "the offspring would eventually adopt new religious affiliations after their fathers [e.g., Catholicism]," and the mothers and relatives "would expose the Kingdom's internal public affairs to foreign countries" (ibid., 17–18). Mixed marriage was thus viewed harshly both as anti-Buddhism and as anti-Siamese treachery. In the reign of King Narai in the second half of the seventeenth century, Siamese women who were involved in mixed marriages, or who had sexual relationships with *farang* or other foreigners, if proven guilty, would be sentenced to death. Their parents or relatives were also subject to punishment. Since *farang* and other foreigners were non-Buddhist evils, having intimate relationships with them would lead to a "state of suffering/misery" (*abaiyathuk*) (*Kotmai Tra Sam Duang*, vol. 5., 1994, 98–99). Prohibiting mixed marriage and interracial sexual intercourse can be said to have been part of Siam's political project of constructing "otherness." In prohibiting, condemning, and punishing mixed marriage, Siam guarded its social and political institutions by erecting fences of racial, religious, and national difference. The apparatus of the state was to this degree used to impose its discourse on the female body and women's sexuality.

In Siamese official discourses during the Ayutthaya and early Bangkok periods, race and religion/Buddhism were made to stand out prominently as the heart and soul of the "body politic" (Loos 2006). Of many kinds of foreigners, white Christian *farang* men had always loomed large in the Siamese imagination. Since the early nineteenth century, *farang* had come to represent, psychologically, Siam's greatest source of security as well as its greatest threat, especially in the eyes of its rulers and other elites. The most consciously articulated statement of the European colonial threat was that of King Rama III (r. 1827–51), announcing from his deathbed in 1851, that, "there will be no more wars with Vietnam and Burma. We will have them only with the West [*farang*]. Take care, and do not lose any opportunities to them. Anything that they propose should be held up to close scrutiny before accepting it: Do not blindly trust them" (Wyatt 1984, 180). *Farang* were non-Buddhists, yet they were very technologically advanced and had great command of modern knowledge and material wealth. Their numbers in Siam were small, yet they were quite powerful economically and politically. Their skin and hair color, and other bodily features, stood in sharp contrast to that of local Siamese and other foreigners of Asian origin.

Farang economic and political domination peaked at the height of European colonization in Asia at the turn of the twentieth century. The fact that Siamese authorities had to issue decrees prohibiting mixed marriage and outline proper economic and cultural contacts with *farang* suggests the degree to which Siamese people on the ground were embracing *farang* as people, as well their traditions and technological inventions. The range of roles they played—as, traders, travelers, mercenaries, and missionaries—gave them an important place in Siamese economy and politics and other aspects of social life. In 1856, a year after Siam signed the Bowring Treaty with the British (with similar treaties with other Western countries soon to follow), when King Mongkut (r. 1851–68) opened up trade with the Siamese domestic market, he issued a decree instructing his subjects that employment, trade, or other business with *farang* "were not only not illegal, but also highly encouraged as means to make a living [in the new economy for Siamese people]" (*Prachum Prakat Ratchakan Thi 4* 2004, 107). The 1909 census reported significant numbers of Euro-American *farang* (predominantly males) working and living in the Thonburi area, including "532 British, 144 French, 47 American, 162 German, 150 Portuguese, and 52 Italian" (Sawitri Thapphasut 1984, 106). Mixed marriage between *farang* men and Siamese women of common origin must have been widely practiced. In order to legalize such marriages, the first royal decree was issued on the topic in 1907 (Dararat 2006).

Mixed marriage between European women and Siamese elites stationed in Europe or studying there was taboo in the early twentieth century. Both King Chulalongkorn (r. 1851–1910) and King Vajiravudh (r. 1910–25) strictly prohibited blue-blooded Siamese and young students or civil servants (*kharatchakan*) from marrying European women, citing the kings' personal preference as well as appealing to nationalism in maintaining "pure blood." King Chulalongkorn and his queen reacted negatively when his son, Prince Chakkrabongse, took a wife in Russia, while undertaking military studies there, and brought her to live in Bangkok in 1907. In 1914, King Vajiravudh issued a royal notification to Siamese embassies and consulates abroad, informing them that the king preferred that his officials and students on royal scholarships not marry foreign women and that anybody wishing to enter such a marriage must request royal approval. In the revised version of the 1924 Royal Succession Law (*Kot Monthianban Wa Duai Kan Sueb Ratcha Santatiwong Pho. So. 2467*), a prince with a foreign wife was effectively disqualified from the succession line (Dararat 2006).

Since the post-1932 Democratic Revolution, and especially in the post-World War II period, mixed marriage between *farang* men and Siamese/Thai women of common stock has been a significant locus for contested discursive practices of race, gender, and class (Jackson and Cook 1999; Van Esterik 2000). Despite strict official regulations, mixed marriage began to gain widespread acceptance. Weisman's 2000 study of racially mixed children (*luk khrueng*) shows that, while cases of mixed marriage between *farang* and Thai elite were sometimes controversial, the frequency, on the ground, of interracial and cross-cultural contact, and of intimate relationships, intensified, and came to seem, increasingly, inevitable. *Farang* presence in Thailand's political, economic, and popular culture has increased remarkably since the 1960s, and Thai people at all levels have had firsthand experience of *farang* and other foreigners. Thailand has become one of the region's centers for communication and commerce, and various kinds of business and industry, including tourism, have flourished. Its deep involvement in the economy of global culture has led to a multi-faceted transformation of contemporary Thai culture and society.

Farang Men and Their Gendered Orientalizing Project

Why have *farang* men felt such strong desire for Thai wives and invested so much effort to find them? What is special about Thai women? What are the key factors that make mixed marriages work from the *farang* perspective? We find some answers on one Internet site providing the following information to Thai wife-seeking British men and other *farang*.

(1) **Alluring reputation**: Thai women are noted for their warmth, beauty, grace, charm, and loyalty. Perhaps that's why so many British [and other *farang*] men find them irresistible. In many cases, that

longing translates into marriage. This is now such a common practice that the Land of Smiles must surely lead the way in global dating. It's a modern social phenomenon.

(2) **Availability**: So many Thai women are in or have escaped unhappy marriages. They have a fantasy that things will be better with a *farang* (foreigner). This is enhanced by the mutual availability of unhappily married or lonely, single Western men. Not all men who beat the hot trail to Thailand seek simple gratification in the bars of Bangkok or Pattaya. They are looking for something better, a loving and beautiful wife.

(3) **Home-maker**: Western men go for Thai women because they know how to take care of their husbands . . . but there can be pitfalls. The Western woman has given up the idea of being a devoted housewife and so the *farang* believes the Thai lady will do a much better job of looking after his needs . . .

(4) **Happy with Older Men**: Another reason the *farang* heads for Thailand to find a wife is because he has heard that Thai women are happy with older men. I know a delightful Englishman in his mid-60s who is happily married to a young lady half his age . . .

(5) **Marriage is about more than love**: Falling in love is about loveable chemistry and, of course, one of the great attractions is the misconception that Thai women are loveably free. Few eligible Thai women are bar girls whose economic circumstances force them to exchange money for love. The *farang*, who thinks that the average Thai lady will bed down with him on their first date, is in for a rude awakening . . .

(6) **Money misunderstandings**: This is probably the biggest cause of all misunderstandings. The exchange rates make the *farang* appear a rich man when he is in Thailand and the Thai lady is often deceived by this illusion of wealth. Little does she realize that, back in his own

country, where the cost of living may be three or four times as much, her man has a very ordinary income...[4]

We take this Internet passage as a graphic narrative of "gendered Orientalizing" (Schien 2005, 76) as well as a form of "manual knowledge" (Reynolds 2005), illustrating how to make Oriental woman the Occident man's lover or wife. Said (1978) would remind us that *farang* men, from their privileged Western, male, wealthy, and pleasure/romance-seeking position, "Orientalize" Thai women as objects of desire. The passage represents "a style of thought based upon an ontological and epistemological distinction made between "the Orient" and (most of the time) "the Occident" and "a Western style for dominating, restructuring, and having authority over the Orient" (Said 1978, 3, 4). An image of Thai women, as well as aspects of Thai culture, is systematically and summarily projected. It represents as mixture of myth, illusion, and reality from the male *farang*'s standpoint. Images of Thai women in the global marriage market are presented both positively and negatively. In *farang* men's eyes, the Thai woman can range anywhere from the warm lover, the ideal homemaker, to the wicked money chaser. In dating or marrying Thai women, there will always be significant potential cross-cultural misunderstanding. Wise *farang* men, therefore, have to be extraordinarily cautious in the business of marrying Thai women.

Farang men can always learn lessons about marrying Thai women from their fellows. There are countless websites providing tips and information about Thai women accessible through popular search engines like Yahoo or Google. On the websites, one finds questions like, "Why are Thai women so explosive?"[5] or, "Do Thai women make good wives? Absolutely!! They are faithful, loyal, somewhat jealous, a bit demanding, sweet, funny, sexy, small, beautiful skin, world's best personal hygiene and tend to treat you better than you've experienced before."[6] In an autobiographical novel, entitled *The Lady of Isan*, Michael Schemmann (2007), a German-Canadian university professor, tells a fascinating real-life love story about his relationship with Iuu, a young Isan woman and ex-bar girl from Amphoe Nong Han, Udon Thani. Michael fell madly in love with Iuu, went the extra mile to win her heart, and finally married her. He gave the following comment on his genuine perspective about mixed marriages between *farang* men and Isan women: "Let us remember that Thai marriages, or at least Isan ones, are not based on the notion of romance and love forever until death does us part, but on economic survival, sex being merely part of the contract" (Schemmann 2007, 129). Schemmann critizes Thai-Isan marriages as being about pure economic survival. He reduces other aspects of marital traditions into a means of survival, as if in jungle rule, and implies that, for Isan women and their relatives, money comes before everything else. Mixed marriage, according to this statement, is portrayed as if it were a business deal.

Farang men's current gendered Orientalist project, perceiving Thai women's irresistible charm, is strongly rooted in post–Vietnam War tourism. Sociologist Erik Cohen (1982, 403–29) points out that the currently dominant pattern of liaisons between young Thai women and foreign men began with the arrival of American troops in 1962, many of whom acquired Thai mistresses, referred to as "hired wives" or "rented wives." The easy availability of sex became one of the chief attractions for American servicemen to use the country for "rest and recreation" (R&R). With more than forty thousand American GIs stationed in Thailand in the late 1960s and early 1970s, their presence shaped the institutions which mediate contact between young Thai women and *farang*: the bar, the nightclub, the massage parlor, and the coffee shop. When the US military left in 1975, tourism to Thailand expanded rapidly, due to a successful campaign by the Tourism Authority of Thailand (TAT). The number of foreign arrivals, which in 1971 stood at 634,000, rose to 1,098,000 in 1976 and reached 1,591,000 in 1979. Males outnumbered females among tourist arrivals two to one, many of whom were "sex-seeking tourists" from Europe, Japan, and the United States. Pasuk Phongpaichit (1982) estimated that between 500,000 to 1 million Thai women were working in the sex industry in the early 1980s. The numbers of visitors to Thailand and of Thai sex workers both increased dramatically in the 1990s and 2000s. According to TAT, the country received 7.2, 9.5, and 11.5 million international tourists in 1997, 2000, and 2005, respectively. International tourist revenues for the same years were 6.9, 9.0, and 11.6 billion US dollars, respectively.[7] In 2007, TAT estimated the total tourist revenues from European and US markets at US$8.7 billion ("Paomai raidai kan thongthiao pi 2551" [2008 International Tourist Revenues Targets] *Matichon Weekly*, 2007, 26). Going beyond the kinds of purchasable sexual intimacy emerging in the 1960s and 1970s—e.g., hired or rented wives, and sex workers—another study by Cohen (1986) shows how relationships between *farang* male tourists and Thai bar girls developed patterns of more extended and emotional relationships in what he calls "the paradoxes of intimacy-at-a-distance." Many *farang* tourists, especially middle-aged married or divorced men, encountered the paradox of extended relationship with the young women, because they want to safeguard their girlfriends' fidelity and attachment during the long separation between vacations. In his analysis of correspondence between *farang* men and Thai bar girls, he argues that, though sexually intensive, the relationship is usually superficial. Bar girls, on the micro-personal level and in their expert management of their correspondence with *farang*, "are adroit at manipulating their absent boyfriends and may be in a position of dominance in the relationship-at-a-distance" (Cohen 1986, 115). Traces of these kinds of skillful manipulative strategies are undoubtedly found in mixed marriages between *farang* men and Isan village women, particularly those of ex-bar girls who worked in tourist destinations like Bangkok, Pattaya, and Phuket.

"Romances" in the Contact Zones

The *farang* men's journey pursuing the quest of their gendered Orientalist vision in Isan villages usually begins with a popular mode of modern tourism. Almost all of our thirty-four *farang* interviewees made their first trip to Thailand as tourists and met their mates in tourist places, particularly Pattaya. More than fifteen years ago, Jan, sixty-five—a Flemish speaking Belgian who settled in a village in Amphoe Kranuan, Khon Kaen, with his wife Pen—visited Pattaya like other European tourists and met his wife there. She worked in a bar. After they met, he stayed with her the entire vacation. Jan had never stayed with any Thai woman before. He was a widower. His Belgian wife passed away long ago. His children were all grown and had their own families. He met his wife when he was forty-nine years old; she was then around thirty years old. She had three teenage children from a Thai husband whom she had divorced. Jan and Pen lived in Belgium for almost nine years after they met in Pattaya.[8] In 2001, Bob, fifty, an English carpenter, first came to Thailand to take his annual vacation in Pattaya with three friends, and met his wife, Nok, in a bar there. He began coming to Thailand annually. He spoke some Thai by then. He was attracted to Nok and decided to spend one week with her in her home village in Amphoe Wang Nam Khiao, Nakhon Ratchasima. As their romance grew, Bob asked Nok if he could stay in her village. He came back to marry her a year later and Nok gave birth to his daughter. He was previously married for a long time but had divorced and had no children from the marriage. He has been married to Nok for almost six years now, but has to stay away from the family for three months every year. He works in Britain during the summer, when carpentry work is plentiful, and then returns to his family in Wang Nam Khiao. His brother-in-law is also a carpenter and he sometimes helps to line up summer carpentry jobs for him as well. Bob is fifty-six years old and he is not eligible for retirement with a pension.[9]

The "contact zones" where *farang* men enacted their gendered Orientalism were popular tourist-oriented entertainment establishments. Typical *farang* men entering serious relationships with Thai bar girls are of relatively advanced age with a stable career and income, and divorced. Because of their age and with the savings they have accumulated, they are in a position to travel extensively. They come to Thailand looking for tourist-type pleasures at entertainment establishments like bars, nightclubs, and pubs, where they meet and develop relationships with their future wives. John, an Englishman from Manchester, told us that he had visited Bangkok and Pattaya almost every summer for seven years. According to him, "In Pattaya, I have seen so many *farang* men living with Thai women. They are from Britain, Germany, and so on. Some of these *farang* men are alcoholic and fail in their intimate relationships with their Thai women. Pattaya is the favorite destination for *farang* on their holidays."[10]

Purchasing escort services and sex from Thai bar girls in Bangkok, Pattaya, or Phuket is common practice among *farang* male tourists (Cohen 1982, 1986). However, developing serious relationships with their partners is a rather complex process. *Farang* men make their decision based on a series of factors, going beyond physical appearance or romantic attachment. For them it is a carefully calculated move. Since most of these *farang* men are approaching or already in retirement, they have to make a decision that will represent a wise investment of their savings or pensions. John, the Englishman who married a woman from Amphoe Pak Thong Chai, Nakhon Ratchasima and settled in a village near there, offers the rationale behind his decision to marry his Isan wife. This is his story.

> Khorat is an isolated place. Holiday *farang* men do not come here like they go to Pattaya. However, unlike Pattaya, the rental fee is cheap. I only pay 3,500 baht per month to rent this brand new two-bedroom house with a small yard in the front and back where I can put up a small vegetable garden too. It is a nice and quiet new estate and close to the Khorat market town. If I want to buy it, it will cost me 2.2 million baht. I am not sure whether I want to invest that much money on this property. No, I do not think that I will invest that much money on it. I used to own one 20 million baht home in Britain. I also used to run my own cosmetic company. My ex-wife was an accountant. My company used to bring in around 14 million baht profit each year after paying 75 staff. The highest profit is around 19 million baht. My company had zero bank loans when I sold it before I decided to come to live in Thailand.[11]

John's journey as a son in-law of Isan was quite stormy. He had already been married twice when we interviewed him in early 2007. He got to know his first "lady" (he did not use the term "wife") through a marriage broker, but his relationship was not smooth. His first lady was a young university student, but, according to John, she and her parents were in the mixed marriage for money. John finally ended up with his second lady, who is a much older food seller (*mae kha somtam*) and divorcee with three children to support. Below is John's story of how he ventured into his relationships with Isan women.

> I came to this area because my Thai ex-lady and her family live in this area. She is an opinionated lady. She used to label my present lady, Nui,

as "an ugly woman." My first lady is beautiful and educated. She is a university student and speaks good English. However, I did not wish to take her as my lady in the first place. The Thai internet marriage broker insisted that I meet her first when I got to Khorat. She is a good lady from a good family. I found out later that her good parents were in need of cash, lots of it. I even specifically told the Internet marriage broker that I wished to meet an older woman. Anyway, after meeting my first beautiful university lady and her parents, we agreed that we could try to live together for a few months. I rented a hotel room for weeks. I did not pay 60,000 baht for the marriage brokering fee yet. Her family began to ask me for cash. I gave them 100,000 baht plus I bought one 60 cc motorcycle for her. She demanded more money for other expenses. We quarreled. She spent less time in my hotel room with me. Finally, she said that she no longer wanted to have anything to do with me. We split. By that time, I got to know Nui, my present lady. My first lady took me to eat *kai yang* [grilled chicken] *somtam* [green papaya salad] at her restaurant. I saw her all the time. She worked very hard and was still very pleasant to all of her customers. We cannot talk because she does not speak any English. I would go to eat at her restaurant by myself and got to talk to her through her brother who helped her selling *somtam*. Her brother understood some English words. I also learned Thai with Thai ladies who know English through the Internet. I discovered that they are all looking for *farang* husbands. I do not find anyone whom I really wish to have a long-term relationship with like Nui or my *kai yang somtam* lady. It took me a few months to settle our agreement to live together.[12]

Each marriage has its own story. Romantic love and a strong sense of commitment to the marriage are notable characteristics found among a significant number of *farang* men who decide to marry their Isan women and rebuild their new families in rural villages. This is the deep emotional feeling that Mark, a sixty-two-year-old Belgian bus driver, continues to treasure for his late wife, Amporn, a village woman from Amphoe Kranuan, Khon Kaen. It is a case of true romantic love "til death do us part," as Amporn tragically died from cancer. Mark has kept Amporn's name plaque in memory of his late wife. He told us this story.

I am a retired bus driver from Belgium. I am the only child in my family and had to take care of my mother until she passed away. I met Amporn in my hometown when she went to visit her younger sister, who married another driver whom I knew well. It was love at first sight. I fell in love with her right away. I knew that she was a widow with a few grown-up children who lived in Kranuan. With some help from Amporn's younger sister, I was able to confess my love to her and proposed marriage in Belgium. Amporn was on a three-month social visit then. With all of her proper paper works from Kranuan, I was able to get my marriage registered without difficulty. Amporn had to return to Kranuan before her social visit visa expired. While waiting in Belgium, she moved in to live with me. I at that time lived alone. With her younger sister's help, Amporn was able to take care of my house with no difficulty. Amporn did not speak Flemish or English but our life together in Belgium was smooth. I took her to buy food and visited places around the town when I had days off. She could talk to her younger sister every day whenever she had questions to ask. I was very happy with Amporn in my life. She was also happy living with me in my house. Despite the language barrier, we got along well.

    I came to live in Kranuan with a bus driver friend and his wife after I retired at sixty. I stayed with Amporn in her Isan house, while having the present house built by local builders. Again, with my Belgian driver friend and his wife's help, Amporn and I got the house built with no difficulty. All the specifications on my house, walling, electrical wiring, kitchen counter and cabinet, bathroom, toilet, and everything else were carried out without any major difficulty. I was able to buy one four-door pickup under Amporn's name. The lot for the house was under her name, too. It belonged to her. I would get my visa renewed by driving over to Nong Khai in order to cross the Mekong River to visit Laos and get my visa stamped for another three months. Our marriage was very happy until Amporn got sick with cancer. I wanted her to receive the best medical service in Belgium. She was eligible for the service because she was my wife. We decided to return to Belgium where she received treatment for a few months. She asked the doctor to let her go home because she could not communicate with him and other people adequately. She believed that she could get similar medical treatments at Khon Kaen University (KKU) Hospital, where she could talk directly to doctors and nurses. With her younger sister's help, I agreed to bring her back to Kranuan. The Belgian doctors agreed with our decision and gave us their approval of the medical treatments at the KKU hospital from their evaluation of her medical record. We returned to Kranuan. She was admitted for her medical treatment at the KKU hospital right away. I paid extra medical costs even though Amporn had a 30 baht health care card. I was happy that she was happy during her last fight against cancer. She passed away a few months after I brought her back to Kranuan.[13]

Mark's story is very moving. He himself is an emotional person. He cried while he talked to us. It was the biggest loss in his life. He was disappointed with how Amporn's adult children behaved. They did not pay much attention while their mother was sick with cancer. They only came to visit her once in a while but never stayed to take care of her while she was at home or at the hospital. They only showed interest in the things (properties and money) that were under her name after her death. Mark has now married another Isan woman and lives in a village in Amphoe Chonnabot, Khon Kaen.

Stories of genuinely emotional, romantic love by many *farang* men for their Isan/Thai girlfriends or wives often surfaced. To quote Schemmann's account on his estranged relationship with Iuu, he once visited a Thai Buddhist monk and received this advice, "If you love a woman, you have to be smart" (2007, 112). However, many "lovelorn *farangs*" (Cohen 1982) or love-seeking *farang* men do not keep their head when they enter love affairs with experienced Isan women. Schemmann himself, even in his advanced age, is a strong believer in romantic, true love. He insists that, "love that was built over three years of living together as husband and wife, sharing almost every moment, cannot die over night . . ." (ibid.). However, not all mixed marriages have happy endings. Many stories are filled with harsh disappointment and disaster. In some respects, they replicate the short-term unions between *farang* tourists and Thai bar girls in which "the *farang* seeks authenticity in their relationships with the girls, [which] varies widely from a mere desire to enjoy their bodies to a quest for a genuine sexual experience or even an extended love relationship" (Cohen 1986, 413). The details of the stories about marriage from John and Mark, with some comments from Schemmann (2007) and Cohen (1982; 1986), can be taken as representative of the wide range of experiences of *farang* men marrying Isan women and settling in the cultural settings of their in-laws.

Stories of the Women from Isan

Like *farang* men, Isan village women enter cross-border marriage with their own agendas, perceptions, and approaches, which we call "gendered Occidentalism." By this, we mean a style of thought or widely regarded belief, together with a common pattern of responses, that Thai-Isan women have adopted in their marital life with *farang* men. Western men, young and old, have acquired some rather positive images for Thai, especially women. In the popular, manual-style book, *Faen farang, sami farang* (*Farang* boyfriends and *farang* husbands), *farang* men are seen as better than their Thai counterparts. According to the book by Chomrom Mia Farang ([Farangs' Wives Club] 2006, 25–30), *farang* men are more desirable than Thai men because:

> they lead their own life without copying anyone's else lifestyle. They do not rope in sister-in-law if one is offered . . . They are tall and good looking. If they are not, they always have sex appeal, anyway. They are rich. The Western currencies are always dependable. They do not mind about the past of their wives. They are open-minded even though their women have children from previous marriages and are no longer virgins. They always honor their wives and prefer them to be independent and clever. They love their wives with open heart. They are not womanizers. They have generous heart that is as wide as river and give total freedom to their women. They take good care of their own women and are utterly romantic . . .

The *farang* is automatically associated with an abundance of material wealth. Isan villagers assume that *farang* husbands will be rich and generous. They have thus become the ideal choice for a husband, especially for older women or divorcees. Findings such as the following are not surprising:

> The marriage [between *farang* men and Thai-Isan women] is one livelihood strategy for the rural poor... At the household and village levels, fellow villagers have constructed vastly different images of these women. From being sex workers, mistresses, and minor wives (*mia noi*), they are considered as women with luck and fortune. They do not have to work in the rice field. Their life has drastically turned around. With their generous support to their parents and relatives, they have been admired as morally dutiful and model daughters (Buaphan 2005, 73).

One village elder in Khon Kaen Province pronounced boldly that having a generous *farang* son-in-law is equivalent to an unexpected arrival of reliable source of fortune for his daughter and his own family. In his own words, "[Having a *farang* or foreign son-in-law] is even greater luck than winning a lottery. You will get your lottery fortune only once and it is gone" (Buaphan 2005, 70).

Marrying a *farang* husband is considered to be a good strategy for village women of poor rural backgrounds. As the country is deeply embedded in the global cultural economy, contemporary Thai women are encouraged to "go inter [national]." The international space has become a source of wealth for many. *Farang* men are particularly desirable to Thai women who have had failed marriages and women who have never married. They are seen as an alternative to "bad, wife-beating" Thai men. Such popular perceptions are often seen in tabloids, magazines, and sensationalist books like *Faen farang, sami farang* (*Farang* boyfriends and *farang* husbands). This book includes quotations like: "Thai women do not want to be treated badly by vicious Thai men"; "It is better to become the wife of an old *farang* man than the sole, major, or minor wife of a Thai man"; "It is a pity that nice, good-looking Thai men are all married. The unmarried, handsome men available are homosexual (*gay*)"; and "Do not be sad with our wounded past, keep going forward and looking for a *farang* husband!" (Chomrom Mia Farang 2006, 1–2).

Most of the Isan village women in this study met their future husbands in transit, when they themselves were migrant workers away from home villages. Some were introduced to their *farang* men through female relatives married to *farang* men. Only a small number of them (mostly those with good education backgrounds and living in urban areas for an extended time) hire private matchmaking companies. Piya, a forty-two-year-old woman who sells beef in the local market in Amphoe Kumphawapi, Udon Thani, is married to an Englishman and told us the following story, which represents a common pattern of how a village woman meets and marries a *farang* husband.

> I worked as a waitress in a *farang*-owned restaurant in Bangkok. My *farang* boss's name is Martin. He has an Isan wife from Sisaket. However, his wife has never worked in the place. This restaurant is located in Din Daeng. *Farang* customers come to eat there all the time. My boss is a nice man. He speaks Thai well. I worked there for six months. It was very hard work. I had to do everything such as, serving food, cleaning tables, washing dishes, and preparing food in the kitchen. I got 3,000 baht per month plus food and a free room to sleep in. Yes, there were some extra tips too. My boss is a very fair and good-hearted person (*chai di*).
>
> My husband, Paul, came to visit Thailand for the first time when we first met three or four years ago. He came to eat in the restaurant with many *farang* males and Thai female friends. He did not have a Thai female friend with him. Thai females who come with other *farang* males are "working girls for *farang* clients" (*phuying ha ngoen*). I served them food and drink. I never spoke to my husband. I did not speak English but could take food and drink orders in English from the menu. After that time, my husband returned to eat there alone many times.
>
> One day, my boss called me into his office. I was frightened but had to face him. However, my boss told me that I had done nothing wrong. My future husband liked me very much. He had learned about me from my boss. He asked my boss that I take him with me to visit my family in Udon. He also asked my boss to tell me that he was serious about getting to know me and my family on this trip. He also asked my boss to grant me leave. My boss and my husband decided that I

should take him on an air-con bus from Bangkok to Udon so that he could enjoy the Isan countryside scenery all the way. My *farang* boss allowed me to take one week off from work.[14]

Piya was twice divorced when she met her husband. She was no longer young or favorably eligible in the local marriage market. She was also a grandmother since her married eighteen-year-old daughter already had her own three-year-old son. Piya told us that her family was poor, and she had to go to Bangkok to look for a job to support her seventy-eight-year-old mother. Luck was on her side in marrying Paul, who is now sixty years old. "My husband and I spent his money to buy a 100-square-meter plot of land. We then built an eight-room, one-story shop house. We rent out rooms to store owners. Each room brings us a 1,200 baht monthly rental fee. Our new house is built on another plot of land. My husband has invested the total amount of 8–9 million baht since our marriage, which took place three years ago. We also bought one pickup truck and one motorcycle."[15]

Poverty and failed marriage due to maltreatment by Thai husbands are often cited as key reasons why Isan women make the decision to marry *farang* men if they have the chance. From their perspective, marriage to *farang* men is a true hypergamy-type journey. For Piya, Dave was like a savior. Marriages like this not only save women from economic misery, but create totally new opportunities for middle-aged women from rural backgrounds. They are indebted to their *farang* husbands for their financial contributions and for enabling them to travel abroad and visit European countries; they could have only gone there in their dreams if they had not married *farang* men. Their socioeconomic status in their home villages improved due to the financial support their husbands contributed to their immediate families and other relatives, and to other public activities in the village.

However, no marriages anywhere are free from tension and anxiety. Not every mixed marriage is happy. Some unfortunate women ended up divorcing their bad-tempered, poorly adapted *farang* husbands. Many women also have to live with domestic tensions stemming from the complications of children or ex-husbands, parents, or overly demanding *farang* husbands. The story of Fai and Dan, a *somtam* vendor from

Pakthongchai and her English husband, is a case in point. Fai divorced her previous husband before she married Dan. She had three sons from her previous marriage. However, her ex-husband was sick and had to rely on her. He lived in her house with the children, even though they were no longer husband and wife. When Dan approached her about this, she told him all about her family. Dan said he did not mind having her ex-husband living under the same roof. However, there were times he was jealous and did not trust her words. Fai described in detail the family tension, which she dealt with along with a demanding job selling food from dawn to dusk.

> My *farang* husband is a good man. He loves my sons. He teaches them computer and English. He likes to have them stay with us. He loves to cook a breakfast of scrambled eggs for them. He does not add any fish sauce, just some salt in it. My son does not eat it much. I cannot force them to eat it. He sometimes cooks steak for my relatives, who do not like it either. He only uses salt and pepper on the steak to serve to them. Sometimes he cooks it too rare. He puts western steak sauce on steak before he eats it. My relatives and I do not eat meat this way. It is so unlike our roasted chicken (*kai yang*) that is well seasoned with lots of garlic, fish sauce, and some other Thai seasonings. He complains to me that they do not like his cooking—so unlike his new *farang* friends who praise him for how well he cooks steak when they are invited to his dinner party. He once said, "I am a good cook. My *farang* friends like my cooking but not you and your family." I try my best to explain to him they are more familiar with Thai seasonings but not with the British way. He now accepts this fact. My *farang* lover is very generous. He spent over 600,000 baht buying all new household furniture. He paid for an annexed kitchen in the back of the rental house because he likes to have an open-air kitchen. He also pays quite a bit to have a gas stove and oven for the kitchenette and a big ice box. He drives my two sons to school and picks them up every day now.
>
> My ex-husband's older sister does not like my *farang* lover. She tells me to leave him. She will ask her younger sister and her Dutch husband to find a nice Dutch man for me. She realizes that I do need

a *farang* husband who can help me take care of my three sons. She says that my *farang* lover is moody (*khi mo ho*) and not enough of a gentleman (*phu di*). After drinking beer, he speaks too loud. I agree with her impression. However, my former sister-in-law does not know the good and generous side of him. Yes, he can be too demanding. For an example, he wants me to give him a hug and a kiss as soon as I get home from work in the evening. He tells me that I do not love him enough to give him kisses and hugs. I try my best to explain to him that I am very tired because I am on my feet from dawn to dusk. My hair, clothes, and entire body smell like roasted chicken. I do not want to get him dirty with all the smell. Besides, I am not a *farang* wife whose way is what he is familiar with and does this kind of thing every day, just like in some Hollywood movies. Yes, he complains that I work too much and have no day off. He tells me that he will help me take care of my three sons. But, I still have to save money for them too. Soon, I will close our restaurant for a few days so that I can go on a vacation with my *farang* lover. He wants to take me to Pattaya with him.[16]

For some Thai women and many Thai in general, *farang*-ness, as associated with their husbands, implies superior racial whiteness. *Farang* men bring in money and other kinds of material wealth and make other kinds of contributions. They do not mind their wives' pasts, e.g., working as bar girls or prostitutes, or the fact that they come from poor family backgrounds. They certainly do not have a negative view of female non-virginity. They do not subscribe to the Thai way of imposing social stigma on women. More and more village women, and other villagers, view them as a quick way to earn easy money. However, these Isan villagers, especially the women, realize as well that *farang* men, although very generous and wealthy, have their own standards of what is reasonable and strongly prefer transparent behavior. They hate people telling lies and cheating them. They make themselves well prepared when they have to deal with legal matters. Some *farang* men refuse to pay a dowry, which is essential to any Thai marriage. One woman sums up the situation clearly from her own direct experience. She said, "*Farang* are not stupid (*Farang mai ngo*). You cannot deceive them easily."

Conclusion

The narratives of mixed marriage we have given above represent a type of cross-border hypergamy. We have told stories from the perspective of both *farang* men and Thai-Isan women. Although we tend to give priority to the under-represented narratives of *farang* men, our goal is to approach global hypergamy by showing what cross-border mixed marriage can mean to the different parties involved through an analysis of "gendered agency" (Constable 2005, 13) and "gendered geographies of power" (Massey 1994; Constable 2005, 14–15). In other words, marriage between *farang* men and Isan village women cannot be taken as conventional in the classic anthropological approach to marriage. At least, such marriage is not about an exchange of women between parties of men or between the bride-givers and the bride-takers (Levi-Strauss 1969). It is not about acts of bargaining or the maintenance of political power among neighboring groups, nor is it about the reproduction of new community members, because both the men and the women are already at advanced ages and have their own children from previous marriages. It is a special kind of marriage—and an indication of how deeply and intimately the Thai state has acted to embed the nation in the world's global cultural economy in the past three decades. At the individual level, the stories of the marriages and family relations of *farang* men and Isan women reveal how, on either side, agency is structurally gendered. Balancing stories from both sides helps us understand critical aspects of complex border-crossing processes—channels of mobility and the negotiation of intimacy—taking concrete form in Thailand's least developed region.

Reworking Edward Said's (1978) notion of "Orientalism," we argue that *farang* men coming to the hot, dry region of northeastern Thailand and marrying women there demonstrates a certain degree of a "masculine Orientalizing" style of thought in rationalizing their behavior, whereas Isan women and their relatives have countered the *farang* men's project to compromise and/or dominate with their own subtle strategies of "Occidentalizing" (Pattana 2004) vis-à-vis the *farang* husbands. The mixed marriage is, therefore, best understood as a project of power negation and negotiation, or of the production and counter-production of cultural meaning vis-à-vis constructed otherness among the men and women involved. The predominantly advanced-aged middle-class *farang* man with the Isan village woman represents what seems like a strange couple, but they are indeed highly complementary as candidates for global cultural match-making as it brings together two stereotyped identities: the Occidental, romantic, and wealthy family man, in contrast to the exotic, faithful, care-giving, and family-oriented Oriental woman. In other words, *farang* men are determined to fulfill their exotic dream of Oriental wives, while Isan women find themselves strategically "marrying up" (Freeman 2005) to Occidental husbands in order to escape poverty and realize their "Cinderella fantasies."[17]

Our mixed-marriage stories show "... a nuanced appreciation of the play of structural forces and personal agency" (Abelmann and Kim 2005, 102). They demonstrate how males and females from different nations and cultural backgrounds have acted and interacted with one another, negated and negotiated, communicated and learned, in an emerging cross-border marital "space." In this context, agency is structurally and practically engendered. Marriage defines roles on each side based on culturally conditioned sexual and gendered attributes. Both *farang* men and Isan village women have their own methods and conceptual frameworks when they enter intimate relationships. We argue, on the one hand, that *farang* bring with them their gendered Orientalization project when they marry Isan village women. They expect to have exotic, Oriental wives whom they can financially support, to enjoy marital intimacy, and to build a post-retirement life and family away from their homes. On the other hand, Isan women have developed their own methods and their own ways of viewing their *farang* husbands. *Farang* are "Occidentalized" as generous, rich, and rational men. Women are prepared to play the traditional role of Thai wives serving their Western husbands in their own home, while *farang* husbands are expected to contribute to the family financially and socially. Since *farang* men expect cultural authenticity from their Thai-Isan wives, their marriages confirm dominant cultural and gender norms for men and women in Thai society, despite the fact that the marriages involve new actors (i.e., *farang* men) and a transnational cultural economy. In short, mixed marriage in Isan is deeply rooted in unequal, stereotyped relationships of power in the context of the global cultural economy.

Notes

1. Our informants' nationalities are consistent with the samples studied by NESDB (2004), in which 162 out of 219 husband (73.97%) were European men, from countries like Belgium, Denmark, England, France, Germany, Italy, Norway, Scotland, Sweden, Switzerland, and the Netherlands.

2. For instance, on February 17–18, 2006, Sisaket's Provincial Administration Organization organized a *sukhwan* ceremony, entitled "*Khoei Thai-Saphai Thet*" (Thailand's sons-in-law and foreign countries' daughters-in-law) as part of the province's annual fair. Similar events were also held in Nakhon Ratchasima and Khon Kaen (Amphoe Kranuan) the same year.

3. Nevertheless, we should keep in mind that mixed marriage is neither a new social phenomenon, nor a cultural experience particular to certain geographical areas.

4. We adjusted and cited this set of information from this Internet source: http://www.jucee.org/japan-travel/Thaiing-the-Knot-farang-marriages.html.

5. http://www.thaigirl2004.blogspot.com/2007/07/why-are-thai-women-so-explosive.html.

6. http://www.whyretireinthailand.com/thai%20women.html.

7. http://www.tourism.go.th/doc.php?datatype=stattourism.

8. Suriya Smutkupt, interview with Jan, Amphoe Kranuan, Khon Kaen, March 27, 2005. This name and subsequent names have been changed to protect the privacy of the individuals interviewed, both Thai and foreign.

9. Suriya Smutkupt, interview with Bob, Amphoe Wang Nam Khiao, Nakhon Ratchasima, January 21, 2007.

10. Suriya Smutkupt, interview with John, Amphoe Pak Thong Chai, Nakhon Ratchasima, January 21, 2007.

11. Suriya Smutkupt, interview with John, Amphoe Pak Thong Chai, Nakhon Ratchasima, January 21, 2007.

12. Suriya Smutkupt, interview with John, Amphoe Pak Thong Chai, Nakhon Ratchasima, January 21, 2007.

13. Suriya Smutkupt, interview with Mark, Amphoe Kranuan, Khon Kaen, March 27, 2005.

14. Suriya Smutkupt, interview with Piya, Udon Thani, February 27, 2007.
15. Suriya Smutkupt, interview with Piya, Udon Thani, February 27, 2007.
16. Suriya Smutkupt, interview with Fai, Nakhon Ratchasima, January 20, 2007.
17. *"Khu Sang Khu Som"* (lit., soulmates), a Thai-language, popular tabloid-style magazine focusing on sensational love stories and family affairs, has regularly featured stories of "Thailand's Cinderella" (*sinderela Mueang Thai*). Such stories often show happy-ending, successful marriages between poor village women from the Thai countryside and their well-to-do European or American *farang* husbands. It has published real-life drama stories of *"farang* husbands" (*sami farang*) written and mailed in by the *"farang*'s wives" (*mia farang*). For example, Phanumat Songsri (2006, 20) tells a story of a Thai Cinderella named Nok, a woman from Khon Kaen, who worked in Phuket as a laundry lady and met her Italian husband there. They married and she has lived in Italy with her engineer husband for the past eleven years.

References

Abelmann, Nancy, and Hyunhee Kim. 2005. "A Failed Attempt at Transnational Marriage: Material Citizenship in a Globalizing South Korea." In *Cross-Border Marriages: Gender and Mobility in Transnational Asia*, edited by Nicole Constable, 101–23. Philadelphia: University of Pennsylvania Press.

Buaphan Phromphakping, Asok Phonbamrung, Nilwadee Phromphakping, Suphawadee Bunchua, Sumalai Phuangket, Kitiyawadee Sida, Phonphen Pankham, Phatharaphorn Sriphrom, and Ketsaraphorn Klangsaeng. 2005. *Kan taeng-ngan kham watthanatham khong phuying nai chonnabot Isan* [Cross-cultural marriage of women in the northeast of Thailand]. Khon Kaen, Thailand: Khon Kaen University, Faculty of Humanities and Social Sciences, Department of Social Development.

Chaiphon Phonyiam. 1999. *Withi chiwit phuying Isan thi taeng-ngan kap chao tang chat: Suksa korani changwat Roi Et* [Lives of Isan Women Marrying Foreigners: A Case Study of Roi Et Province]. MA thesis, Mahasarakham University.

Chomrom Mia Farang [The Club of Farang's Wives] (2006?) *Faen farang, sami farang* [*Farang*'s girlfriends, *farang*'s wives]. Bangkok: A. I. Printing.

Cohen, Erik. 1982. "Thai Girls and *Farang* Men: The Edge of Ambiguity." *Annals of Tourism Research* 9: 403–28.

———. 1986. "Lovelorn *Farang*s: The Correspondence between Foreign Men and Thai Girls." *Anthropological Quarterly* 59 (3): 115–27.

Constable, Nicole. 2005. "Introduction: Cross-Border Marriages, Gendered Mobility, and Global Hypergamy." In *Cross-Border Marriages: Gender and Mobility* in *Transnational Asia*, edited by Nicole Constable, 1–16. Philadelphia: University of Pennsylvania Press.

Dararat Mettariganond. 2006. "Kan taeng-ngan kham watthanatham: Thai kap farang nai prawatsat" [Cross-cultural marriage: Thai and *farang* in Siam's social history]. *Silapa Watthanatham* [Art and Culture Magazine] 27 (5).

Freeman Caren. 2006. "Marrying Up and Marrying Down: The Paradoxes of Marital Mobility for Chosonjok Brides in South Korea." In *Cross-Border Marriages: Gender and Mobility in Transnational Asia*, edited by Nicole Constable, 80–100. Philadelphia: University of Pennsylvania Press.

Jackson, Peter A., and Nerida M. Cook, eds. 1999. *Gender and Sexualities in Modern Thailand*. Chiang Mai: Silkworm Books.

Kotmai Tra Sam Duang [The Laws of Three Seals], vol. 4. 1962. Bangkok: Khuru Sapha Business Organization.

Kotmai Tra Sam Duang [The Laws of Three Seals] vol. 5. 1994. Bangkok: Khuru Sapha 1994.

Levi-Strauss, Claude. 1969. *The Elementary Structures of Kinship*. Translated by James H. Bell, John R. von Sturmer, and Rodney Needham. Boston: Deacon.

Loos, Tamara. 2006. *Subject Siam: Family, Law, and Colonial Modernity in Thailand*. Ithaca: Cornell University Press.

Massey, Doreen. 1994. *Space, Place, and Gender*. Minneapolis: University of Minnesota Press.

Mills, Mary Beth. 1999. *Thai Women in the Global Labor Force: Consuming Desires, Contested Selves*. New Brunswick: Rutgers University Press.

National Economic and Social Development Board (NESDB). 2004. A Survey of Thai Women Marrying Foreigners in Northeastern Thailand. Unpublished report.

Niphaphorn Yongkhampom. 2004. *Krabuankan ha khukhrong thi pen chao tang chat khong phuying Thai nai chonnabot: korani suksa Ban Kutphangkrua, Tambon Thakrasoem, Amphoe Namphong, Changwat Khon Kaen* [A process to court foreigners as potential spouses by Thai rural women: A case study of Ban Kutphangkrua, Tambon Thakrasoem, Amphoe Namphong, Changwat Khon Kaen]. Term paper, Office of Graduate Volunteers, Thammasat University.

Pattana Kitiarsa. 2010. "An Ambiguous Intimacy: *Farang* as Siamese Occidentalism." In *The Ambiguous Allure of the West: Traces of the Colonial in Thailand*, edited by Rachel V. Harrison and Peter A. Jackson, 57–74. Hong Kong: Hong Kong University Press.

Pasuk Phongpaichit. 1982. *From Peasant Girls to Bangkok Masseuses*. Geneva: International Labour Organization.

Phanumat Songsri. 2006. "Chiwit khu khue kan long ruea lam diao kan" [Married life is a ride together in the same boat]." *Khu san khu som* [Soulmates] 27, (537), July 20–31: 59–61.

Prachum Prakat Ratchakan Thi Si [Collected Proclamations of King Mongkut], edited by Charnvit Kasetsiri. Bangkok: Toyota Thailand Foundation, 2004.

Matichon Weekly. 2007. "Paomai raidai kan thongthiao pi 2551" [2008 international tourist revenue targets]. 27 (1409), August 17–23: 26.

Oxfeld, Ellen. 2005. "Cross-Border Hypergamy? Marriage Exchanges in a Transnational Hakka Community." In *Cross-Border Marriages: Gender and Mobility in Transnational Asia*, edited by Nicole Constable, 17–33. Philadelphia: University of Pennsylvania Press.

Ratana Tosakul Boonmathya. 2005. "Women, Transnational Migration, and Cross-Cultural Marriages: Experiences of '*Phanraya farang*' from Rural Northeastern Thailand." Paper presented at the Association for Asian Studies Annual Meeting (AAS), Chicago, April 3, 2005; and the 9th International Conference on Thai Studies, Northern Illinois University, DeKalb, Illinois, April 3–6, 2005.

Reynolds, Craig J. 2005. *Sediments and History*. Singapore: Singapore University Press.

Said, Edward. 1978. *Orientalism*. New York: Vintage Books.

Sawitri Thapphasut. 1984. "*Khwam samphan rawang chumchon chao Thai, Chin, lae tawantok nai Krungthep, pho so 2398–2453*" [Relationships among Thai, Chinese, and Western communities in Bangkok, 1855–1910]. MA thesis, Chulalongkorn University.

Schemmann, Michael. 2007. *Lady of Isan: The Story of a Mixed Marriage from Northeast Thailand*. 2nd. ed. Bangkok: ThaiSunset Publications.

Schein, Louisa. 2005. "Marrying Out of Place: Hmong/Miao Women Across and Beyond China." In *Cross-Border Marriages: Gender and Mobility in Transnational Asia*, edited by Nicole Constable, 53–79. Philadelphia: University of Pennsylvania Press.

Suphaphon Ngamwan. 2005. *Phonlawat phap mao ruam khong phuying Thai thi taeng-ngan kap chao tang chat* [The dynamic stereotypes of Thai women marrying foreigners]. MA thesis, Office of Graduate Volunteer Studies, Thammasat University.

Suphawatthanakorn Wongthanawasu, Wanapa Niwasavat, and Khanitta Nuntaboot. 2005. *Phon krathop khong kan taeng-ngan kham chat to sathaban khrobkhrua Thai nai phak tawan-ok chiang nuea* [Impacts of transnational marriage on family in northeastern Thailand]. Khon Kaen, Thailand: Faculty of Nursing, Khon Kaen University.

Van Esterik, Penny. 2000. *Materializing Thailand*. London: Berg.
Weisman, Jan R. 2000. *Tropes and Traces: Hybridity, Race, Sex, and Responses to Modernity in Thailand*. PhD diss., University of Washington.
Wyatt, David K. 1984. *Thailand: A Short History*. Chiang Mai: Silkworm Books.

CHARLES F. KEYES:
His Life and Work

This volume, like the conference from which it came, honors Charles Keyes as a mentor, colleague, and friend whose scholarship has touched us, the contributors to this volume, and influenced the direction of our work. It honors, in an even broader sense, a life of engagement with anthropology, Southeast Asia, and the many institutions over the years that he has worked with and helped build.

Keyes, a native of Nebraska who grew up in Idaho, completed his undergraduate work at the University of Nebraska, graduating in 1959 with a double major in anthropology and math, and then going on to do doctoral work in anthropology at Cornell University, the pre-eminent center for Southeast Asian Studies in the United States. At Cornell he studied with G. William Skinner, an anthropologist of China who had also worked on the ethnic Chinese community in Thailand. Although Skinner chaired Keyes's doctoral dissertation committee, Lauriston Sharp was more influential in mentoring Keyes in the study of Thailand. Sharp, together with Lucien and Jane Hanks, had begun in the late 1940s the Cornell Thailand project, initially focused on studies in the village of Bang Chan on the rural perimeters of Bangkok. The Bang Chan project was the beginning of what became significant American anthropological work in Thailand.

While at Cornell, Keyes met and married Jane Godfrey, a British graduate student who was also in the Southeast Asian Studies program. It was together with Jane that he conducted his first fieldwork in Thailand and much subsequent work; she has over the years been an important interlocutor of his scholarship. He joined the faculty of the University of Washington in 1965, two years before completing his doctorate, and has stayed there since. He continues to remain actively engaged with the department even since his retirement in 2007.

Keyes has pointed out the significance of the fact that his early anthropological career was at a time when anthropology was still shifting away from its pre–World War II focus on small-scale "primitive" pre-modern societies, and beginning to look more intensively at peasant society. The Cornell project at Bang Chan and a similar Harvard project in Indonesia were typical of this new direction. Although Keyes's initial research represents a somewhat later wave than the Bang Chan project and took place in what was then considered to be the more remote area of northeastern Thailand, it can be seen as continuation of the Cornell Thailand project in orientation. Anthropologists were searching for ways to reconcile the directions the discipline was taking—to see peasant society in relation to and in contrast with small-scale societies and to understand the relation of the peasant village to the modern nation-state of which it was part.

Keyes would subsequently carry out fieldwork in northwestern Thailand near the frontier with Burma. Here he expanded his first interest in the ethnicity of lowland-dwelling Thai-Lao in northeast Thailand to include upland-dwelling peoples, most notably the Karen, of northwestern Thailand. He would later go on to carry out fieldwork on ethnic groups in northern Laos, and northern and southern Vietnam. A third strand of his research interests also can be traced to his first fieldwork when he sought to understand the role Thai religion, and especially Buddhism, played in shaping the ways in which Thai were confronting the modern world.

The questions that underlie Keyes's work have, thus, included the transformation of peasant communities in modern nation-states, the shaping of ethnic identities of non-dominant peoples in nation-states, and the role of religion and national identities. For Keyes, the study of

Weber gave him theoretical tools for dealing with such questions. In the 1950s, most American anthropologists who were influenced by Weber were products of the Harvard Department of Social Relations, where Talcott Parsons had championed Weber's work. Keyes describes his own interest in Weber as deriving originally from conversations with Thomas Kirsch, then a Harvard anthropology graduate student who came to Cornell to study the Thai language. Kirsch, who would become a long-term friend, as an anthropologist of the same generation working on Thailand, introduced Keyes to Parson's *The Structure of Social Action*. Like Kirsch, Keyes would go on to develop his own understanding of Weber.

Keyes's view of the anthropological project is characterized by what he writes about Weber:

> Weber was not interested in ideas per se but in ideas that become practically realized. That is, he was interested in those ways of giving meaning to action within the world that after having been advanced become incorporated into the understandings (culture) by which people assert their lives. In other words, it is not sufficient for an idea to be thought up; it must become the basis for practical action (2002b, 4).

Keyes himself followed Weberian models in exploring for Thailand the ways modernization involved the relation between politics, economics, and religion. Weber was also, if less famously, an early theorist of ethnicity, and Keyes's way of looking at ethnicity, as cultural identity worked out in practical politics, can be said to be rooted in Weberian theory.

If we were to look for a single key to explain Keyes's lifework, however, it would probably be the importance of his fieldwork experience. A student once asked Keyes what kept him going over the years, and he replied that it was his fieldwork. Keyes was one of those anthropologists who developed a passionate love for the place where they did fieldwork. Over the course of his career, he jumped at any opportunity to go to Southeast Asia and loved being in the community of those who shared his passion for the region. At the most practical level, this means he worked tirelessly to promote Southeast Asian Studies in the United States; he also worked very hard to give Southeast Asian countries the tools of social science.

If his work was shaped by Weber and the directions that anthropology was taking, it was likewise shaped by what he experienced on the ground in Thailand (and, later, in Vietnam and other Southeast Asian countries). That is, he was engaged with a country experiencing rapid post–World War II modernization. Thailand fit the schemes Migdal described, as being a country that in the 1950s and 1960s had faith in modernization and inspired faith in observers. Modernization has continued despite increasing awareness of the social complexities involved in precisely the areas on which Keyes focused: ethnic relations, uneven rural development, and the social permutations of the Thai national project of modernizing religion.

The underlying ironies to all of this, as Midgal and others tell us, was that modernization was not taking place *sui generis*, but was part of a number of global processes relating to the development of a community of nation-states in the context of the Cold War, and the new institutions and ideologies of development associated with the UN, as well as changes in the global economic structure. Scholarship develops with its own logic and can never be reduced to political-historical formulas, but it is legitimate to say that the development of social sciences within Southeast Asia, and the development of social science about Southeast Asian countries, had a significant connection to the very processes that social scientists were observing. Within the American academy, area studies flourished in this context. Keyes has been very conscious of this dynamic and, for example, has described (2007) the transformation of his University of Washington anthropology department from one focused on Boasian study of Northwest American Indian cultures to one with more of an area studies focus—a change which coincided with the rise of the Jackson School of International Studies at the University of Washington. Keyes, whose love for Southeast Asia was nurtured in the context of his training in the particularly rich Southeast Asian studies program at Cornell, worked assiduously to develop Southeast Asian studies at the University of Washington, at universities in a consortium in the Pacific Northwest, and in North America more generally.

Keyes's involvement in Southeast Asia included stays at Southeast Asian universities. He had three extended residencies at Chiang Mai University, and also affiliations with Mahasarakham University (where he was granted an honorary doctorate in 2004) and Khon Kaen University. He was, likewise, from 1998 to 2001, the co-director of a Ford Foundation-funded program preparing Thai and Vietnamese researchers for work among upland minorities in their own countries.

While teaching at Chiang Mai University in 1972–74, Keyes found that he needed to develop, under the guidance of Thai colleagues, a new scholarly discourse to represent Western ideas in Thai. This experience, together with his awareness of the controversy in American anthropology over American anthropological presence in Thailand and the context of the Vietnam War, led him to embrace the objective of "de-Orientalizing" anthropology. This commitment led him to actively recruit Asian (mainly Thai and Vietnamese, but also Japanese, Chinese, and Afghan) graduate students for training both at the University of Washington and in cooperative programs. Of the forty-one doctoral students and twenty MA students he supervised at the University of Washington, more than one third were from Thailand, Hong Kong, and Vietnam. He supervised the doctoral studies of more Thai anthropologists than any other scholar and of more Vietnamese anthropologists than anyone else outside of Vietnam.

Keyes's level of proficiency in the Thai language was such that he could readily teach in Thai, and he has been over the years very much an interlocutor of Thai scholars and intellectuals—a significant factor in the level of respect with which he is regarded in Thailand. The transnational articulation of scholarly institutions is a complex issue full of nuances and contradictions, and Keyes would be the first to acknowledge its practical importance in the negotiation of a framework of meaning by which people—academics, clearly, but also the general population—come to live their lives. Keyes, in this context, has been a firm advocate for Southeast Asia and for dialogue with Southeast Asian academics.

For those of us who were anthropology graduate students at the University of Washington—including several contributors to this book—Keyes was first and foremost a teacher and a mentor. We may have coincided with the period when he was chair of the anthropology department (1985–90), the director of the Southeast Asian Studies Program (1987–96), or the director of the Northwest Regional Consortium on Southeast Asia (1986–2001). When we were doing our fieldwork, we may have met him on one of his frequent trips to Southeast Asia. As we read more of his writing, we became more aware of its depth and breadth: he has authored, edited or coedited fourteen books, monographs, or special issues of journals, and published over ninety articles. It was sometimes harder to put our finger on the role he was playing at the national level with his participation in numerous committees and editorial boards, and his frequent consultancies. He was a member of various different committees of the Association for Asian Studies, the American Council of Learned Societies, the Social Science Research Council, the Council for International Exchange of Scholars, the Council on International Educational Exchange, and the executive board of the Southeast Asian Studies Summer Institute. He was on the editorial boards of many of the key journals of Asian studies and Southeast Asian studies. At different times, he was a consultant to the American Council of Learned Societies, the Social Science Research Council, the Ford Foundation, and the Vietnamese National Academy of Social Science and the Humanities. That is, he was very much a player in the key institutions influencing the direction of Southeast Asian studies in the United States and sometimes in Southeast Asia itself. The culmination of all this activity was his 2001/2 stint as president of the Association of Asian Studies.

In a talk Keyes gave in the anthropology department near the time of his retirement, he expressed the desire to contribute to "an intellectual and social history" of the department. To my knowledge, there has been as of yet no attempt to record the intellectual and social history of Southeast Asian studies in the United States, but in any such history, Charles Keyes would figure prominently.

This long list of achievements perhaps does not adequately convey the respect and affection Charles Keyes inspires as a person—for his scholarship, yes, but also for his capacity for enthusiasm—and the profound generosity and equanimity which seems so consistent with his study of Thai Buddhism.

John Marston

QUESTIONS FOR CHARLES KEYES

Editor's note: It seemed important that the volume included the voice of Charles Keyes himself, and we exchanged ideas about how to do this. Finally we decided that, instead of having him write an essay, it would make sense to have him respond to my written questions in "interview" format. This was completed at the end of 2010. My hope is that this will help illuminate the development of his thinking and his role as a scholar as well as provide further context to how his thinking relates to the chapters in this book.—John Marston

JM: You've written about your debt to Lauriston Sharp and the Hanks, but perhaps less about the influence of the Cornell Southeast Asia Program (SEAP) as a whole. Could you describe the atmosphere at Cornell when you were a graduate student and how it shaped your vision of Southeast Asian studies?

CFK: I discovered Southeast Asia when I went to Cornell. I had a rather vague interest in Asia when I entered Cornell, but shortly after I arrived in the fall of 1959, I was advised to meet the senior members of the Department of Anthropology in order to choose a mentor. I was very impressed by Lauriston Sharp and made a rather quick decision to begin the study of Thai and of Southeast Asia. My decision was also led by the fact that the Southeast Asian studies program at Cornell was recognized as one of the preeminent area studies programs in the United States.

Having made my decision, I not only enrolled in Thai language study, but I also began to take the interdisciplinary seminars offered by SEAP. These seminars fostered discussions focused usually on a particular country among historians, political scientists, anthropologists, economists (yes, there were economists in area studies in those days), art historians, rural sociologists, and others. I was deeply impressed by these seminars and realized that understanding social phenomena required transcending disciplinary boundaries even as one remained rooted in a discipline. This was the primary influence that shaped my subsequent career and established my commitment to area studies in the Cornell mode.

JM: The idea of area studies has been questioned by some scholars, and some funding institutions have made the decision to give less emphasis to it, but you have continued to champion it. From your perspective, what does "area studies" or "Southeast Asian Studies" imply and why is it of continuing importance?

CFK: By the late 1980s, area studies had gone out of fashion in many North American universities (they had never had the same character in European or Asian institutions). This was partially a consequence of the increasing competitiveness for academic positions that were allocated by disciplinary departments. Thus, to be successful in competing for a position in a major department one had to prove that one was working on the cutting edge of the discipline. Those who blurred the lines between disciplines were likely to be less successful. One pursued a theoretically derived problem in a particular place, but one did not seek to acquire a broader understanding of that place.

Nonetheless, some anthropologists and historians (but many fewer political scientists and sociologists, and increasingly fewer and fewer economists) who were motivated initially by a theoretical problem that might have been pursued almost anywhere in the world realized that the most impressive (to one's peers) interpretations of such a problem necessitated having more than just a limited knowledge of the language of the place in which one carried out research. Investments by individuals and institutions in language learning proved to be the salvation of area studies. But the question of how one should understand the "area," that is, the "place," in which one worked no longer made sense to many in terms of the area studies configurations that had emerged following World War II.

Thus, while I have always remained deeply committed to area studies, I no longer think of Southeast Asian studies in the way I first encountered it at Cornell. The Cornell model was rooted in the political-economic perspective on the world that had developed in and after World War II and contrasted to the "Orientalist" perspective that had existed before the war, especially in Europe. This earlier perspective accentuated the Indian and Chinese roots of Southeast Asian cultures and, thus, was linked to Indology and Sinology. The newer perspective emphasized the transformations of Asia because of Western colonialism and the emergence of nationalist movements. At Cornell, Southeast Asian studies was defined with reference to boundaries that then divided the countries into distinct nation-states. Thus for example, rather than seeing the dominant culture of Vietnam as linked to that of China, Vietnam was seen primarily as a new state that had been created following the dissolution of French Indochina. As such it had much in common with Indonesia, Malaysia, the Philippines, and Burma, as well as Cambodia and Laos, which had also been included in Indochina.

At a 1990 SSRC-sponsored conference on the state of Southeast Asian studies in the Wingspread center in Wisconsin, I strongly questioned continuing to think of Southeast Asia in the way I had been introduced to Southeast Asian area studies at Cornell. In my presentation at the conference (and in the published version, "A Conference at Wingspread and Rethinking Southeast Asian Studies"), I began by asserting that "Southeast Asia does not exist as a place." After a long critique of the inherited version of Southeast Asian studies, I concluded as follows:

> Southeast Asian studies is no longer a colonial enterprise entailing the study of "them" by "us." On the contrary, "they"—the Thai, the Indonesians, the Vietnamese, the Filipinos, the Malays, and so

on—are engaged in pursuing research on their own and sometimes neighboring societies that is much deeper and richer than any carried out by Americans. Only by undertaking collaborative projects—conferences, training workshops, joint research—and establishing institutional linkages between programs in the United States and centers and institutes in Southeast Asia can the field of Southeast Asian studies in the United States continue to develop.

I have sought to further this vision in a number of ways. First, I undertook to teach in several institutions in Southeast Asia and to work with colleagues and funders to develop some of these institutions. More importantly, I had already by the late 1980s begun to recruit Southeast Asians as students. I take pride in the fact that I have trained significant cadres of Thai and Vietnamese anthropologists as well as several from other countries as is apparent from some of the contributors to this book. Finally, I also began to insist that my English-speaking graduate students learn not only an Asian language for purposes of research but also, where possible, for engaging the indigenous scholarly literature. All those contributing to this book, albeit in their own ways, exemplify the post-Orientalist/post-colonial approach to Southeast Asian studies.

JM: You have written about the importance of Weber to your work and how you see Bourdieu as in some ways the logical extension of the work of Weber. I have wondered to what extent this direction was a decision not to follow movements in anthropology that stressed Marx or, later, Foucault. Put in broader terms, how has being a Weberian situated you in relation to the field of anthropology as a whole?

CFK: Very much. Because anthropology at Cornell was linked with area studies, I was led early in my career toward seeking to make sense of empirical experience with the aid of social theory rather than seeking empirical materials that could be used to demonstrate the superior merit of one theory over others. My mentors at Cornell were very skeptical of the then prevalent Euro-American Marxism that they considered was used to fit historical actuality into a procrustean mold. It was only after I came to the University of Washington that I discovered that Marx's ideas could be detached from polemics and could lead one to very fruitful thinking. I still recall how taken I was with Marx's "Eighteenth Brumaire of Louis Napoleon," and his characterization of French peasants because of their individualism as not constituting a class or sharing a single community or political movement. In other words, although he did not frame the argument in such terms, in this and other of his work he allowed that the role of the individual could be very socially significant.

By the time I had begun to discover another Marx, I had already developed an understanding of the transformation of social life that was "developmental" rather than "evolutionary" that came from my engagement with Weber. I still remain very skeptical of teleological approaches that give too much credit to social forces as distinct from human agency, although I have always recognized that people do act with reference to social conditions that are mostly not of their own making.

Weber did not relegate culture to the superstructure, and from Weber I developed my understanding of the dialectical relationship between meaning and actual social practices. I have read many other theorists since my first encounter with Weber and subsequent reading of Marx, and have found a number of others—notably, Ricoeur, Bourdieu, and Foucault, the latter two also being influenced by Marx—expand on this same basic approach. I have thus, as my article on Weber demonstrates, reinterpreted the Weberian theoretical stance with reference to the thinking of these more recent social theorists.

The "anthropology" I came to identify with was not, however, determined by Weberian theory. Rather, the grounding of my approach has always been ethnographic, or, perhaps more accurately, a consequence of my engagement with people's lives under particular historical circumstances. As I said in an unpublished talk I gave in 2004, my intellectual roots lie primarily in my first fieldwork in a village in northeastern Thailand. It was here that I came to understand that "kinship," "gender," "religion," "ethnic identity," "peasant," "development," "state," and "nation" could not be understood only in theoretical terms, but made sense only if they were thought through with reference to actual sociocultural practices. In sum, I have always seen myself primarily as an ethnographer cum historian who makes use of theory for deepening one's understanding rather than one who seeks to be recognized for one's theoretical reflections.

All those who have contributed to this book share my commitment to making ethnography rather than theory the foundation of their work.

JM: Looking back at your scholarship on religion, is there any of it you would now frame with greater emphasis on the state, as you have come to do with your writing on ethnicity?

CFK: I see "religion," again following not only Weber but also historians of religion such as Paul Mus, as constituting a distinctive domain of human experience that cannot be reduced to being a reflection or representation of social structure or economic relationships. As all who have passed through my classes on the anthropology of religion know, I maintain that the fundamental characteristic of religion derives from the universal human effort through thought and especially practices to confront the ultimate conditions of their existence. The most significant of such ultimate conditions are manifest in the problems of suffering and death and the establishment of order.

These meanings and practices have their roots in particular traditions or lineages. That is, different religions have developed different sets of meanings and practices whereby their followers confront, cope, and adapt to these ultimate conditions. Prior to going to Thailand, I had only the vaguest knowledge of Buddhism, but I soon became aware during my first fieldwork that I must undertake to understand how Buddhism as a religion is practiced.

My fieldwork also led me to see that Buddhism as institutionalized in the Sangha, the order of monks, has been articulated with other social institutions, very much including the state. Although I have written a number of articles about the distinctive way Thai Buddhism offers followers ways of confronting suffering and death, I have also from early in my career written about Buddhism and the state (e.g., "Buddhism and National Integration in Thailand") and continue to do so in some ongoing work (e.g., a forthcoming paper on "Buddhism, Human Rights, and Non-Buddhist Minorities"). In the introduction to *Asian Visions of Authority*, of which I was the senior author, I also undertake some theoretical reflections on religion and the state, especially in modern societies.

In short, I think that I have made the relationship between religion and the state a central theme in my work, but as I say below, I do not, like some political scientists, privilege the state as being the product of the interests primarily of those who govern. I maintain that for those who govern to gain the support of the governed, there must be shared values, and that these values are often rooted in religious understandings. While in some instances, such as in Iran, such values are derived from particular religions, in others, a "civil religion" has emerged that makes it possible for those who privately follow different faiths to accept the legitimacy of a government that may not be overtly religious.

JM: From the perspective of a former student like myself, the trajectory of your career as a teacher and scholarly writer is fairly clear. Another part of your career has been your participation in numerous scholarly councils, committees, and editorial boards, where you have also had considerable impact in shaping the direction of Asian studies—but it is harder to get a clear sense of the trajectories of this kind of work. What generalizations can you make about this kind of scholarly involvement and the kinds of things you have worked for in this sphere?

CFK: My first image of the academic life was from a movie I saw as a child. I don't remember the movie, but I do remember that it was set in a small liberal arts college and the main character was a professor. I thought his life of teaching and writing was ideal, and I think that my desire to become a professor began then. When I actually joined the academic profession, I soon learned that one is expected to contribute not only through instruction and scholarship but also through professional service.

For some, professional service becomes the primary focus of their careers, and I certainly have found value while at the University of Washington in being the director of Southeast Asian studies and chair of the Department of Anthropology, a member of a number of editorial boards and fellowship committees, and an officer in several professional associations, including being the president of the Association for Asian Studies. I gained some positive recognition for these activities and was approached in the 1980s and 1990s about becoming a candidate for several deanships and directorships, and even a provost-ship. Although some of these were tempting, I finally decided that taking such a position would mean the end of my scholarly and instructional career.

In retrospect, I find I gained most from those professional activities that were closely linked to my primary academic roles. My long involvement with the Joint Social Science Research Council/American Council of Learned Societies committee on Southeast Asia and the SSRC Indochina Studies Committee (which I helped to create) made it possible for me to help, through grants, to foster the scholarship of others in areas in which I had strong interests. The Indochina Studies Program in particular led to my developing new research work in Vietnam and Laos and in establishing links with a number of institutions in Vietnam, Laos, and Cambodia.

I also had a leading role in establishing a cooperative project for training young researchers for work in minority communities in Vietnam and Thailand. The project was funded by the Ford Foundation and SIDA (the Swedish development agency) and involved the Institute of Ethnology in the Vietnamese Academy of the Social Sciences and Humanities, the Department of Anthropology at the Vietnam National University in Hanoi, the Regional Center for Sustainable Development and the Social Sciences at Chiang Mai University, the Department of Anthropology at Gothenburg University, Sweden, and the Department of Anthropology at the University of Washington. This project proved to be very successful in helping recruit and train a new generation of Vietnamese and Thai researchers specializing in the study of ethnic minorities.

A number of conferences that I helped to organize, some of them under SSRC auspices, also offered me the opportunity to frame a number of issues—e.g., the anthropological study of karma, ethnic change, ethnicity and the state, religion and the state, and development and the transformation of Thailand—that have been central to my intellectual projects.

Looking back, I feel fortunate to have been able pursue a career whose primary rewards have come from the pursuit of scholarship and the mentoring of students.

JM: James Scott has been your friend and represents a clear influence on your work, yet I sense that your vision of the state is rather different from his. Could you elaborate?

CFK: Jim Scott has a highly deserved reputation as one of the most creative and provocative of scholars who have made Southeast Asia the focus of their research. I have long valued his friendship and our exchanges even though these have often centered on some fundamental intellectual disagreements.

I have on two occasions pursued these disagreements in print: one in an edited collection in 1983 for the *Journal of Asian Studies*, on what was termed the Scott-Popkin debate about the relevance of moral vs. rational economy approaches for the study of Asian peasantries, and more recently in a long review article of his *The Art of Not Being Governed*. In both I praised his major contributions to the scholarship of Southeast Asia and acknowledged his innovative insights while also offering critical reflections on his theoretical positions. Scott's great strength is bringing within a single purview diverse peoples—all Southeast Asian peasants in the case of *The Moral Economy of the Peasant*, and all minorities in the highland borderlands lying between Southeast Asia, China, and India in the case of *The Art of Not Being Governed*—whose particular characteristics can be shown to be variations on a common theme. This is, I also think, the weakness of his approach.

I would like here to quote a little from my review of his *The Art of Not Being Governed* as it summarizes my dissent from his approach:

> Scott's model of the "state" is, thus, one that is the same across time and across cultures. "If this explicitly political perspective has any merit, its effect is to radically decenter any essentialist understanding of 'Burmanness,' or 'Siameseness,' or, for that matter, 'Hanness.' Identity at the core was a political project designed to weld together the diverse peoples assembled there" (80). Such a premise runs counter to most historical scholarship on mainland Southeast Asia that distinguishes a variety of different types of state.

Since my beginnings as a scholar at Cornell and continuing to the present, I have been and still am very skeptical of political scientists and other social scientists who impose a theoretical model that requires the ignoring or dismissal of significant historical facts. As one originally trained in mathematics and physics, I appreciate the use of Occam's razor to find underlying commonalities among what appears to be marked diversity. At the same time, my Weberian approach leads me to be cautious in ignoring historical contingency.

I share Jim's political judgment about the perfidious actions of particular governments, such as those of the country its leaders insist be known as Myanmar, but I do not share his view that every state should be viewed as evil. The acceptance by people of the authority of a particular state is predicated, I maintain, on a culture of power that makes people view the state as legitimate.

JM: International institutions such as the United Nations or the World Bank, transnational corporations, and even international NGOs, all, in many cases, support the institution of the nation-state but in some cases pursue agendas that put them at odds with it. Do you see this as fitting into your vision of the state and its relationship to ethnicity?

CKF: In a very real way, the UN, its predecessor, the League of Nations, and many international organizations—IMF, ASEAN, NATO, etc.—are predicated on and validate the existence of "recognized" nation-states. The true challenge to this order comes primarily not from international institutions but from peoples who live between worlds.

Several chapters in this volume concern such "border-crossing" peoples—Vietnamese in Laos (Hanh), Shan who feel excluded from Myanmar, but who don't quite find a home with ethnically related Thai (Ferguson), Lahu who are found primarily in China but also in Thailand (Pine), Lao in Thailand (Suchada), and *farang* (Western) husbands in northeastern Thailand (Suriya and Pattana). Pinkaew raises this discussion to a higher level in questioning what *citizenship* actually means.

These studies all point to the necessity of rethinking the relationship between the state and ethnicity—going beyond, in other words, my previous thinking. These papers make me recognize that ethnicity can be an interstitial identity that is only partially constrained by state policies. While I do not see such people as "escaping" the state, as Scott would put it, I do see the assertiveness of distinctive identities by ethnic minorities as compelling states (if not at present, in the near future) to reformulate what citizenship means. International institutions will also have to rethink their agendas to accommodate Hmong, Karen, Shan, and others who find their distinctive heritage still relevant in a world dominated by nation-states. Herein lies a significant research agenda for future anthropologists.

SELECTED PUBLICATIONS OF CHARLES KEYES

BOOKS AND MONOGRAPHS

Single-Authored Books and Monographs

"Peasant and Nation: A Thai-Lao Village in a Thai State," PhD diss., Cornell University, 1966, University Microfilms, no. 67–2710, 1967.

Isan: Regionalism in Northeastern Thailand. Ithaca, NY: Cornell University Southeast Asia Program, Data Paper no. 65, 1967.

The Golden Peninsula: Culture and Adaptation in Mainland Southeast Asia. New York: Macmillan, 1977. Reprinted, Honolulu: University of Hawaii Press, 1995.

Thailand: Buddhist Kingdom as Modern Nation-State. Boulder, Co: Westview Press, 1987; Bangkok: DK Publishers, 1989.

Symposia and Edited Volumes

with W. J. Klausner and S. Sivaraksa, eds. *Phya Anuman Rajadhon: A Reminiscence*. Bangkok: Sathirakoses-Nagapradipa Foundation, 1973.

Ethnic Adaptation and Identity: The Karen on the Thai Frontier with Burma. Philadelphia: Institute for the Study of Human Issues, 1979.

Ethnic Change. Seattle: University of Washington Press, 1981.

with E. Valentine Daniel, eds. *Karma: An Anthropological Inquiry*. Berkeley and Los Angeles: University of California Press, 1983.

"Peasant Strategies in Asian Societies: Moral and Rational Economic Approaches—A Symposium." *Journal of Asian Studies* 42, no. 4 (1983): 753–868.

with Pierre van den Berghe, eds. "Tourism and Ethnicity." Special Issue of *Annals of Tourism Research* 11, no. 3 (1984): 343–502.

with E. Jane Keyes and Nancy Donnelly, eds. *Reshaping Local Worlds: Rural Education and Cultural Change in Southeast Asia*. New Haven: Yale University Southeast Asia Studies, 1991.

with Charles Hirschman and Karl Hutterer, eds. *Southeast Asian Studies in the Balance: Reflections from America*. Ann Arbor, MI: Association for Asian Studies, 1992.

with Laurel Kendall and Helen Hardacre, eds. *Asian Visions of Authority: Religion and the Modern States of East and Southeast Asia*. Honolulu: University of Hawaii Press, 1994.

with Shigeharu Tanabe, eds. *Cultural Crisis and Social Memory: Modernity and Identity in Thailand and Laos*. Richmond, Surrey, UK: Routledge Curzon, 2002.

On the Margins of Asia: Diversity In Asian States—Perspectives on Asia: Sixty Years of the Journal of Asian Studies, Ann Arbor, MI: Association for Asian Studies, 2007.

Articles Published Separately

Who Are the Lue, Revisited? Ethnic Identity in Laos, Thailand, and China. Cambridge, MA: Massachusetts Institute of Technology, The Center for International Studies, Working Paper (1992).

Cultural Differences, The Nation State, And Rethinking Ethnicity Theory: "Lessons" From Vietnam. Bloomington, IN: University of Indiana, Department of Anthropology, 2001 (The David Skomp Distinguished Lecture in Anthropology).

The Destruction of a Shrine to Brahma in Bangkok and the Fall of Thaksin Shinawatra: The Occult and the Thai Coup in Thailand of September 2006. Singapore: Asia Research Institute, National University of Singapore, Working Paper Online Series, 2006.

Bibliographical Studies

Southeast Asian Research Tools: Thailand. Honolulu: Southeast Asian Studies, Asian Studies Program, University of Hawaii, Southeast Asian Paper no. 16, part 6, 1979.

Southeast Asian Research Tools: Laos. Honolulu: Southeast Asian Studies, Asian Studies Program, University of Hawaii, Southeast Asia Paper no. 16, part 7, 1979.

Southeast Asia Research Tools: Cambodia. Honolulu: Southeast Asian Studies, Asian Studies Program, University of Hawaii, Southeast Asia Paper no. 16, part 8, 1979.

"Indigenous Minorities in Northern Mainland Southeast Asia: Selected Sources in English and French." In *Ethnic Communities in Changing Environments*, comp. Chayan Vaddhanaphuti, 306–32. Chiang Mai, Thailand: Center for Ethnic Studies and Development, 1997.

Research Reports

"Some Thoughts on Health Problems in Rural Northeast Thailand." Mahasarakham, Thailand, typescript, June. Incorporated into "Health and Nutrition among Peasants in Northeastern Thailand," 1963.

Field Work in Thailand: Reports to the Foreign Area Fellowship Program, 1962–64. Seattle: Thailand Project, Department of Anthropology, University of Washington, 1968.

Security and Development in Thailand's Rural Areas. Bangkok: United States Operations Mission to Thailand, Research Division, mimeo., 1968.

Tai-Tribal Relations in a Frontier District of Thailand: A Preliminary Report. Seattle: University of Washington, Department of Anthropology, Thailand Project, 1969. Also printed and circulated by the National Research Council of Thailand, Bangkok, 1970.

"Some Thoughts on American Aid to Thailand." Seattle: University of Washington, Department of Anthropology, Thailand Project, mimeo. Paper prepared for a meeting of the Academic Advisory Council to Thailand, Washington DC, February 1970.

"Health and Nutrition among Peasants in Northeastern Thailand." Seattle: University of Washington, Department of Anthropology, Thailand Project, November 1970.

Development of Rural Northeastern Thailand and Programs of Planned Change. Seattle: University of Washington, Department of Anthropology, Thailand Project. Report for the Southeast Asian Office, the Ford Foundation, Bangkok, 1974.

Government Development Assistance for Thailand's Rural Poor: A Social Impact Assessment of the Provincial Development Program. Seattle: University of Washington, Department of Anthropology, Thailand Project, (Report prepared under USDA contract no. 53-319R-9-138), 1979.

Socioeconomic Change in Rural Northeastern Thailand: A Case Study. Seattle: University of Washington, Department of Anthropology, Thailand Project, (Report for the United States Agency for International Development), 1980.

with Suriya Smutkupt, Paitoon Mikusol, and Jane Keyes. *Socioeconomic Change in Rainfed Agricultural Villages in Northeastern Thailand*. Seattle: University of Washington Department of Anthropology, Thailand Project, (Report for the United States Agency for International Development), 1985.

ARTICLES

Articles in Journals

"Thailand, Laos, and the Thai Northeastern Problem." *Australia's Neighbours* 4, no. 17, (July–August 1964).

with Kenneth T. Young, Michael Moerman, David Wilson, Millard Long, Frederick Simmons, Anand Panyarachun, and Jack Shideler. "Thailand: The Northeast." *Asia* 6 (1966): 1–27. Excerpts from an abridged transcript of a group discussion held at Asia House in April 1966, chaired by Ambassador Kenneth T. Young.

"Ethnic Identity and Loyalty of Villagers in Northeastern Thailand." *Asian Survey* 6, no. 7 (1966): 362–69. Translated into Thai and reprinted under "Laksana thong chattiphan lae khwam phakdi khong chao ban nai phak tawanok chiang nuea," In *Sangkhomwitthaya Khong Muban phak tawanok chiang nuea* [Sociology of northeastern villages], edited by Suthep Soonthornpesuch, 229–46. Bangkok: Faculty of Political Science, Chulalongkorn University, 1968. Also reprinted in *The Politics of National Integration*, edited by John McAlister, 355–63. New York: Random House, 1973.

"Buddhism and National Integration in Thailand." *Journal of Asian Studies* 30, no. 3 (1971): 551–68. Reprinted in abridged form in *Visakha Puja 2514*, 22–34. Bangkok: The Buddhist Association of Thailand, Annual Publication, 1971. Translated into Japanese and reprinted in *Kokusai Shūkyō News*. Tokyo, 1972.

"The Power of Merit." In *Visakha Puja B.E. 2516*, 95–102. Bangkok: The Buddhist Association of Thailand, Annual Publication, 1973. Translated into Thai by Warani Osatharom and published under "Phū Mī Bun." In *"Khwamchuea Phra Si An" lae "Kabot Phu Mi Bun" nai Sangkhom Thai* ["Maitreya Beliefs" and "Holy Men Rebellion" in Thai Society], edited by Pornpen Hantrakool and Atcharaphon Kamutphisamai, 44–62. Bangkok: Sangsan, 2527 (1984).

"A Note on the Ancient Towns and Cities of Northeastern Thailand." *Tonan Ajia Kenkyu* (Southeast Asian Studies) 11, no. 4 (1974): 497–506.

"Tug-of-War for Merit: Cremation of a Senior Monk." *Journal of the Siam Society* 63, no. 1 (1975): 44–62. Reprinted in abridged and revised form as "Cremation of a Senior Monk." in *The Life of Buddhism*, edited by Frank E. Reynolds and Jason A. Carbine, 124–35. Berkeley and Los Angeles: University of California Press, 2000.

"Buddhist Pilgrimage Centers and the Twelve Year Cycle: Northern Thai Moral Orders in Space and Time," *History of Religions* 15, no. 1 (1975): 71–89. Translated into Japanese and reprinted in *Kokusai Shūkyō New* (Tokyo) 14, no. 4 1973. (The date of publication is odd because the publication schedule of the journal was delayed.)

"Buddhism in a Secular City: A View from Chiang Mai." In *Visakha Puja BE 2518*, 62–72. Bangkok: The Buddhist Association of Thailand, Annual Publication, 1975.

"In Search of Land: Village Formation in the Central Chi River Valley, Northeast Thailand." *Contributions to Asian Studies* 9, (1976): 45–63.

"Towards a New Formulation of the Concept of Ethnic Group." *Ethnicity* 3, (1976): 202–13. Reprinted in *American Immigration and Ethnicity*, edited by George E. Pozzetta, 228–40. New York: Garland Publishing Co., 1991.

"Millennialism, Theravada Buddhism, and Thai Society." *Journal of Asian Studies* 36, no. 2 (1977): 283–302. Translated into Thai and reprinted under "Khwamchuea rueng samai Phra Si An, Satsanaphut baep Therawat, lae Sangkhom Thai." In *Kabot Chao na* [Peasant rebellions], edited by Wuthichai Munlasin and Thammanit Waraphon, 19–43. Bangkok: Social Science Association of Thailand, 1982. Also translated into Thai under "Khwamchuea Phra Si An, Latthi Therawat lae Sangkhom Thai, by Natthawipha Chalitanon." In *"Khwamchuea Phra Si An" lae "Kabot Phu Mi Bun" nai Sangkhom Thai* ["Maitreya Beliefs" and "Holy Men Rebellions" in Thai Society], edited by Pornpen Hantrakool and Atcharaphon Kamutphisamai, 63–102. Bangkok: Sangsan, 2727 (1984).

"Donning the Yellow Robes: Theravada Buddhist Ordination Rituals in Northern Thailand." In *Visakha Puja* BE 2521, 36–50. Bangkok: The Buddhist Association of Thailand, Annual Publication, 1978.

"Buddhist Economics in Action." In *Visakha Puja BE 2522*, 19–25. Bangkok: Buddhist Association of Thailand, Annual Publication, 1979.

with Phra Khrū Anusaranaśāsanākiarti. "Funerary Rites and the Buddhist Meaning of Death: An Interpretative Text from Northern Thailand." *Journal of the Siam Society* 68, no. 1 (1980): 1–28.

"Introduction." In *Peasant Strategies in Asian Societies: Perspectives on Moral and Rational Economic Approaches*, edited by Charles F. Keyes. *Journal of Asian Studies* 42, no. 3 (1983): 753–68.

"Economic Action and Buddhist Morality in a Thai Village." In *Peasant Strategies in Asian Societies: Perspectives on Moral and Rational Economic Approaches*, edited by Charles F. Keyes. *Journal of Asian Studies* 42, no. 3 (1983): 851–68.

"Mother or Mistress but Never a Monk: Culture of Gender and Rural Women in Buddhist Thailand." *American Ethnologist* 11, no. 2 (1984): 223–41.

"Theravāda Buddhism and Its Worldly Transformations in Thailand: Reflections on the Work of S. J. Tambiah." *Contributions to Indian Sociology* 21, no. 1 (1987): 123–46.

"From Death to Birth: Ritual Process and Buddhist Meanings in Northern Thailand." *Folk* 29 (1987): 181–206.

"Buddhist Politics and Their Revolutionary Origins in Thailand." In *Structure and History*, edited by S. N. Eisenstadt. Special issue of *International Political Science Review* 10, no. 2 (1989): 121–42.

"Cambodia and the Legacy of Angkor." *Cultural Survival Quarterly* 14, no. 3 (1990): 60–63.

"Buddhism and Revolution in Cambodia." *Cultural Survival Quarterly* 14, no. 3 (1990): 60–63.

"Being Protestant Christian in Southeast Asia." *Journal of Southeast Asian Studies* 27, no. 2 (1996): 280–92.

"Weber and Anthropology." *Annual Reviews in Anthropology* 31, (2002): 233–55.

"'The Peoples of Asia': Science and Politics in Ethnic Classification in Thailand, China and Vietnam." *Journal of Asian Studies* 61, no. 4: 1163–1203, November 2002.

Articles in Edited Volumes

"Local Leadership in Rural Thailand." In *Local Authority and Administration in Thailand*, edited by Fred R. von der Mehden and David A. Wilson, 92–127. Los Angeles: Academic Advisory Council for Thailand, 1970. Translated into Thai by Phonchai Theppanya and reprinted under the title, *Phunam thongthin nai chonnabot Thai*. Chiang Mai: Department of Sociology-Anthropology, Faculty of the Social Sciences, Chiang Mai University, 1973. Also reprinted in *Modern Thai Politics*, edited by Clark Neher, 219–50. Cambridge, MA: Schenkman, 1976.

"New Evidence on Northern Thai Frontier History." In *In Memoriam Phya Anuman Rajadhon*, edited by Tej Bunnag and Michael Smithies, 221–50. Bangkok: The Siam Society, 1970. Translated into Thai under "Lakthan mai thang prawatsat chaidaen phaknuea khong prathet Thai." In *Phapa Samakkhi Chaemphon kap Khanadara* [(Offering) of Forest Cloth (by) Taksin Caemphon and a Film Actors Group]. Mae Sariang: Privately Published for Distribution at Ceremony Held at Wat Chaiyalap, Mae Sariang District, Mae Hong Son Province, June 30, 2516 (1973), no page numbers.

"Phya Anuman Rajadhon and the Study of Culture." In *Phya Anuman Rajadhon: A Reminiscence*, edited by C. F. Keyes, W. J. Klausner, and S. Sivaraksa, 31–34. Bangkok: Sathirakoses-Nagapradipa Foundation, 1973.

"Kin Groups in a Thai-Lao Village." In *Change and Persistence in Thai Society: Homage to Lauriston Sharp*, edited by G. William Skinner and A Thomas Kirsch, 275–97. Ithaca, NY: Cornell University Press, 1975.

"Political Crisis and Militant Buddhism in Contemporary Thailand." In *Religion and Legitimation of Power in Thailand, Burma, and Laos,* edited by Bardwell Smith, 147–64. Chambersburg, PA: Anima Books, 1978.

"Ethnography and Anthropological Interpretation in the Study of Thailand." In *The Study of Thailand*, edited by Eliezar Ayal, 1–60. Athens, OH: Ohio University Center for International Studies, Southeast Asia Program, Papers in International Studies, Southeast Asia Series, no. 54, 1978.

"Introduction." In *Ethnic Adaptation and Identity: The Karen on the Thai Frontier with Burma*, edited by Charles F. Keyes, 1–23. Philadelphia: ISHI, 1979.

"The Karen in Thai History and the History of the Karen in Thailand." In *Ethnic Adaptation and Identity: The Karen on the Thai Frontier with Burma*, edited by Charles F. Keyes, 25–62. Philadelphia: ISHI, 1979.

"The Dialectics of Ethnic Change." In *Ethnic Change*, edited by Charles F. Keyes, 4–30. Seattle: University of Washington Press, 1981.

"Charisma: From Social Life to Sacred Biography." In *Charisma and Sacred Biography*, edited by Michael Williams, 1–22. Chico, CA: Scholars Press (*Journal of the American Academy of Religion*, Thematic Series 48/3-4), 1981.

"Death of Two Buddhist Saints in Thailand." In *Charisma and Sacred Biography*, edited by Michael Williams, 149–80. Chico, CA: Scholars Press (*Journal of the American Academy of Religion*, Thematic Series 48/3–4), 1981.

"The Study of Popular Ideas of Karma." In *Karma: An Anthropological Inquiry*, edited by Charles F. Keyes and E. Valentine Daniel, 1–24. Berkeley: University of California Press, 1983.

"Merit-Transference in the Karmic Theory of Popular Theravada Buddhism." In *Karma: An Anthropological Inquiry*, edited by Charles F. Keyes and E. Valentine Daniel. Berkeley: University of California Press, 1983.

"The Observer Observed: Changing Identities of Ethnographers in a Northeastern Thai Village." in *Field Work: The Human Experience*, edited by Robert Lawless, Vinson H. Sutlive Jr., and Mario D. Zamora, 169–94. New York: Gordon and Breach, 1983.

with Pierre van den Berghe. "Introduction: Tourism and Recreated Ethnicity." In "Tourism and Ethnicity," edited by Charles F. Keyes and Pierre van den Berghe. Special issue of *Annals of Tourism Research* 11, no. 3 (1984): 343–52.

"The Interpretive Basis of Depression." In *Culture and Depression: Studies in the Anthropology and Cross-Cultural Psychiatry of Affect and Disorder*, edited by Arthur Kleinman and Byron J. Good, 153–74. Berkeley and Los Angeles: University of California Press, 1985.

"Ambiguous Gender: Male Initiation in a Buddhist Society." In *Religion and Gender: Essays on the Complexity of Symbols*, edited by Caroline Bynum, Stevan Harrell, and Paula Richman, 66–96. Boston: Beacon Press, 1986.

"Tribal Peoples and the Nation-State in Mainland Southeast Asia." In *Southeast Asian Tribal Groups and Ethnic Minorities: Prospects of the Eighties and Beyond*, edited by Benedict O'G. Anderson, 19–26. Cambridge, MA: Cultural Survival, Inc., Cultural Survival Report, 22, 1987.

"Buddhist Practical Morality in a Changing Agrarian World: A Case from Northeastern Thailand." In *Attitudes toward Wealth and Poverty in Theravada Buddhism*, edited by Donald K. Swearer and Russell Sizemore, 170–89. Columbia, SC: University of South Carolina Press, 1990.

"State Schools in Rural Communities: Reflections on Rural Education and Cultural Change in Southeast Asia." In *Reshaping Local Worlds: Rural Education and Cultural Change in Southeast Asia*, edited by Charles F. Keyes, 1–18. New Haven: Yale University Southeast Asian Studies, 1991.

"The Proposed World of the School: Thai Villagers Entry into a Bureaucratic State System." In *Reshaping Local Worlds: Rural Education and Cultural Change in Southeast Asia*, edited by Charles F. Keyes, 87–138. New Haven: Yale University Southeast Asian Studies, 1991.

"Buddhist Detachment and Worldly Gain: The Economic Ethic of Northeastern Thai Villagers," in *Yu mueang Thai: Ruam botkhwam thang sangkhom phuea pen kiat dae Sastrachan Sane Chamrik* [In Thailand: Collected Essays in Honor of Professor Saneh Chammarik], edited by Chaiwat Satha-Anand. Special issue of *Ratthasatsan* (Journal of Political Science, Thammasat University) 16, nos. 1–2 (1991): 271–98.

"A Conference at Wingspread and Rethinking Southeast Asian Studies." In *Southeast Asian Studies in the Balance: Reflections from America*, edited by Charles Hirschman, Charles F. Keyes, and Karl Hutterer, 9–24. Ann Arbor, MI: Association for Asian Studies, 1992.

"Buddhist Politics and Their Revolutionary Origin in Thailand." In *Innovations in Religious Traditions: Essays in the Interpretation of Religious Change*, edited by Michael A. Williams, Collett Cox, and Martin S. Jaffee, 319–50. Berlin and New York; Mouton de Gruyter, 1992.

"Buddhist Economics and Buddhist Fundamentalism in Burma and Thailand." In *Remaking the World: Fundamentalist Impact*, edited by Martin Marty and Scott Appleby, 367–409. Chicago: University of Chicago Press, 1993.

"Why the Thai are Not Christians: Buddhist and Christian Conversion in Thailand." In *Christian Conversion in Cultural Context*, edited by Robert Hefner, 259–84. Berkeley and Los Angeles: University of California Press, 1993.

with Helen Hardacre and Laurel Kendall. "Contested Visions of Community in East and Southeast Asia." In *Asian Visions of Authority: Religion and the Modern States of East and Southeast Asia*, edited by Charles F. Keyes, Helen Hardacre and Laurel Kendall, 1–16. Honolulu: University of Hawaii Press, 1994.

"Communist Revolution and the Buddhist Past in Cambodia." In *Asian Visions of Authority: Religion and the Modern States of East and Southeast Asia*, edited by Charles F. Keyes, Laurel Kendall, and Helen Hardacre, 43–73. Honolulu: University of Hawaii Press, 1994.

"Hegemony and Resistance in Northeastern Thailand." In *Regions and National Integration in Thailand, 1892–1992*. Volker Grabosky, 154–82. Wiesbaden: Otto Harrassowitz, 1995.

"Who Are the Tai? Reflections on the Invention of Local, Ethnic and National Identities." In *Ethnic Identity: Creation Conflict, and Accommodation*, edited by Lola Romanucci-Ross and George A. De Vos, 136–60. 3rd ed. Walnut Creek, CA: Alta Mira Press, 1995.

"Cultural Diversity and National Identity in Thailand." In *Government Policies and Ethnic Relations in Asia and the Pacific*, edited by Michael Brown and Sunait Ganguly, 197–232. Cambridge, MA: MIT Press, 1997.

"The 'Great Transformation' of Upland Peoples in Thailand and Vietnam: Reflections on the Workshop on Ethnic Communities in Changing Environments." In *Ethnic Communities in Changing Environments*. compiled by Chayan Vaddhanaphuti, 1–16. Chiang Mai, Thailand: Center for Ethnic Studies and Development, 1997. Translated into Vietnamese, and published in Hanoi by Institute of Ethnology, National Center for the Social Sciences and Humanities, June 1997.

"Moral Authority of the Sangha and Modernity in Thailand: Sexual Scandals, Sectarian Dissent, and Political Resistance." In *Socially Engaged Buddhism for the New Millennium: Essays in Honor of the Ven. Phra Dhammapitaka (Bhikkhu P.A. Payutto on his 60th Birthday Anniversary*, edited by Sulak Sivaraksa, 121–47. Bangkok: Sathirakoses-Nagapradipa Foundation and Foundation for Children, 1999.

"A Princess in a Peoples' Republic: A New Phase in the Construction of the Lao Nation." In *Civility and Savagery*, edited by Andrew Turton, 206–26. Richmond, Surrey, UK: Curzon, 2000.

with Shigeharu Tanabe. "Introduction." In *Social Memory and Crises of Modernity: Politics of Identity in Thailand and Laos*, edited by Shigeharu Tanabe and Charles Keyes, 1–42. Richmond, Surrey, UK: Curzon, 2002.

"National Heroine or Local Spirit? The Struggle over Memory in the Case of Thao Suranari of Nakhon Ratchasima." In *Social Memory and Crises of Modernity: Politics of Identity in Thailand and Laos*, edited by Shigeharu Tanabe and Charles Keyes, 113–36. Richmond, Surrey, UK: Curzon, 2002.

"The Politics of Language in Thailand and Laos." In *Fighting Words: Language Policy and Ethnic Relations in Asia*, edited by Michael E. Brown and Sumit Ganguly, 177–210. Cambridge, MA: MIT Press, 2003.

"Afterword: The Politics of 'Karen-ness' in Thailand." In *The Karen in Thailand*, edited by Claudio Delang, 210–18. Singapore: Singapore University Press and Bangkok: White Lotus, 2003.

"Vietnamese and Thai Literature as 'Indigenous Ethnography.'" In *Southeast Asian Studies for the 21st Century*, edited by Anthony Reid, 193–232. Tempe, AZ: Arizona State University, Southeast Asian Studies, 2003.

"The Anthropology of Thailand and the Study of Social Conflict." In *Watthanatham rai akhati chiwit rai khwam runraeng* (Culture free of prejudice, life free of violence), 1–36. Bangkok: Princess Maha Chakri Anthropology Centre, Proceedings of the 4th Annual Conference of the Princess Maha Chakri Anthropology Centre, vol. 1, 2006.

"Dẫn luận: Sự thăng trầm của nghiên cứu học về tôn giáo (Selected Essays: Approaches to Research in the Study of Religion)." In *Những Vấn Đề Nhân Học Tôn Giáo* (Issues in the study of religion), edited by Hội Khoa Học Lịch Sử Việt Nam (Association of Vietnamese Historians), 7–27. Đà Nẵng: Nhà Xuất Bản Đà Nẵng, Tạp Chí Xưa và Nay, 2006. Translation of an essay originally entitled "The Decline and Rise of the Anthropological Study of Religion."

"The 'Other' Asian Peoples in Asia." In *On the Margins of Asia: Diversity in Asian States —Perspectives on Asia: Sixty Years of the* Journal of Asian Studies, edited by Charles Keyes, 9–30. Ann Arbor, MI: Association for Asian Studies, 2007.

"Monks, Guns and Peace: Theravada Buddhism and Political Violence." In *Belief and Bloodshed*, edited by James Wellman, 147–65. Lanham, Maryland: Rowman & Littlefield Publishers, Inc., 2007.

"Ethnicity and the Nation-States of Thailand and Vietnam." In *Challenging the Limits: Indigenous Peoples of the Mekong Reigon*, edited by Prasit Leepreecha, Don McCaskill, and Kwanchewan Buadaeng, 13–54. Chiang Mai, Thailand: Mekong Press, 2007.

"Buddhists, Human Rights, and Non-Buddhist Minorities." In *Religion and the Global Politics of Human Rights* (Working title), edited by Tom Banchoff and Robert Wuthnow. Oxford: Oxford University Press. Forthcoming.

"Communism, Peasants and Buddhism: The Failure of 'Peasant Revolutions' in Thailand in Comparison to Cambodia." In *Community and the Trajectories of Change in Cambodia and Thailand*. Forthcoming.

"Northeastern Thai Ethnoregionalism Updated." In *Culture and Discourse, Language and Power, Text and Ritual Practice: Reflections on the Anthropology of Thailand through the Work of Andrew Turton* (working title), edited by Nicholas Tapp and Philip Hirsch. Forthcoming.

"Buddhists Confront the State." In *Buddhism and the Crises of Nation-States in Asia* (working title), edited by Pattana Kitiarsa. Forthcoming.

Papers in Conference Proceedings

"The Basis of Relations between Ethnic Groups in Contemporary Nation-States." In *Ethnic Processes in USSR and USA: Material of the Soviet-American Symposium*, vol. 1, edited by Kozlov. Moscow: INION, The Academy of Sciences, 1986. In Russian. Translation of a paper presented at a symposium on "Contemporary Ethnic Processes in the USA and the USSR." New Orleans, 1984.

"A Tale of Two Villages: Rural Northeastern Thailand on the Eve of 'Development' and 'Revolution.'" Paper prepared for a symposium honoring Professor A. Thomas Kirsch, Cornell University, Ithaca, New York, February 1999. Published in the proceedings of the symposium in honor of Professor Kirsch, Chiang Mai: Chiang Mai University, Faculty of Social Sciences, 2000.

"The Thái of Vietnam in Thai Thought." Paper presented at the International Conference on Vietnamese Studies, Hanoi, July 1998. Published in the proceedings of the conference, Hanoi: Hanoi National University of Social Sciences and Humanities, Faculty of History, 2001.

"Buddhism Fragmented: Thai Buddhism and Political Order since the 1970s." Keynote address presented at the 7th International Thai Studies Conference, Amsterdam, July 1999. Published in the proceedings of the conference, Amsterdam: University of Amsterdam, 2001.

"Migrants And Protestors: 'Development' in Northeastern Thailand." Keynote address at the 8th International Studies Conference, Nakhon Phanom, Northeast Thailand, January 2002. Published in the proceedings of conference, Bangkok: Ramkhamhaeng University, 2002.

"The Village Economy: Capitalist AND Sufficiency-based—A Northeastern Thai Case." Keynote address at the 10th International Thai Studies Conference, Bangkok, January 2008. Published in the proceedings of conference, Bangkok: Thammasat University, 2008.

Articles in Encyclopedias

"The Thai Peoples." *Encyclopaedia Britannica* 22 (1966): 935–36.

"Hinduism in Southeast Asia." In *Abingdon Dictionary of Living Religions*, edited by Keith Crim, et al., 321–24. Nashville: Abingdon Press, 1981.

"Tribal Religions in Southeast Asia." In *Abingdon Dictionary of Living Religions*, edited by Keith Crim, et al, 709–13. Nashville: Abingdon Press, 1981.

"Buddhist Pilgrimage in South and Southeast Asia." In *The Encyclopedia of Religion*, vol. 11, edited by Mircea Eliade, 347–49. New York: Macmillan, 1987.

"Thai Religion." In *The Encyclopedia of Religion*, vol. 14, edited by Mircea Eliade, 416–21. New York: Macmillan, 1987.

"Southeast Asian Religions: Mainland Cultures." In *The Encyclopedia of Religion*, vol. 13, edited by Mircea Eliade, 512–49. New York: Macmillan, 1987.

"Ethnic Groups, Ethnicity." In *The Blackwell Dictionary of Anthropology*, edited by Thomas J. Barfield, 152–54. Oxford: Basil Blackwell, 1997.

"Leach, Edmund R. (1910-88)." In *The Blackwell Dictionary of Anthropology*, edited by Thomas J. Barfield, 280–81. Oxford: Basil Blackwell, 1997.

"Nation, Nationalism." In *The Blackwell Dictionary of Anthropology*, edited by Thomas J. Barfield, 335–38. Oxford: Basil Blackwell, 1997.

"Nativistic Movements." In *The Blackwell Dictionary of Anthropology*, edited By Thomas J. Barfield, 339–40. Oxford: Basil Blackwell, 1997.

"The Buddha." In *Encyclopedia of Politics and Religion*, edited by Robert Wuthnow, 80–81. Washington, DC: Congressional Quarterly Books, 1998.

"Buddhism, Theravada." In *Encyclopedia of Politics and Religion*, edited by Robert Wuthnow, 81–86. Washington, DC: Congressional Quarterly Books, 1998. Revised for second edition.

"Ethnicity." In *Encyclopedia of Politics and Religion*, edited by Robert Wuthnow, 237–39. Washington, DC: Congressional Quarterly Books, 1998. Reprinted in second edition.

"Nhat Hanh, Thich." In *Encyclopedia of Politics and Religion*, edited by Robert Wuthnow, 563–64. Washington, DC: Congressional Quarterly Books, 1998. Revised for second edition.

"Vietnam." In *Encyclopedia of Politics and Religion*, edited by Robert Wuthnow, 767–70. Washington, DC: Congressional Quarterly Books, 1998. Revised for second edition.

"Thailand." In *Encyclopedia of Politics and Religion*, edited by Robert Wuthnow. Washington, DC: Congressional Quarterly Books. Completed for publication in second edition.

with Ralph Nicholas. "Anthropology in Asia," in "Anthropology." In *Encyclopædia Britannica*. Last retrieved from Encyclopædia Britannica Online, March 2006.

With Jane E. Keyes. "Thailand." In *Encyclopædia Britannica*. Last retrieved from Encyclopædia Britannica Online, February 2007.

Short Articles and/or Popular Articles

"Value and Form in Modern Jazz." *Scrip* (University of Nebraska Literary Magazine) 2 no. 1 (1959): 18–23.

"Chotmai chak Isan" (Letter from the Northeast). *Social Science Review* (Bangkok) 6, no. 1 (1968): 89–94. In Thai. Published anonymously under the name of "Our Special Correspondent." The English original, entitled "Where Can I Turn for Help? The Story of a Northeastern Villager," was prepared in mimeographed form in Seattle (University of Washington, Department of Anthropology, Thailand Project, 1968).

"Peoples of Indochina." *Natural History* 79, no. 8 (1970): 40–54.

"Boonsanong Punyodyana (1936–1976)." *Journal of Asian Studies* 36, no. 2 (1977): 331–32.

Comment on Judith Nagata's Review of *Ethnic Adaptation and Identity*, *Reviews in Anthropology* 6, no. 1 (1979): 121–25.

"Some Reflections on Contemporary Burma." In *Military Rule in Burma since 1962: A Kaleidoscope of Views*, edited by F. K. Lehman, 79–81. Singapore: Institute of Southeast Asian Studies, 1981.

"Still More on Peasant Strategies in Asian Societies: A Reply to Edwin Moise." *Journal of Asian Studies* 43, no. 3 (1984): 501–2.

"Lucien M. Hanks (1910–1988)." *Khosana* (Bulletin of the Thailand/Laos/Cambodia Group of the Association for Asian Studies), 1989. Reprinted in *Crossroads* 7, no. 1 (1992): 1–5.

"Christianity as an Indigenous Religion in Southeast Asia." *Social Compass* 38, no. 2 (1991): 177–85.

"Yunnan Approached from Thailand." Published in abridged form as "Quick Look at Yunnan." *seaspan* 4, no. 3 (1991): 1–3.

"Report on an International Colloquium on 'Regions and National Integration in Thailand (1892-1992),' University of Passau, Germany, June 25–27, 1992." *Khosana* [Newsleter of the Thailand/Laos/Cambodia Studies Group of the Association for Asian Studies] 27, nos. 4–6 (1993).

"Lauriston Sharp and the Anthropological Study of Thailand: Some Reflections." *Thai-Yunnan Project Newsletter* (Australian National University) 25, nos. 1–5 (1994).

"On the Margins of Modernity." SEASPAN 10, nos. 1–3 (Autumn 1996).

"Foreword." In *The Organization of Thai Society in the Early Bangkok Period 1782–1873*, by Akin Rabibhadana, vii–ix. Reprinted, Bangkok: Wisdom of the Land Foundation and Thai Association of Qualitative Researchers, 1996.

"From Ethnology to the Politics of Ethnicity." *Minpaku Anthropology Newsletter* (National Museum of Ethnology, Osaka) 7, nos. 5–7 (1999).

[contributor to] *Weighing the Balance: Southeast Asian Studies Ten Years After*. New York: Social Science Research Council, Southeast Asia Program, 2000.

"Remembering Mely Tan's Early Encounter with America." In *Multikulturalisme, Peran Perempuan & Integrasi Nasional: Persembahan untuk Mely G. Tan*, edited by Efendi, et al., 341–44. Jakarta: Penerbit Universitas Atma Jaya, 2008.

Review Articles

with James N. Anderson. "Perspectives on Loosely Organized Social Structures." Review of *Loosely Structured Social Systems*, edited by Hans-Dieter Evers. *Journal of Asian Studies* 29, no. 2 (1970): 415–19.

"Religious and Social Change in Southern Laos." Review of *The New Year Ceremony at Basak (South Laos)*, by Charles Archaimbault. *Journal of Asian Studies* 31, no. 3 (1972): 611–14.

"Northeastern Thai Village: Stable Order and Changing World." Review of *Little Things*, by Prajuab Thirabutana, and *Reflections in a Log Pond*, by William J. Klausner. *Journal of the Siam Society* 63, no. 1 (1975): 177–207.

"Structure and History in the Study of the Relationship between Theravāda Buddhism and Political Order." Review of *World Conqueror and World Renouncer*, by S. J. Tambiah. *History of Religions* 25, no. 2 (1978): 156–70.

"Tribal Ethnicity and the State in Vietnam: A Review Article." Review of *Sons of the Mountains,* and *Free in the Forest*, by Gerald Cannon Hickey, 1983. *American Ethnologist*, 11, no. 1 (1984): 176–82.

Review of *The Legend of King Aśoka: A Study and Translation of the Aśokāvadāna*, by John S. Strong. *Religious Studies Review* 12, no. 1 (1986): 133–37.

Reviews

Over fifty reviews, published in journals such as: *American Anthropologist, American Ethnologist, The Asia Pacific Journal of Anthropology, Development and Change, Ethnic and Racial Studies, History of Religions, Journal of the American Oriental Society, Journal of Asian Studies, Journal of Asian and African Studies, Journal of the Siam Society, Journal of Southeast Asian Studies, Medical Anthropology Quarterly, Pacific Affairs, Religion*

CONTRIBUTORS

DUONG BICH HANH received her doctorate in anthropology at the University of Washington in 2006. She is currently the Culture Program Coordinator at the UNESCO Office in Vietnam. Her dissertation is entitled *The Hmong Girls of Sa Pa: Local Places, Global Trajectories, Hybrid Identity*.

JANE M. FERGUSON is a research fellow in the Department of Anthropology at the University of Sydney. Her research interests include issues of ethnic conflict, energy politics, popular culture production, historical memory, and passenger aviation, in Burma/Myanmar and Thailand.

PATTANA KITIARSA taught anthropology, popular Buddhism, and Thai studies in the Department of Southeast Asian Studies, National University of Singapore. He completed his doctorate in anthropology at the University of Washington in 1999. His book *Mediums, Monks and Amulets: Thai Popular Buddhism Today* was published by Silkworm Books in 2012.

PINKAEW LAUNGARAMSRI is Assistant Professor at the Department of Sociology and Anthropology, Faculty of Social Sciences, Chiang Mai University. Her book *Redefining Nature: Karen Ecological Knowledge and the Challenge to the Modern Conservation Paradigm* was published by Earthworm Books in 2002.

JOHN A. MARSTON completed his doctorate in anthropology at the University of Washington in 1997 and has taught since then at the Center for Asia and African Studies of El Colegio de México. He is coeditor of *History, Buddhism, and New Religious Movements in Cambodia* (University of Hawaii Press/Silkworm Books) and editor of *Anthropology and Community in Cambodia: Reflections on the Work of May Ebihara* (Monash University Press.)

JUDITH M. S. PINE is a linguistic anthropologist, and currently Assistant Professor of Anthropology at Western Washington University. She has conducted fieldwork on Lahu language and culture since 1996. Her current project, building on the intersection of ethnicity and modernity in a Lahu context, explores the use of Lahu language media in performance of a Lahu modernity.

SURIYA SMUTKUPT has been an independent researcher in Chiang Mai, Thailand, since 2003. Prior to that he taught at Khon Kaen University and Suranaree University of Technology. He studied anthropology under Charles F. Keyes at the University of Washington, 1976–82.

SUCHADA THAWEESIT completed her PhD in sociocultural anthropology at the University of Washington. She is Assistant Professor at the Institute for Population and Social Research, Mahidol University, Nakhon Pathom, Thailand.

RATANA TOSAKUL is a senior lecturer of anthropology teaching at Thammasat University in Bangkok, Thailand. Her research interests include rural agricultural community studies, diaspora, and transnationalism with gender sensitivity. She holds a PhD in sociocultural anthropology from the University of Washington in Seattle.

ALLISON TRUITT is Associate Professor of Anthropology at Tulane University in New Orleans, Louisiana. She is the author of *Dreaming of Money in Ho Chi Minh City* (University of Washington Press) and several articles about the social life of money in Vietnam.

INDEX

A Sha Fu Cu, 125, 129, 131–32
area studies, 248, 252–54
Bamrung Kayotha, 104, 116–18, 120
Bangkok
   as center of government, 131, 147, 219–20
   labor migration to, 49, 110, 114, 176, 181, 184, 234–35
   missionaries based in, 129–30
   nightlife in, 223, 226–27
Baptist denomination, 125, 127–29, 131–33, 135–36, 138–39
   See also Protestantism
Bhumibol Adulyadej, King, 53, 119
Bourdieu, Pierre, 66, 254–55
Bowring Treaty, 130, 221
Buddha, 47–48, 68, 72, 77–78
Buddhism, 63, 130, 136, 246, 256
   in Cambodia, 14, 65–93
   Mahanikay order, 68, 75, 82, 84, 90
   Mahayana, 81, 83–85, 129
   and Thai identity, 146, 184, 186, 220
   Thammayut order, 69, 75–76, 78–79, 82, 90–91
   Theravada, 14, 47, 65, 67–68, 83–85, 92, 136
Burma. *See* Myanmar

Buu Chon, Ven., 84–85, 87–89, 92, 95n20, 95n22
Cambodian military, 71, 77, 91, 93
capitalism, 8, 11, 15, 103–4, 106, 115, 119
ceremony. *See* ritual
Chan Sang, 69, 73–75, 78, 80–82, 91, 93
Chea Sim, 87–88, 95n19, 97n37
Chiang Mai, 49, 51, 130, 135–36, 138, 169
Chiang Mai Province, Thailand, 143, 152, 159
Chiang Mai University, 248–49, 258
Chiang Rai Province, Thailand, 152, 154–55, 159, 172
China, 3
   and Lahu, 125, 128–29, 131–33, 135, 260
   and Southeast Asia in general, 253, 259
   and Vietnam, 13, 28, 81
Chinese (ethnic populations in Southeast Asia), 146–47, 152–53, 159, 194, 245
Christianity, 127–29, 131, 140n3
Chulalongkorn, King, 108, 110, 130–31, 145, 221

Chuon Nath, Samdech, 79, 84
citizenship
　and border-crossing populations, 11, 16–17, 49, 51, 193–95
　categories of, 4, 15–16, 143–49, 151–54, 156–61, 260–61
　cultural, 35
　lack of, 132, 165–69, 172–73, 175–80, 182–87
Cohen, Erik, 225–26, 232
colonialism, 7, 9, 110, 145, 166, 253
communism
　fear of, 147, 150, 171
　in Laos, 170–71, 183, 185
　Thai movements, 108–9, 151
　Vietnamese Communist Party, 13, 86–87
Democratic Kampuchea
　aftermath of, 8, 13–14, 67, 93
　living conditions under, 70, 75, 79, 80
　monks defrocked during, 66, 69, 73
　monks maintaining robes during, 71, 76, 78, 80, 86, 88
diaspora, 11, 13–14, 24–25, 31, 33–34, 37, 49, 51
Do Trung Hieu, 80–85, 87–89, 92–93, 95n21, 95n25, 96n27, 96n32
ethnicity
　and border crossing, 9, 16–17
　concept of, 1–4, 12, 49, 247–48, 255–56
　ethnic identity, 15, 60, 63, 126, 133–34, 138–39, 180–83
　ethnic Khmer in Vietnam. See Kampuchea Krom
　ethnic nationalism, 13, 45–46
　missionaries and, 130
　state categorization, 14, 29, 132, 143–61, 165–66, 168, 170, 261
　stereotypes, 55, 205–6
Fang, Chiang Mai Province, Thailand, 135–37
Foucault, Michel, 3, 10, 254–55
France, 76, 90, 170, 194, 216, 240n1

Gioi Nghiem, Ven., 84, 87–88, 95n20, 97n36
global capitalism, 8, 11–12, 105, 107–9, 112, 115, 216
　rejection of, 103, 107, 120
global culture, 18, 215, 218, 222, 233, 238, 240
global labor market, 217
global marriage market, 215, 219, 223–24, 238–39
globalization, 16, 29–30, 38, 127, 248
　and mobile populations, 9–11, 16
Hai Duong Province, Vietnam, 198–99, 205–6
Hanoi, 32, 84, 191, 209
Hickey, Gerald, 135, 137
Hmong, 154, 170–71, 187, 261
Ho Chi Minh, 23, 30, 39, 201
Ho Chi Minh City, 30–32, 38, 83, 88–89, 192
Hue, 191–92, 203, 205, 212
Hung Temple, 30–32, 38, 40n4
Hung Yen Province, Vietnam, 191, 199, 206, 209
hybridity, 15, 83, 126, 139
hypergamy, 219, 235, 238
identity. See national identity
Ieng Sary, 73, 86, 88
India, 47, 81, 85, 253, 259
Indochina, 35, 180, 193–94, 253
In-Plaeng Network, 104, 197–98, 112–15, 118
Internet, 88, 169, 222, 224, 229
Isan, 134, 137, 246, 255
　displaced persons in, 166, 170–71, 174–85
　rural population in, 103–11, 113–14, 116–18
　women, marriage to *farang*, 215–19, 224–26, 228–35, 237–39, 260
Japan, 107, 116, 134, 219, 225, 249
Kaet Vay, Ven., 73, 86, 88–89, 96n27
Kalasin Province, Thailand, 104, 116, 118

Kampong Cham Province, Cambodia, 69–71, 73, 75–76, 96n32
Kampong Thom Province, Cambodia, 71, 78, 86, 88, 96n32
Kampot Province, Cambodia, 74–75, 94n5
Kampuchea Krom (ethnic Khmer areas of Vietnam), 74, 83, 85–86, 88, 95n20, 95n25, 95n26
Karen, 246, 261
Kaysone Phomvihane, 199, 201
Keane, Webb, 127, 131
Keyes, Charles F.
  and Association for Asian Studies, 3, 165, 250, 257
  and Buddhism, 14, 63, 65, 67, 128, 246, 256
  at Cornell University, 245–48, 251–54, 260
  and education in Southeast Asia, 136–37
  and ethnicity, 1–3, 12, 17, 24, 49, 60–61, 133, 139, 144–45, 165, 247, 255, 259, 261; and Laos, 246, 258
  and modernity, 12, 105, 125–26, 248
  and nation states, 4, 12–13, 24, 165, 246, 255, 260
  and northeastern Thailand, 103, 105, 108, 113, 180, 246, 249
  and northern Thailand, 246, 248
  and peasantry, 105, 107, 109, 114, 120, 246, 255, 259
  and religion, 12–13, 92, 246, 255–57
  and Social Science Research Council, 250, 253, 258
  and Southeast Asian Studies, 247, 249–50, 252–54, 257
  at University of Washington, 246, 248–49, 254, 257–58
  and Vietnam, 28, 246, 248, 258
  and Weber, 247–48, 254–56
Khmer Rouge Period. *See* Democratic Kampuchea
Khmer Rouge insurgency, 74, 89, 91
Khon Kaen Province, Thailand, 216, 226, 229, 231, 233
Khon Kaen University, 213, 130, 249
Khorat Plateau, 180, 217
labor
  corvée, 147
  rural, 110, 118
  See also migrant labor
labor market, 54, 207
Lahu
  Christianity, 127–29, 131–32
  identity, 15, 126–27, 133–34, 137, 139
  missionaries and, 128–31, 136
  in Thailand, 134–38
"Lahu Baptist Chronicle," 132
Laos, 8, 253, 258
  ethnic Lao in Thailand, 17, 105, 166, 179, 180–82, 246
  ethnic minorities in, 135, 246
  immigrants from, 108, 154–55, 168, 170–86
  Lao People's Democratic Republic, 157, 173
  Royal Lao Government, 170–71, 185
  Vietnamese migrants to, 191–213
Loei Province, Thailand, 154, 172
Loh Lay, Samdech, 72–73, 79, 85, 91, 96n28
Louisiana, 34–35, 37–39, 40n7

Mae Hong Son Province, Thailand, 49, 54–55, 152
marriage and border-crossing
  farang and Isan women, 215–40
  Lao migrants to Thailand, 171, 174, 176–77, 179–80, 183, 184, 187
  on Thai-Malay border, 159
Marxism, 10, 254–55
McGilvary, Rev. Daniel, 130–31, 140n1
Mekong River, 108, 180–82, 184–85, 230
Migdal, Joel, 4, 7, 8, 10, 248
migrant labor
  in Laos, 191–97, 199–204, 206, 209–10, 212–13
  in Thailand, 61–62, 150, 155–56, 160, 170, 174

migrant workers, 63, 150, 155, 160, 168, 174–75, 178
modernization, 8–9, 105, 108, 119, 247–48
Mongkut, King, 129–30, 221
Mukdahan Province, Thailand, 118, 154, 172
Myanmar, 53, 133, 220, 246, 253, 259
  border-crossing between Thailand and, 51, 135–36, 143, 152, 154, 159–60, 174
  insurgency, 45–46, 61, 150
  missionaries in, 128, 131
myth, 67, 125, 131, 183, 224
  national, 12–13, 23–25, 28, 33

Nakhon Phanom Province, 154, 183
Nan Province, Thailand, 153–54, 172
nation-state
  and citizenship, 157–58, 165–66, 168–69, 187
  and cross-border movement, 110, 206
  ethnic groups in, 2, 24, 132, 144–46, 165, 245, 261
  and modernity, 8–9, 61, 246, 248, 253, 260–61
  and religion, 12–13, 129
  and state authority, 4
  Thailand as, 130, 148–49, 181–82
national identity, 158, 259
  ambivalence of, 92, 145, 161
  Thai, 138, 146–48, 180, 187, 259
  Vietnamese, 28–29, 31, 35, 37–38
  See also ethnicity
Nationality Act, Thailand, 145, 146, 166–67, 175, 177, 188n5
Nel Mony, 69, 71–75, 77, 80–82, 86–88, 90–91, 93
NGOs, 11, 15, 104–7, 111, 119, 260
Nong Khai Province, Thailand, 154, 172, 185, 230
Noun Nget, Samdech, 72–73, 86, 90–91, 96n28, 97n39

orientalism, 145, 225–27, 238, 253–54

Paen Sen, Ven., 75–76, 78, 92n10
Pakse, 194, 203

Pattaya, 223, 226–28, 237
peasantry, 5, 109, 118, 246, 255, 259
Pen Sovan, 86, 96n27
Phnom Penh, 71–73, 75, 77, 78&, 86, 88, 90
Phu Phan Mountain, 108–10, 112
Po Diep, Ven., 76, 79
Pol Pot period. *See* Democratic Kampuchea
Prak Ing, 86–89, 95n21, 95n23, 96n28, 97n36
Prey Veng Province, Cambodia, 70–71, 86
prostitution, 135, 218, 225–26, 233, 237
Protestantism, 15, 126–31, 136, 139
  See also Baptist denomination

Quang Tri Province, Vietnam, 192, 195, 198, 203, 207

refugees
  Cambodians in Vietnam, 70, 74, 94n5
  in Thailand, 150, 168, 170: Burmese, 160, 168; Cambodian, 93; Lao, 154, 170, 172, 176, 183–85, 187; Vietnamese, 151
  Vietnamese in United States, 34
Ricouer, Paul, 105, 255
ritual
  Buddhist ordination, 45–63, 65–93
  and culture, 82–83, 105
  described, 35–37, 47–51, 70–78, 87–90
  and ethnic identity, 45–47, 55, 60–63, 186
  and national myth, 25–26, 33
  and politics, 53, 80–81
  and the state , 4, 12–14, 25–26, 39, 67–68, 92–93, 217

Said, Edward, 224, 238
Sakon Nakhon Province, Thailand, 104, 109, 111, 118, 154
Schemmann, Michael, 224–25, 231–32
Scott, James
  and ethnicity, 3, 261
  and peasantry, 109, 259
  and the state, 5, 8–9, 11, 82, 93, 144, 259

Shan
  in Burma, 45
  insurgency, 46, 61
  language, 128
  music, 46, 51, 53, 55, 57–61, 63
  ritual, 45, 47–51, 55–56
  in Thailand, 45, 49, 51, 54–56, 62, 153, 160
Sharp, Lauriston, 245, 251
Sieu Viet, Ven., 84, 88, 95n20, 95n23, 97n36
Sri Lanka, 67, 81, 84–85
sustainable development, 104, 106–7, 111–12, 258

Tak Province, Thailand, 154–55, 160
Takeo Province, Cambodia, 69, 71, 73, 75–76, 78, 86
Tep Vong, Samdech, 73, 86, 89–90, 96n27, 97n39
Thai military, 107, 119, 171
Thailand, northeastern. *See* Isan
Thailand Lahu Baptist Convention, 125, 136
Thien Tam, Ven., 85, 87, 95n19, 96n20, 95n21, 96n34
tourism
  Lahu as tourists in China, 139
  in Louisiana, 34
  in Thailand, 49, 53, 216, 225–27, 231
  in Vietnam, 30
transnationalism, 9–11, 249, 260
  Lahu identity, 133
  of marriage, 215, 239
  migration, 200–1, 206, 218
  Vietnamese identity, 24, 30, 32

Ubon Ratchathani Province, Thailand, 154, 172, 177, 184
Udon Thani Province, 118, 216, 224, 234
United States, 13, 33–35, 37, 170, 194, 216, 225
US military, 170, 216, 218, 225,
Uttaradit Province, Thailand, 154, 172

Vajiravudh, King, 145–46, 221
Van Lang kingdom, 25, 27

Vickery, Michael, 65, 80
Vientiane, 185–86, 183–84, 203
Viet Kieu, 17, 29, 192–98, 207
Viet Lieu, 193, 196
Vietnam
  Buddhist crossborder activitity with Cambodia, 66–69, 74, 76–77, 80–90, 92
  diasporic communities: in Laos, 192–203, 205, 208–9, 211, 260; in Thailand, 151; in United States, 2–5, 31, 33–39
  ethnic policies, 3, 24, 249
  modernization, 81, 248, 253
  relation to Thailand, 220
  Socialist Republic of Vietnam, 25, 30, 33, 38
  state holidays of, 23–24, 26–31, 33, 38–39
Vietnam War, 216, 225, 249
Vietnamese military, 36–37, 70, 77, 89
Vinaya, 68, 71

Walker, Andrew, 117, 119
Wat Lanka, Phnom Penh, 84, 95n22
Wat Mahamontrey, Phnom Penh, 73, 85
Wat Sansom Kosol, Phnom Penh, 71–73, 77
Wat Saravan, Phnom Penh, 77, 82, 91
Wat Unnalom, Phnom Penh, 71, 76, 86–88, 90–91
Weber, Max, 4, 10, 92, 247–48, 254–56, 260

Yawnasan, Rev., 125–27, 129, 139
Young, William, 128–29, 131, 140n2
Yunnan Province, China, 125, 129, 154